ad vivum delin.^t G. Bew.

The dotted Line shews the place where the Arm was Amputated.

MEMOIRS

OF THE

LITERARY

AND

PHILOSOPHICAL SOCIETY

OF MANCHESTER.

VOL. I.

WARRINGTON,

PRINTED BY W. EYRES,

FOR T. CADEL IN THE STRAND, LONDON,

MDCCLXXXV.

TO THE

KING,

THESE VOLUMES ARE HUMBLY INSCRIBED

BY THE MEMBERS OF THE

LITERARY AND PHILOSOPHICAL SOCIETY

OF *MANCHESTER,*

WITH THE

PROFOUNDEST RESPECT AND LOYALTY:

AND WITH PECULIAR GRATITUDE

FOR HIS GRACIOUS PATRONAGE OF THE

FIRST FRUITS OF THEIR

INSTITUTION.

THE
PREFACE.

THE numerous Societies, for the promotion of Literature and Philosophy, which have been formed in different parts of Europe, in the course of the last and present centuries, have been not only the means of diffusing knowledge more extensively, but have contributed to produce a greater number of important discoveries, than have been effected in any other equal space of time.

The progress that has been made in Physics and the Belles Lettres, owes its rapidity, if not its origin, to the encouragement which these Societies have given to such pursuits, and to the emulation which has been excited between different academical bodies, as well as among the individual Members of each institution. The collecting and publishing the more important communications which have been delivered to them,

them, have saved from oblivion many very valuable discoveries, or improvements in arts, and much useful information in the various branches of science. These their modest authors might have been tempted to suppress, but for the respectable sanction of societies of men of the first eminence and learning in their respective countries, and the easy mode of publishing, which their volumes of Transactions afford.

Though, in France, Societies for these purposes have been instituted in several of the provinces, in England, they have almost been confined to the Capital; and however great have been the advantages resulting from the researches of the learned bodies, who are incorporated in London, it seems probable, that the great end of their institutions, the promotion of arts and sciences, may be more widely extended by the forming of Societies, with similar views, in the principal towns in this kingdom.

Men, however great their learning, often become indolent, and unambitious to improve in knowledge, for want of associating with others of similar talents and acquirements: Having few opportunities of communicating their ideas, they are not very solicitous to collect or arrange those they have acquired, and are still less anxious about the further cultivation of their minds.—But science, like fire, is put in motion by collision.—Where a number of such men
have

have frequent opportunities of meeting and conversing together, thought begets thought, and every hint is turned to advantage. A spirit of inquiry glows in every breast. Every new discovery relative to the natural, intellectual or moral world, leads to a farther investigation; and each man is zealous to distinguish himself in the interesting pursuit.

Such have been the considerations that have led to the institution of the Literary and Philosophical Society of Manchester.—Many years since, a few Gentlemen, inhabitants of the town, who were inspired with a taste for Literature and Philosophy, formed themselves into a kind of weekly club, for the purpose of conversing on subjects of that nature. These meetings were continued, with some interruption, for several years; and many respectable persons being desirous of becoming Members, the numbers were increased so far, as to induce the founders of the Society to think of extending their original design. Presidents, and other officers were elected, a code of laws formed, and a regular Society constituted, and denominated, THE LITERARY AND PHILOSOPHICAL SOCIETY OF MANCHESTER.

This Society now presents the first fruits of its institution to the public; and from the assiduity of the Members, and the correspondence of others, there is reason to presume, that a volume may be regularly sent to the press, every second or third year. The selection of the papers has been made with as much impartiality, and as strict attention to their comparative merits, as could be expected, in decisions of so delicate a nature. Yet the committee are sensible that a majority of votes, delivered by ballot, is not an infallible test of excellence, in literary or philosophical productions. This consideration, they trust, will give them a reasonable claim to the candour of the reader, if there should be found occasion for its exercise: And they hope that Gentlemen, who have favoured the Society with valuable communications, will deem it no injustice or disparagement, that their Essays have not been inserted, through the imperfection of necessary forms and regulations. They are preserved in the Archives of the Society, and may again come under review, when subjects of a similar nature, to those on which they treat, are offered for discussion.*

No systematic order has been observed, in the disposition of the miscellaneous materials, which compose these volumes; because such an

---

* Several Dissertations, by Dr. Percival, Mr. Henry, and others, enumerated in the printed Report of the Society, were published by their respective authors, long before these Memoirs were committed to the press.

arrangement would have required the completion of the work, before any part of it could have been committed to the press.

The sanction which the Society gives to the work, now published, under its auspices, extends only to the novelty, ingenuity, or importance of the several memoirs which it contains. Responsibility concerning the truth of facts, the soundness of reasoning, or the accuracy of calculation, is wholly disclaimed; and must rest alone, on the knowledge, judgment, or ability of the authors, who have respectively furnished such communications.

LAWS AND REGULATIONS

FOR THE GOVERNMENT OF THE

LITERARY AND PHILOSOPHICAL SOCIETY OF MANCHESTER;

TOGETHER WITH A

LIST OF THE MEMBERS.

LAWS.

I. THAT the number of the Members of this Society, invested with the privilege of voting, electing members, &c. be limited to fifty.

II. That Honorary Members, residing at a distance from Manchester, be eligible into this Society, provided no Gentleman be recommended, who has not distinguished himself by his literary or philosophical publications; or favoured the Society with some paper, which shall have received the approbation of the Committee of Papers.

III. That every Candidate for admission into the Society, whether as an Ordinary or Honorary Member, shall be proposed by at least three Ordinary Members, who shall sign a Certificate of his being, from their knowledge of him, or of his writings, a fit person to be admitted into it: which certificate shall be read at four successive meetings of the Society, previously to the election—Such election, with respect to an Ordinary Member, to be void, if he do not attend within four meetings afterwards, unless he can plead some reasonable apology.

IV. That every election shall be conducted by ballot; That the majority of votes shall decide; thirteen Members at least being present; and that the President shall have a casting voice, if the number of votes be equal.

V. That two Presidents, four Vice-Presidents, two Secretaries, a Treasurer, and a Librarian, be elected annually, by the majority of members present, on the last Wednesday in the month of April: The election to be determined by ballot.

VI. That a Committee of Papers shall be appointed, by ballot, at the same time, which shall consist of the Presidents, Vice-Presidents, Secretaries, Treasurer and Librarian, together with six other members of the Society: And that this Committee shall decide, by ballot, concerning the insertion in the Register, or the publication, of any paper which shall have been read before the Society; and shall be authorized to select, with the consent of the author, detached parts of any paper, the whole of which may not be deemed proper either for insertion or publication: But that the presence of seven members of the Committee shall be necessary for such discussion, or decision.

VII. That Visitors may be introduced by any Member to the meetings of the Society, with the permission of the Chairman.

VIII. That the subjects of conversation comprehend Natural Philosophy, Theoretical and Experimental Chemistry, Polite Literature, Civil Law, General Politics, Commerce,

Commerce, and the Arts. But that Religion, the Practical Branches of Physic, and British Politics, be deemed prohibited; and that the Chairman shall deliver his *Veto*, whenever they are introduced.

IX. That each Member, who shall favour the Society with any interesting facts and observations, respecting Philosophy, Polite Literature, &c. which may occur to him, either from reflection, experiment, reading, or correspondence, shall send his paper to one of the Secretaries, the Monday before the meeting of the Society.

X. That the Secretary, to whom the paper shall be delivered, shall, with the approbation of one President, or two Vice-Presidents, have the power of suspending the recital of it, if deemed improper to be read, until the pleasure of the Committee of Papers be known, a meeting of which shall be called by the Secretary to inspect it: And, if the Committee disapprove of its being introduced to the Society, they shall be empowered to reject it.

XI. That all papers which shall be delivered to the Secretary, and not prohibited as above, shall be read by him, or the author, according to the order of succession in which they were presented.

XII. That each paper shall be read to the Society without interruption; and that more than thirty minutes shall not be allowed to the reading of any single paper: If more time be required in the delivery of it, the remainder shall, except the Society determine otherwise, be deferred to the succeeding evening. No paper, however, shall engage more than two evenings, without the consent of the Society expressed by a ballot.

XIII. That a second paper shall not be read, before the subject of the former one has been discussed.

XIV. That

REGULATIONS.

XIV. That the Society shall meet every Wednesday evening, except during the Months of June, July, August, and September: And that each meeting shall commence at half past six, and be concluded at half past eight o'clock.

XV. That each Member shall pay one guinea annually, at half yearly payments, into the hands of the Treasurer, to defray the rent of the room, and other incidental expences; and also, to establish a fund for the benefit of the Society. And if any Member shall refuse or neglect to pay his subscription, he shall be excluded the Society. Each Member, on his election, to pay his subscription for the current half year, together with one guinea, admission fee.

XVI. That it be recommended to each Member to enter the Society's room with silence, and without ceremony.

XVII. That no Laws shall be enacted, rescinded, or altered, but at the quarterly meetings, on the last Wednesdays in the Months of January, April, and October: And that notice shall be given, at least fourteen days, previous to those meetings.

REGULATIONS.

I. THAT the Society shall publish a volume of miscellaneous papers, every two years: And that, at stated times, the Committee shall select from the papers, which shall have been read to the Society, such as shall appear to be most worthy of publication: But that no papers shall be published, against the consent of the authors.

II. That

REGULATIONS.

II. That a Library be formed for the use of the Members of this Society; and that the Librarian be authorized to purchase such books, as shall be ordered at the quarterly meetings of the Society: But that no books shall be taken out of the Library, without a written order from one of the Secretaries, limiting the time of keeping it to seven days.

III. That the resolution to establish a Library be announced to the Honorary Members of the Society; and that it be intimated to them by the Secretaries, that donations of their past and future publications will be highly acceptable.

IV. That a gold medal, of the value of seven guineas, be given to the Author of the best Experimental Paper on any subject relative to Arts and Manufactures, which shall have been delivered to the Secretaries, and read at the ordinary meetings of the Society before the last Wednesday in March 1786.

V. That the adjudication of this premium be referred to the Committee of Papers; that their decision shall be made by ballot; and that the medal shall be delivered by the President, to the person to whom it shall have been adjudged, or to his representative, at the first meeting of the Society in October 1786.

VI. That if the person, to whom the medal shall have been adjudged, be not one of the Society, his name shall be enrolled in the list of Honorary Members.

VII. The regular attendance of members being essential to the prosperity and usefulness of the Institution, that if any Member shall absent himself during the space of three months, from the meetings of the Society, notice shall be sent to him, at a quarterly meeting, that the Society considers his absence as a mark of disrespect,

and

and that a more punctual observance of the Laws is expected from him.

VIII. To encourage the exertions of young men, who attend the meetings of the Society, as visitors, that a silver medal, not exceeding the value of two guineas, be annually given to any one of them, under the age of twenty-one years, who shall, within the year, have furnished the Society with the best paper on any subject of Literature or Philosophy; and that such adjudication shall be made by the Committee of Papers.

A LIST OF THE MEMBERS.

* James Massey, Esq.
* Thomas Percival, M. D. F. R. S. & S. A. & Reg. Soc. Med. Par. Soc. } Presidents.

* The Rev. Samuel Hall, A. M.
* Charles White, Esq. F. R. S. Honorary Mem. R. M. S. & Cor. Mem. R. S. A. in Scotland, &c.
* George Lloyd, Esq.
* Mr. George Bew, } Vice-Presidents.

* The Rev. Thomas Barnes, D. D.
* Mr. Thomas Henry, F. R. S. } Secretaries.

Mr. Isaac Moss,   Treasurer.
Mr. Thomas Robinson,   Librarian.
Mr. Joseph Atkinson.
Mr. John Barrow.

A LIST OF THE MEMBERS.

Thomas Butterworth Bayley, Esq. F. R. S.
* Mr. John Bill.
Mr. John Birch.
Mr. Charles Frederick Brandt.
Mr. Ashworth Clegg.
Mr. Robert Darbey.
Mr. James Dinwiddie.
Mr. John Drinkwater.
* Mr. George Duckworth.
Alexander Eason, M. D.
Mr. Edward Hall.
Mr. Richard Hall.
* The Rev. Ralph Harrison.
Mr. Samuel Hibbert.
* Mr. Thomas Kershaw.
Mr. John Lawrence.
Mr. James Macaulay.
Peter Mainwaring, M. D.
John Mitchell, M. D.
Mr. John Orme.
Mr. George Philips.
Mr. John Philips.
Mr. Robert Philips.
* Mr. John Leigh Philips.
Mr. Thomas Philips.
* Mr. James Potter.
Mr. John Powel.
The Rev. Frederick Robert Slater.
Mr. George Wakefield.
Mr. George Walker.
Mr. John Wilson.

*Those marked thus * are of the Committee of Papers.*

HONORARY MEMBERS.

John Aikin, M. D.
Felix Vicq d'Azyr, R. S. Med. Par. Sec. & R. A. Sc. Soc. &c.
Sir George Baker, Bart. F. R. S. Medic. Regin.
James Beattie, LL. D.
Patrick Brydone, Esq. F. R. S.
Mr. John Buchanan.
The Right Rev. Beilby, Lord Bishop of Chester.
Edwood Chorley, M. D.
Mr. Thomas Cooper.
James Currie, M. D.
Erasmus Darwin, M. D. F. R. S.
Edward Hussey Delaval, Esq. F. R. S. Reg. S. S. Gotting. & Upsal, & Instit. Bologn. Soc.
The Hon. Sir John Talbot Dillon, Knight and Baron of the Holy Roman Empire.
Rev. William Enfield, LL. D.
William Falconer, M. D. F. R. S.
Anthony Fothergill, M. D. F. R. S.
Benjamin Franklin, LL. D. R. S. L. & R. Acad. Scient. Par. Soc. &c.
The Rev. —— Frossard, D. D. of Lyons, in France.
William Hawes, M. D.
John Haygarth, M. B. F. R. S.
Mr. George Hibbert.
Thomas Houlston, M. D.
Alexander Hunter, M. D. F. R. S.
James Johnstone, M. D.
Monsieur Lavoisier, Reg. Ac. Scient. P. Soc.

The

A LIST OF THE MEMBERS.

The Right Rev. Richard, Lord Bishop of Landaff, F.R.S.

John Coakley Lettsom, M. D. F. R. S. & S. A.

Mr. J. Hyacinth Magellan, F. R. S. & R. Acad. Petrop, & Paris. Corresp.

Mr. Patrick Mac Morland.

Henry Moyes, M. D.

The Rev. John Pope.

The Rev. Joseph Priestley, LL. D. F. R. S. Acad. Imp. Petrop, R. Holm. & Med. & Reg. Acad. Scient. P. Soc.

Mr. William Rathbone.

Mr. William Roscoe, Liverpool.

Benjamin Rush, M. D. Professor of Chemistry at Philadelphia.

Dorning Rasbotham, Esq.

Samuel Foart Simmons, M D. F. R. S. & R. S. M. P. Soc. & R. S. Monspel. Corresp.

The Rev. William Turner.

The Rev. George Travis, A. M.

Mr. Alexander Volta, Professor of Experimental Philosophy at Como, &c.

Martin Wall, M. D. Clinical Professor in the University of Oxford.

Mr. John Warltire.

The Rev. Gilbert Wakefield, B. D.

Josiah Wedgwood, Esq. F. R. S.

The Rev. John Whittaker., B. D. F. S. A.

CONTENTS

OF THE

FIRST VOLUME.

SOME REMARKS *on the* OPINION *that the* ANIMAL BODY *possesses the* Power *of* GENERATING COLD. *By* GEORGE BELL, M.D. Page 1.

On the Advantages of LITERATURE *and* PHILOSOPHY *in general, and especially on the* CONSISTENCY *of* LITERARY *and* PHILOSOPHICAL, *with* COMMERCIAL, PURSUITS. *By* THOMAS HENRY, F. R. S. - - - P. 7.

On CRYSTALLIZATION. *By* ALEXANDER EASON, M. D. - - - - P. 29.

On the PRESERVATION *of* SEA WATER *from* PUTREFACTION *by Means of* QUICKLIME. *By* THOMAS HENRY, F. R. S.—*To which is added, an Account of a newly invented Machine for* IMPREGNATING WATER, *or other* FLUIDS *with* FIXED AIR, *&c. Communicated to Mr. Henry by* J. HAYGARTH, M. B. F. R. S. - P. 41.

On

CONTENTS.

On the NATURE and Essential CHARACTERS of POETRY, as distinguished from PROSE. By THOMAS BARNES, D. D. - Page 54.

On the AFFINITY subsisting between the ARTS: with a PLAN for promoting and extending MANUFACTURES, by encouraging those ARTS on which MANUFACTURES principally depend. By THOMAS BARNES, D. D. - - - P. 72.

REMARKS on the different SUCCESS with Respect to HEALTH, of some ATTEMPTS to pass the WINTER in HIGH NORTHERN LATITUDES. By JOHN AIKIN, M. D. - - - P. 89.

On the PLEASURE which the MIND receives from the EXERCISE of its FACULTIES; and that of TASTE in particular. By CHARLES DE POLIER, Esq. - - - P. 110.

On ŒCONOMICAL REGISTERS. By Mr. J. WIMPEY. P. 134.

On the PLEASURE which the MIND, in many Cases, receives, from contemplating SCENES of DISTRESS. By THOMAS BARNES, D. D. - P. 144.

OBSERVATIONS on BLINDNESS, and on the Employment of the OTHER SENSES to supply the LOSS of SIGHT. By Mr. GEORGE BEW. - P. 159.

On SALT-PETRE. By JAMES MASSEY, Esq. P. 184.

An ATTEMPT to shew, that a TASTE for the BEAUTIES of NATURE and the FINE ARTS, has no INFLUENCE favourable to MORALS. By the Rev. SAMUEL HALL, A. M. - P. 223.

OBSERVATIONS *on the Use of* ACIDS *in* BLEACHING *of* LINEN. *By* ALEXANDRER EASON, M. D. Page 240.

Conjectural REMARKS *on the* SYMBOLS *or* CHARACTERS, *employed by* ASTRONOMERS *to represent the several* PLANETS, *and by* CHEMISTS, *to express the several* METALS: *in a* LETTER *to* THOMAS PERCIVAL, M. D. &c. *By* MARTIN WALL, M. D. CLINICAL PROFESSOR *in the University of* OXFORD. - - - P. 243.

REMARKS *on the* KNOWLEDGE *of the* ANCIENTS. *By* WILLIAM FALCONER, M. D. F. R. S. *Communicated by Dr. Percival.* - - P. 261.

An INQUIRY *concerning the* INFLUENCE *of the* SCENERY *of a* COUNTRY *on the* MANNERS *of its Inhabitants. By* WILLIAM FALCONER, M. D. F. R. S. - - - - P. 271.

A TRIBUTE *to the* MEMORY *of* CHARLES DE POLIER, *Esq. By* THOMAS PERCIVAL, M. D. &c. P. 287.

THOUGHTS *on the* STYLE *and* TASTE *of* GARDENING *among the* ANCIENTS. *By* WILLIAM FALCONER, M. D. F. R. S. - - P. 297.

On the REGENERATION *of* ANIMAL SUBSTANCES. *By* CHARLES WHITE, *Esq.* F. R. S. &c. P. 325.

On the DIVERSIONS *of* HUNTING, SHOOTING, FISHING, &c. *considered as compatible with* HUMANITY. - - - P. 341.

OBSERVA-

CONTENTS.

Observations on Longevity. By Anthony Fothergill, M.D. F.R.S. - Page 355.

On the Influence of the Imagination and the Passions upon the Understanding. By Thomas Barnes, D.D. - - P. 375.

On the Ascent of Vapour. By Alexander Eason, M.D. - - - P. 395.

On the Comparative Merit of the Ancients and the Moderns with Respect to the Imitative Arts. By Mr. Thomas Kershaw. P. 405.

On the Impropriety of allowing a Bounty to encourage the Exportation of Corn, &c. By Mr. Joseph Wimpey. - - P. 413.

On the Natural History of the Cow, so far as it relates to its giving Milk; particularly for the Use of Man. By Charles White, Esq. F.R.S. &c. - - - P. 442.

On the Natural History and Origin of Magnesian Earth, particularly as connected with those of Sea Salt, and of Nitre; with Observations on some of the Chemical Properties of that Earth, which have been, hitherto, either unknown, or undetermined. By Thomas Henry, F.R.S. - - - P. 448.

EXPLANATION OF THE PLATES
in Vol. I.

PLATE I.

Machine for impregnating Liquors with Fixed Air.

E The Effervescing-Vessel.
T t The Tubes through which the Air is conveyed.
A The Air-Vessel.
O The Opening through which the Common Air is expelled.
B The Bellows.
W The Water-Vessel.
P p The Pipe through which the Air is drawn into the Bellows.
c c A Pipe forming the communication between the Air and Water-Vessels.

PLATE II.

Symbols used by the Astronomers and Chemists.

PLATE III.

A Representation of the Stump of the Humerus mentioned in page 337.

The dotted Line shews the Part where the Arm was amputated.

NOTE

This volume has a very tight binding and while every effort has been made to reproduce the centres, force would result in damage

Fig. 1.   ♃   **JUPITER** *Tin.*

Fig. 2.   ♀   **VENUS.** *Copper.*

Fig. 3.   ♄   **SATURN.** *Lead.*

Fig. 4.   ♂   **MARS.** *Iron.*

Fig. 5.   ☿   **MERCURY.** *Quicksilver.*

Published as the Act directs Sept.r 29. 1785 by T. Cadell in the Strand.

MEMOIRS

OF THE

LITERARY AND PHILOSOPHICAL

SOCIETY OF MANCHESTER.

Some REMARKS *on the* OPINION *that the* ANIMAL BODY *possesses the Power of* GENERATING COLD. *By* GEORGE BELL, M. D. *Read May* 16, 1781.

A CURIOUS and important discovery was announced to the world in the LXV. vol. of the Philosophical Transactions. We are there informed, that Dr. Fordyce and other gentlemen, several different times, went into a room, the air of which was heated to a degree far above that of the human blood; and though they remained there, sometimes for the space of half an hour, yet the heat of their bodies was not increased by more than 3 or 4 degrees. From hence they concluded, that the living body possesses a peculiar power of generating cold by some occult operation. The experiments seem to have been made with sufficient accuracy; but the conclusion drawn from them is liable to strong objection. For, in forming it, several circumstances have been overlooked, which, in my opinion, afford an easy explanation of all the phenomena, on principles already known, without referring them to a new law of the animal body, which probably does not exist. These circumstances I shall endeavour to point out.

I. The first cause which prevented their bodies from receiving a greater increase of heat was, *The rarefaction of the air with which they were surrounded.*

The quantity of heat which different substances contain, is, in general, in proportion to their density; and, in this proportion, they communicate more or less of it to others. A cubical foot of water, contains a much greater quantity of heat, than a cubical foot of air, of the same temperature: and, if a third substance be added, its temperature will be considerably changed by the hot water, while by the hot air it will hardly be changed in any perceptible degree. Many facts may be adduced, which serve to illustrate, and, at the same time, are explained by this cause. Thus, the steam of boiling water will scald a person's hand, which can support the heat of air, of the same temperature. And thus perhaps

haps the weather, when hazy and loaded with vapour, seems to our feeling, hotter than when pure and rare; although by the thermometer it is found to be equally warm in both instances.

This also was the true reason, why, in making those experiments, Dr. Fordyce always found that he could bear a greater degree of heat in dry, than in moist air. But nothing shews more clearly the slowness with which heat is imparted to a denser substance, from one that is highly rarefied, than a circumstance mentioned in the paper in question: " that even the small quantity of mercury, contained in a thermometer which the gentlemen carried with them into the room, did not arrive at the degree to which the air was heated, during the whole time they remained there."

II. Another cause which, in the given situation, would diminish the effect of the heated air, is, *The evaporation made from the surface of the body.*

That evaporation produces a considerable absorption of heat, is well known: and, in making the experiments, there is reason to believe, that it took place in a considerable degree. Dr. Fordyce, anxious perhaps to establish his general law, seems unwilling to allow its influence. But when it is considered, that by the operation of the heat, the force of the circulation was increased, the pores of the skin relaxed, and the pressure of the internal air diminished; when we are told, that a turgescence of the veins, and an universal redness of the surface of the body, took place; we are compelled to refuse credit to the assertion, even of Dr. Fordyce, that there was no evaporation. The evaporation must have been great, and would diminish the effect of the external heat by surrounding the surface with a cool atmosphere, from its temperature fit for the absorption of heat, and from its rarity, unfit for the ready transmission of it into the body.

III. But another very powerful cause of the body's having preserved its temperature in the given situation, remains to be noticed; which is, *The successive afflux of blood to the surface, of a temperature inferior to that of the surrounding air.*—By this means, the small quantity of heat which penetrated the skin would be immediately carried off, and transferred throughout the body: and it would have required the space of many hours, before the whole mass could have received any considerable increase of heat.*

It has been adduced, in proof of the existence of the power of the living body to generate cold, that frogs, lizards, and other animals of the same

---

* It may here be remarked, that the two last mentioned causes act more powerfully in moderating the heat of the external air, according to the necessity there is for their action: for both the evaporation from the surface, and the velocity of the circulation of the blood, are in proportion to the degree of heat applied.

sort possess it; for if touched, they feel cold. This proves only, that their heat is less than that of the hand, with which they are felt; and perhaps less than that of the air, when the trial is made.

But it is extremely probable, that no animal whatever can live in health, for any considerable time, in an atmosphere of a temperature superior in heat to that of its own blood. Thus we find, that the animals in question hide themselves in the day-time among thick grass, where there is a great evaporation; and in places, into which the rays of the sun cannot penetrate. Worms, in hot weather, during the day, lie deep in the ground; but in the night-time, when it is cool, rise to the surface to refresh themselves in the dew. When frogs, worms, and such other animals are exposed to air warmer than their blood, its influence is counteracted by the same causes which counteract its influence on the human body, the evaporation from the surface of their bodies, and the coldness of their blood. Such accidental exposure happens more frequently to them, than to the human species; and, from the inferiority of their size, they would be sooner heated through, and less able to resist the noxious effects of the hot air, were not their power of resisting it made up in another respect. In such situations, the evaporation from the surface of their bodies is greater; for their skin is more lax, and is always covered with moisture. It is, perhaps, for this purpose also, that it is rough and uneven; which, by extending the surface, causes a greater evaporation.

These may be said to be the means through which the human body is preserved, in nearly the same temperature, when it happens to be placed, for a time, in an atmosphere of a superior degree of heat. They seem to me so adequate to this effect, that I would even venture to impute the increase of the temperature of the body, from 96 to 100 degrees, which happened in the experiments, rather to the acceleration of the blood, than to the influx of heat from the external air. While the cause of animal heat remains unknown, it would be presumption to assert, that these are the only means, by which the body is enabled to resist the effects of external heat. There may be others; and it is not unreasonable to suppose, that as external cold, perhaps by its tonic influence, increases the power of the body to generate heat, so external heat may diminish that power, and thus lessen the quantity of heat generated within, while the evaporation, produced by the same cause, guards it against receiving any accession from without.

On the Advantages of LITERATURE *and* PHILOSOPHY *in general, and especially on the consistency of* LITERARY *and* PHILOSOPHICAL *with* COMMERCIAL PURSUITS. *By* THOMAS HENRY, F.R.S. *Read October* 3, 1781.

> To either India see the merchant fly,
> Scar'd at the spectre of pale poverty!—
> See him with pains of body, pangs of soul,
> Burn thro' the tropic, freeze beneath the pole!
> Wilt thou do nothing for a noble end,
> Nothing to make philosophy thy friend?
> Pope's Imitations of Horace, Epist. I. Book I.

THE pursuit of knowledge, when properly directed, and under due influence, is of the greatest importance to mankind. In proportion as a nation acquires superior degrees of it, her state of civilization advances, and she becomes distinguished from her less enlightened neighbours by a greater refinement in the manners of her inhabitants, and a departure from those ferocious vices, which mark the features of savage countries. Vices she will, indeed, still be addicted to, but of a different complexion from those of her more uncultivated days. Wherever a love of learning and the arts makes any considerable progress, even crimes themselves lose something of their atrociousness, and, though still offensive, are divested of those strong marks of brutality, which generally accompany ignorance. The horrors of war itself are softened: an enemy is treated with humanity and kindness: the milder virtues find admittance amongst the clash of arms; and men, when compelled to hostilities, seek victory not to *enslave* or destroy, but in the moment of triumph seek opportunities to evince their clemency and generosity to the vanquished foe.

That this picture is not too strongly coloured will appear from an appeal to history. In the earlier ages, we see a conquering army hurling destruction and desolation, murder and rapine around them, and with unrelenting fury, scarcely distinguishing between friends and enemies. In these more polished times, and the polish may be fairly attributed to the diffusion of learning and philosophy, such cruel excesses are discountenanced and prohibited by the general consent of every civilized people.

Nor are these improvements confined to national manners: those of individuals have been equally benefited. The natural tendency of a cultivation of polite learning, is, to refine the understanding, humanize the soul, enlarge the field of useful knowledge, and facilitate the attainment of the comforts and accommodations of life.

How great is the contrast between the characters of the elegant scholar, and the man whose uncultivated mind feels no restraint, but those which

the

the laws of his country impose! A taste for polite literature, and the works of nature and of art, is essentially necessary to form the Gentleman, and will always distinguish him more completely from the vulgar, than any advantage he can derive from wealth, dress, or titles. These external decorations, without those refined manners which proceed from a proper study of books and men, serve only to render his ignorance more conspicuous; whereas a man of a polite imagination, not only secures himself a favourable reception in the world, but as Mr. Addison observes, " is let into a great many pleasures, that the vulgar are not capable of receiving. He can converse with a picture, and find a companion in a statue. He meets with a sweet refreshment in a description, and often feels a greater satisfaction in the prospect of fields and meadows, than another does in the possession. It gives him a kind of property indeed in every thing he sees, and makes the most rude and uncultivated parts of nature administer to his pleasures."*

Affluent circumstances and abundant leisure give the Gentleman great advantages over his inferiors, in the more refined studies. The cold and heavy hand of poverty chills and represses the efforts of genius; wealth cherishes, and, if I may be allowed the metaphor, *manures* and

---

* Spectator, No. 411.

pushes

pushes it forward to maturity. Sometimes, indeed, in so rich a soil, weeds will spring, which, if not timely rooted up, may endanger the safety and health of the nobler plant. But a careful cultivator will exterminate them early, and sedulously prevent their deleterious effects.

The importance of the Gentleman will still rise higher, his mind be enlarged, and his pleasures be increased, if, to the accomplishments of the polite scholar, he add the knowledge of the philosopher, and endeavour with a noble ambition,

> Thro' vast immensity to pierce;
> See worlds on worlds compose one universe;
> Observe how system into system runs,
> How other planets circle other suns.*

Descending from this stupendous elevation, he will find this globe, which we inhabit, an ample field for physical enquiries. Besides, that man himself is the proper study of mankind, he will find the whole universe replete with subjects for his contemplation. The air, the ocean, the vegetable and animal creation, the surface of the earth, and her most profound cavities to which human industry has reached, will all supply abundant food for his intellectual powers, furnish him with infinite sources of amusement, shew to his wondering eye

> All matter quick and bursting into birth. †

---

* Pope's Essay on Man, Ep. I.   † Ibid.

and teach him to admire that wife, that omniscient Being, whose superintending providence inspects and regulates the whole, even the most minute parts of his creation,

> And sees with equal eye, as God of all,
> A hero perish, or a sparrow fall. *

I believe, few will controvert the advantages I have pointed out, as arising to the Gentleman and professionalist from the study of the Belles Lettres and philosophy; but I am sorry to say, many are the adversaries we have to encounter, if these arguments be extended to another wealthy class of men—The Merchant and Manufacturer. The commercial man, say they, should confine his knowledge to trade. His compting-house should be his study; his ledger his hourly amusement. Gold and silver are the only metals with which he ought to be acquainted; and of these to know no more, than the different coins into which they are formed, and the current price of bullion. For poetry, painting and music he must have no attachment, no taste for engravings, but those of bank bills, and, if a single philosophical idea should ter his head, these inveighers against knowledge would expect to see his name immediately in the list of bankrupts.

* Pope's Essay on Man, Ep. I.

To be serious—So far have these prejudices extended, that many parents entertain the most dismal apprehensions of their sons acquiring a taste for literature, and look on an inclination to natural philosophy as highly dangerous to their progress in trade. Behold, say they, that wealthy manufacturer! Without any knowledge, beyond that of the goodness of his raw materials, and of judging whether his wares were properly fabricated and finished, joined with a tolerable acquaintance with figures, and a most cautious prudence, he has amassed an affluent fortune. On the other hand, see that *man of erudition!* Instead of attending to the manufacture of his goods, his time was employed in reading history; instead of keeping his books, and stating his accounts, he was solving problems in Euclid, or making chemical experiments in order to effect new discoveries, when he might have availed himself of those already made, by the labour and at the expence of others. His refined ideas had taught him that suspicion is mean, and his learning and credulity have plunged him into ruin.

These are specious but deceitful representations. That an imprudent young man may, by devoting those hours to philosophical or literary pursuits which ought to have been given to business, have precipitated himself into poverty and distress, cannot be denied. But the mischief arises, not from a taste for those studies, but from the improper arrange-

arrangement of time. Want of œconomy in this point is equally, if not more injurious, than in pecuniary matters.

It will be also allowed, that the profession in which each individual is engaged, should, next to the more important interests of religion, attract and employ his principal attention. But the mind of man, and especially of young men, must be provided with amusements. The young tradesman of fortune has generally many hours of leisure, and, if amusements be necessary to sooth the rugged paths of business, shall we choose those which lead to dissipation, to extravagance, to vice, or such as tend to civilize the mind and improve the understanding, by developing the operations of nature, explaining the nice connection which subsists between the lowest and higher order of beings,

<blockquote>To man's imperial race,
From the green myriads in the peopled grass;</blockquote>

and tracing the hand of Omnipotence through every link of that

<blockquote>Vast chain of being, which from God began,
Nature's etherial, human, angel, man,
Beast, bird, fish, insect, what no eye can see,
No glass can reach.*</blockquote>

Will not the time he can spare from business be more usefully employed in the study of history,

---

* Pope's Essay on Man, Ep. I.

and the reading of our beſt authors; or at an air pump, an electrical machine, or a microſcope, than, as is too often the caſe with thoſe youths who have not received that culture which their fortunes entitled them to, at the tavern, the gaming table, or the brothel; or, if their minds be not ſufficiently active, and paſſions ſtrong, to impel them to theſe exceſſes, in idleneſs, low company, and mean and degrading purſuits? "There are indeed, but very few," ſays an excellent obſerver of human nature, "who know how to be idle and innocent, or have a reliſh of any pleaſures that are not criminal; every diverſion they take is at the expence of ſome one virtue or another, and their very firſt ſtep out of buſineſs is into vice or folly. A man ſhould endeavour, therefore, to make the ſphere of his innocent pleaſures as wide as poſſible, that he may retire into them with ſafety, and find in them ſuch a ſatisfaction, as a wiſe man would not bluſh to take."

The arguments which have hitherto been adduced in favour of commercial men endeavouring to attain liberal knowledge, have been principally confined to thoſe, whoſe parents have already acquired ſuch fortunes, as raiſe their ſons above the level of the more neceſſitous tradeſman, in whom a greater degree of aſſiduity in buſineſs is neceſſary. But, even in this caſe, if his diligence and application degenerate into an inordinate deſire of accumulating wealth, and this

ruling

ruling paffion be allowed to *conquer reafon*, to suppress every wish of the mind for improving and fitting itself for higher enjoyments in this life, and the participation of still more exalted pleasures in a future state, it then becomes criminal, and ought to be resisted.

But it may be said, that all men are not intended by nature for scholars or philosophers; and that there are stations in life that will not admit of profound study and investigation. Yet there are few, whose minds may not receive a bias to some useful research, whereby they may be pleasingly and usefully employed. And we may be bold to assert, that, though it is not in the power of every man to shine as a distinguished literary character, yet there is scarcely any one so meanly situated, as to render some share of learning inconvenient to him; or who will be a worse man, or a worse member of society, by having advanced a few steps higher in the scale of human knowledge.

> Nemo adeo ferus est, ut non mitescere possit,
> Si modo culturæ patientem commodat aurem.*

It is one thing, to be a *profeffed* scholar or philosopher, and another, to possess such a degree of information on a subject, as is compatible with our other avocations. To be a *complete* astro-

---

* Horatii, Epist. I. Lib. 1.

nomer would almost monopolise the business of a man's life. To procure a *general*, but satisfactory idea of the motions of the planetary system; of the distance of the sun from the earth, and of the yet more immense distance between us and the fixed stars, &c. only a moderate degree of application is requisite.

Among those objects of study which may be recommended to the attention of the young tradesman, some may be considered as ornamental, while others deserve to be classed in a higher rank, with respect to the utility he may expect to receive from the cultivation of them; and of these again, some may be more particularly adapted to some branches of trade than others.

A knowledge of history is an indispensible accomplishment to the opulent tradesman. History has been elegantly and emphatically described by a poet, who is an honour to the age and country in which he writes;

> Nature's clear mirror! life's instructive guide!
> Her wisdom soured by no preceptive pride!
> Age from her lesson forms its wisest aim,
> And youthful emulation springs to fame. *

That of our own country, in particular, should attract the regard of the commercial student. Few histories afford more interesting matter than that of this island. How must the heart of a Briton

* Hayley's Essay on History.

burn

burn within him, when he reads of the glorious struggles which our ancestors, through many ages, have made to secure to us that liberty we now so amply enjoy! How closely should he grasp that inestimable jewel which has been purchased by the blood of so many heroes! How must he glory in that constitution which renders Great Britain the object of universal envy and admiration!

Nor are the objects of history confined to the atchievements of war, the revolutions of governments, and the intrigues of statesmen. The origin and progress of commerce and of arts, come also within her province. And the philosophical historian does not content himself with the mere relation of facts; he endeavours to trace effects to their causes, to shew the principles by which commerce should be actuated; how the various interests, situations and connections of different countries should lead to different kinds of traffic; and in what manufactures the particular genius of a people may fit them to excel. Such disquisitions as these have lately tended to the establishment of a new system which may be, not improperly, denominated commercial philosophy. Here the tradesman is more immediately concerned. These are subjects which come directly within the sphere of his inquiries.

The English Classics will be a rich fund of entertainment and improvement. Shakespeare, Milton, Pope, Addison, Thomson, Gray, Mason, with a long lift of excellent writers in profe and verfe, will yield him charming refrefhments, after the fatigues of the day. He may even indulge himfelf in fweet converfe with the fair fex. A Montague, a Carter, a Barbauld and a Seward, juftly demand his notice, and will prove moft delightful companions, refine his tafte, polifh his manners, and meliorate his morals.

The fciences of Natural Hiftory and Botany require fo much time to be devoted to the ftudy of them, and fuch minute inveftigation, that, however *pleafing*, they may be juftly confidered as *improper* objects for the man of bufinefs to purfue *fcientifically*, fo as to enter into the exact arrangement and claffification of the different bodies of the animal, vegetable, and mineral kingdoms. But reading, and perfonal obfervation, will fupply him with ample matter for reflection and admiration. He will fee the great univerfal caufe actuating every part of nature. He will fee animals, which a lefs accurate obferver beholds with the moft contemptuous eye, executing works far above human abilities to perform. He will behold them acting, and conducting their affairs, with a prudence and forefight, which, whether it be the effect of reafon or of inftinct, may juftly humble the pride of human wit. With what attention has Providence beftowed, on the various claffes of animals, thofe endowments which are particularly adapted to

their

their respective functions! Perhaps man, that lord of the creation, as he vainly boasts himself, is indebted for many useful lessons to very inferior animals. The voice of Nature is thus described as crying out to him,

> Go from the creatures thy instruction take;
> Learn from the birds what food the thickets yield;
> Learn from the beasts the physic of the field;
> The arts of building from the bee receive;
> Learn of the mole to plow, the worm to weave;
> Learn of the little nautilus to sail,
> Spread the thin oar, and catch the driving gale.

But several branches of Natural Philosophy seem peculiarly adapted to fill up the vacant hours in which the tradesman can withdraw from his employments. A general knowledge of all will tend to open and enlarge his understanding, at the same time that it affords him the most rational amusement. While the study of some, *in particular*, may not only tend to effect these desirable purposes, but supply him with a kind of information which may turn to good account, by furnishing him with the means of extending his commercial concerns, and conducting them to greater advantage; of improving those manufactures in which he is already engaged, or inventing new fabrics, which may give additional life and spirit to trade.

As Pneumatics, or the doctrine of the nature and properties of air, display an ample field of investigation to the philosopher, so will they also supply to the more superficial inquirer much instruction and entertainment. Every man is interested in the properties of a fluid to which he is so intimately related, and without which, he cannot subsist a moment. Its various degrees of gravity, elasticity, heat, moisture, and purity, all affect the human race. Many of the most dire diseases which affect mankind, are occasioned by noxious impregnations of the atmosphere, or cured by more favourable states of it. And many of the operations of nature and art are essentially influenced by the changes which are continually occurring in it.

Philosophy has lately made most rapid advances in discovering the constitution of common air. The ingenious Dr. Priestley has even taught us the art of fabricating it artificially, of producing it in a degree of purity far exceeding that of the most salubrious climate, and of reducing it to the state in which we commonly breathe it when debased by exhalations from the various bodies which it surrounds. From him we have also learned a mode of judging of the different degrees of purity in air, by means of the eudiometer, as of its gravity and heat by the barometer and thermometer. This excellent philosopher, to whom, as a learned foreigner has observed, "Nature takes delight in revealing her secrets," has also first discovered, and Dr. Ingenhouse, treading in his paths, has more completely

completely demonstrated the method by which Nature makes use of the leaves of vegetables to purify the atmosphere, when contaminated with putrid or phlogistic vapours. When in this state, every leaf acts as a strainer to the air, imbibing and applying to the nurture of the plant, such parts as are unfit for animal respiration, and throwing it out again, thus filtered and suited to act again as a menstruum for the phlogiston, which is continually evolving by the breathing of animals, the corruption of vegetables, and by the many various processes which are by nature and by art continually carrying on.

Electricity is another branch of science which has afforded great light to the operations of nature. A knowledge of its leading principles, and a dexterity in making a number of entertaining experiments, may be attained by moderate application, and thereby, a field of amusement opened to the mind, at an easy expence of time and money.

To obtain a perfect acquaintance with the science of Optics, much attention and close application would be requisite. Such a knowledge of it, however, as is sufficient for general purposes, is easily arrived at. The nature of the reflection and refraction of the rays of light, of vision, and of colours, the properties of lenses, are useful and entertaining objects of inquiry. But the very minute divisibility of the rays of light fills the mind with astonishment. When we are informed, that there proceeds more than 6,000,000,000,000, times as many particles of light from a candle, in a second of time, as the whole earth contains grains of sand, supposing each cubic inch of it to contain 1,000,000; when we are told, that light in its passage from the sun to the earth, moves with the immense velocity of 95,173,000 miles in seven minutes and a half, we are impressed with the most profound veneration for that Almighty Being, who has so wisely adjusted the proportions between the bulk and velocity of these rays, as to make them answer all his benevolent intentions to mankind; whereas, an increase or decrease in the one or the other, might have been fatal to the animal and vegetable world.

By the Telescope and Microscope our eye is enabled to reach far beyond the limits of our natural vision. By the former, objects, at considerable distances, are brought, as it were, within our grasp, and we can soar upwards into other worlds. By the latter, we are impowered to search into the minutiæ of nature, to admire the delicacy of her operations, and the wonders of creation, exhibited in the perfect fabrics of the smallest animals and plants.

The acquisition of knowledge in the sciences which we have already recommended, may perhaps be considered rather as amusing and ornamental,

mental, than necessary. But there are other branches of natural philosophy which may be deemed highly useful and important to commercial men. These are Geography, Mechanics, and Chemistry.

Geography is so closely connected with commerce, that it would be almost as great a reflection on the merchant to be ignorant of it, as of the rules of Arithmetic. Shall the man, whose vessels traverse every quarter of the globe, be unacquainted with its form, its motion, its divisions, its kingdoms, seas, rivers, lakes, islands and mountains? Shall he be uninformed of the nations and people with whom he traffics, their persons, manners, customs, governments and religion? Are not the flux and reflux of the tides, the situation and course of currents in particular seas, and the direction of those winds, which prevail in certain seasons and latitudes, phenomena, into the nature and causes of which he is interested to inquire? And, above all, should he not endeavour to know the produce of every country, and the articles, which, not being supplied in their own climate, may be most acceptable objects of commerce to the inhabitants?

The remaining branches come more immediately within the province of the manufacturer. Manufactures bear so intimate a relation to the Mechanical Powers, as to be incapable of subsisting, in any degree of vigour, without their support. How tedious, how expensive, and how imperfect would many operations be found, if performed by the mere efforts of human strength, or manual skill, unassisted by mechanical aid! The mechanic powers facilitate their performance, and render their products more complete. How much do we owe to them for the improvement and extension of the manufactures of this town! I am addressing a society, *all* of whom are daily eye-witnesses of the beneficial consequences which have arisen from these improvements; *some* of whom are reaping the fruits of them. It would be superfluous, it would be impertinent to enlarge on the subject: for it must be evident, that as mechanics are so essentially necessary to manufactures, a knowledge of their principles must be useful to every man engaged in such branches of trade.

With mechanics, Hydrostatics and Hydraulics are so closely connected, that a knowledge of them may be considered as a necessary adjunct. For, on the principles of these sciences often depends the first movement of the most complete machines; and fire and water engines, mills, aqueducts, pumps, and other mechanical structures, can only be brought into action by their assistance.

Nor is the utility of Chemistry more confined, or less connected with manufactures, than mechanics.

chanics. Indeed chemiſtry may be, not improperly, called the corner ſtone of the arts. They not only are ſupported by her, but many of them derive their very exiſtence from this ſource. She even furniſhes inſtruments to every one of the branches of natural philoſophy we have enumerated. The truth of this propoſition will be evinced, when it is conſidered that metals cannot be ſeparated from their ores, nor glaſs produced without her aid. She ſupplies the aſtronomer with his lenſes, and the mathematician with his inſtruments. The air pump, electrical, hydroſtatical and hydraulic machines cannot be conſtructed without her intervention; and ſcarcely a piece of mechaniſm is formed, to which ſhe does not contribute ſomething.

In the finer arts the influence of chemiſtry is very conſpicuous. To her the painter owes moſt of thoſe colours, by which he is enabled to give the reſemblances of diſtinguiſhed perſonages to the inquiring eye of a grateful poſterity; to place before their view, more clearly than words can expreſs, the martial deeds of the hero, and the firm virtue of the patriot; and to repreſent thoſe beauteous ſcenes of nature, to the deſcription of which, language is inadequate. Without chemiſtry, the fine colouring of a Titian could never have delighted the enraptured beholder. Nay, even the works of the philoſopher, the

hiſtorian

historian and the poet, are indebted to her for their diffusion and permanency.

To shew the advantages arising from this science in all the arts through which they might be traced, would carry me far beyond the limits of my present design. It may be sufficient to point out the connection which subsists between chemistry, and those manufactures which are the pride and glory of this respectable commercial town.

Bleaching is a chemical operation. The end of it is to abstract the oily and phlogistic parts from the yarn or cloth, whereby it is rendered more fit for acquiring a greater degree of whiteness, and absorbing the particles of any colouring materials to which it may be exposed.

The materials for this process are also the creatures of chemistry, and some degree of chemical knowledge is requisite to enable the operator to judge of their goodness. Quick-lime is prepared by a chemical process. Pot-ash is a product of the same art; to which also vitriolic, and all the acids owe their existence. The manufacture of soap is also a branch of this science. All the operations of the whitster; the steeping, washing and boiling in alkaline lixiviums; exposing to the sun's light, scouring, rubbing and blueing are chemical operations, or founded on chemical principles. The same may be be said of the arts of dying and printing, by which those beautiful colours are impressed on cloths, which have contributed so largely to the extension of the manufactures of this place. How few of the workmen, employed in them, possess the least knowledge of the science to which their profession owes its origin and support! If random chance has stumbled on so many improvements, what might industry and experience have effected, when guided by elementary knowledge? The misfortune is, that few dyers are chemists, and few chemists dyers. Practical knowledge should be united to theory, in order to produce the most beneficial discoveries. The chemist is often prevented from availing himself of the result of his experiments, by the want of opportunities of repeating them at large: and the workman generally looks down with contempt on any proposals, the subject of which is new to him. Yet under all these disadvantages, I believe it will be confessed, that the arts of dying and printing owe much of their recent progress to the improvements of men who have made chemistry their study. Much however remains to be done; and perhaps in no respect are the manufactures of this country more defective than in the permanency of their colours. Sensible as our manufacturers are of this defect, is it not strange, that so few of them should attempt to acquire a knowledge of those principles which would

would most probably supply them with the means of improving and fixing their dyes?

This subject would afford matter for very extensive disquisition; but I fear I have already trespassed on the patience of the society. Suffer me, therefore, only to request your indulgence while I point out one other source of improvement and pleasure, consistent with the pursuits, and frequently advantageous, and even necessary to the business of the tradesman.

A taste for the Polite Arts, especially those of drawing and design, should appear a desirable acquisition to the manufacturer of the finer and more elegant wares. If not possessed of this, he is always dependent on others for the patterns of his fabrics. Whereas, were he capable of inventing them himself, he would possess considerable advantages over his less accomplished neighbours. His imagination would continually supply him with something new; and of what importance novelty is, in these times of fashion and fancy, every day's experience furnishes convincing proofs. It is this supereminent taste that has distinguished the productions of a Wedgwood and a Bentley above all their competitors in the same line of business. Such a taste would doubtless be equally beneficial to the manufacturer of the fine cotton and silk goods of Manchester; and he would be enabled to equal in elegance of pattern, as he excels in strength of fabric, the manufactures of our neighbouring and inimical rivals.

On Crystallization. *By* Alexander Eason, M. D. *Read November* 14, 1781.

ALTHOUGH Nature always acts by general and not by partial laws, yet the particular mode of her operations is frequently removed beyond the limited powers of the human understanding. The truth of this observation is strongly confirmed by all the phenomena in the crystallization of salts and other substances, which, under proper circumstances, never fail to shoot into masses or crystals, with more or less regularity, according to the manner in which the process may have been carried on.

Most bodies, during their passage from a fluid to a solid state, seem to discover a tendency to form themselves into regular masses of a constant or given form. This tendency is highly conspicuous in the various kinds of saline substances, and perhaps is dependent on a law of nature which exerts itself, in a more general manner, than philosophers are apt to imagine.

To me it seems highly probable, that the crystallization of salts, the freezing of water, the formation of precious stones, basaltes, &c. are all the effects of the same cause; and if we conjecture that the setting of metals is a species of crystallization, we shall not be wide of the truth. This much is certain, that all the semi-metals, when broken, discover a laminated texture, and in each particular metal these lamina are always of a given or constant form.

That we may, therefore, proceed with due perspicuity, it will be necessary to take a nearer view of the subject, and to consider, shortly, the phenomena attending the crystallization both of simple and compound bodies. The crystallization of a simple crystallizable body may be affected merely by removing the cause of its fluidity, since by this means, its component parts will have an opportunity of arranging themselves into masses more or less regular and transparent, according to the nature of the body, and the law of its crystallization.

The least reflection will serve to discover, that bodies may be converted from a solid to a fluid state, in two different ways, viz. either in the way of solution, or fusion by heat.

Of the first, we have endless examples from the solution of salts in water, and other fluids; and the second may be very well illustrated by the process of making glass.*

* In the LXVI. vol. of the Phil. Transf. No. 34, Mr. Keir gives an account of glass forming crystals when it passes from a fluid to a solid state by slow degrees.

In the first of these cases, the crystallization is carried on by the separation of the fluid which keeps the crystallizable body in a state of solution; and in the second, the same effect is produced by the cooling of the materials, or the extraction of their heat. If, for instance, a solution of the fossil fixed alkali in water be first evaporated to a pellicle, and afterwards be suffered to cool gradually, without being disturbed, the salt will shoot into beautifully transparent crystals; and in like manner, if water be deprived of that degree of heat which is requisite to preserve it in a fluid state, it will shoot into radii or needle-like crystals, which, at their union, form constant angles of 60 degrees. If, however, the water in the first case, and the heat in the second, be separated with too much rapidity, the crystals will be small, and more or less irregular, according to the celerity with which the process may have been conducted. The same observations are equally applicable to all bodies of the crystallizable kind.

Although, in general, every crystallizable substance discovers a manifest tendency to shoot into masses or crystals of a peculiar form, yet we must here observe, that the forms of those crystals are liable to great variation from various circumstances attending their formation.

Gypsum, for example, is well known to be a vitriolic salt with a calcareous basis, and yet
the

the substance is presented to us by nature in five different shapes, to each of which naturalists have given different names; first, the Lapis Specularis. 2dly. Striated Gypsum. 3dly. Gypseous Alabaster. 4thly. Selenites, properly so called. 5thly. A Gypseous Spar, frequently found adhering to the sides of veins in mountains, particularly those inclosing the ores of metals. All these substances when chemically examined, exhibit precisely the same phenomena, and are, in reality, nothing but different crystallizations of the same compound salt.*

Besides the gypsums, there is another substance, which though classed by naturalists with earthy bodies, is nevertheless a compound salt, and, like the gypsums, has a natural tendency to crystallize or shoot into masses of regular forms. This substance strongly promotes the fusion of earthy substances, particularly these of the calcareous and argillaceous kind, and on this account is generally denominated a fluor or flux, but,

---

* La nature fournit beaucoup de matiere saline de même espece que celle dont nous parlons (viz. selenite) mais qui a differentes formes, & à laquelle les naturalistes ont donne differentes noms comme gypse ou miroir d'Ane, pierre a platre, albâtre, spath gypseux, &c. mais toutes ces matieres sout un seul & meme sel, & nous les considererons comme telles.

Chymie Experimentale & Raisonneè, par Mr. Baumé, Tom. I. p. 154.

in England, is better known by the name of Derbyſhire Spar. All the bodies belonging to this claſs have lately been ſhewn to conſiſt of a calcareous earth, and an acid of a very peculiar nature, which has the property of corroding glaſs, and of converting water into flint. Flint, therefore, is probably not a ſimple earth, as philoſophers have generally ſuppoſed, but a compound ſubſtance, conſiſting of water, and this lately diſcovered acid.

The vitrifiable, or flinty earths, bear, neverthelefs, ſtronger marks of a ſimple ſubſtance, than any body hitherto known; and we are now certain, that it forms the baſis of rock cryſtals,* and a part of the whole tribe of precious ſtones, except the diamond. All theſe ſtones have evidently been formed by the cryſtallization of the matters which enter into their compoſition; and all the phenomena relating to their figure,

---

* Il feroit d'ailleurs difficile de pénetrer aſſez profondement dans l'intérieur du globe pour recueillir de la terre primitive, & qui n'auroit eprouvé aucune alteration. Il paroît certain, que ſi l'on pouvoit ſe procurer de cette eſpece de terre, & un degré de feu ſuffiſant pour la faire entrer en fuſion, on la reduiroit en une maſſe auſſi belle que le beau cryſtal de roche, & qu'on ne pourroit diſtinguer l'un de l'autre.

Chymie Experimentale & Raiſonneé, par Mr. Baumé, Tom. I. p. 104.

transparency, &c. bear a strong analogy to those of the saline crystals already described.

Each saline substance, of which there is a great variety, shoots, as already observed, into crystals of a figure and degree of transparency peculiar to itself: and the same thing is true, in general, with regard to gems or precious stones. Thus, the diamond is naturally of one form, the ruby of another, the sapphire of a third, &c. and each of them possesses a degree of transparency different from all the rest.

Among philosophers it has long been a question, from what state the precious stones have crystallized? that is, whether their particles were originally suspended in water, or reduced to a fluid state by the action of a very intense heat? Each of these opinions has been espoused by men of the first abilities and reputation, and several arguments have been urged on both sides of the question.

From analogy, and several facts, which will afterwards appear, there is room, I am persuaded, to conjecture, that all precious stones, with many other mineral bodies, have been originally in a state of fusion, by means of heat, from which they have been formed by the law of crystallization.

Pure vitrifiable earth, indeed, cannot be brought into fusion by the heat of our furnaces; but black flint has been melted without addi-

tion

tion by the concentrated rays of the sun; and, perhaps, there are, or have been, degrees of heat in nature, sufficient to produce the same effect. Is it not possible, that those immense fires, which seem to be the cause of earthquakes and burning mountains, are sufficiently strong to bring into fusion the purest kind of vitrifiable earth? Is it not probable, that from fusions thus effected the whole tribe of precious stones have been formed by crystallization?*

If this conjecture has any foundation in nature, it will enable us to account in a very satisfactory manner for all the peculiar properties observable in this class of bodies. If the melted matter, in which the vitrifiable earth is diffused, be sufficiently fluid, and if the crystallization be carried on with due regularity, the crystals will be well formed, and will exclude from their composition all heterogeneous matters. If, however, the melted matter be too tenacious, or, if the process be carried on with too much rapidity, the crystals will be irregular, and involve in their composition more or less heterogeneous matters, according to

* The difficulty of accounting for the fusion of the earth, constituting the precious stones, is obviated by the experiments of the celebrated Bergman, whose analysis of these substances had not been seen by the author, at the time of writing this paper: For, from these it appears, that the gems contain not only vitrifiable, but argillaceous and calcareous earth.

circumstances, which need not be mentioned.* Thus, for instance, an admixture of metals may give to the crystal different colours, such as the ruby, the emerald, the topaz, or the amethyst;† and, when the crystal is perfectly pure, it constitutes the colourless rock crystal.

Is not this hypothesis strongly supported by the dissipation of the colours of the precious stones? And is not the restoration of those colours a striking proof, that this hypothesis is founded in nature?

Three principles, at least, seem to enter into the composition of precious stones, viz. vitrifiable earth, the metallic calces on which their colours depend, and the particular matter determining the figure into which they crystallize; the variety of which might be instanced by several examples. The presence of the principle just mentioned is still further indicated by the different degree of hardness observable in precious stones. The rock crystal, although as colourless and transparent as the purest diamond, is, nevertheless, the

---

* When crystals are found irregular and not pure, the vulgar expression is, that they are not ripe; but the truth is, they never could ripen, though left to the end of time, on account of some heterogeneous matters having entered into their composition.

† Bergman has shewn that all these colours may be imparted to gems by iron only.

softest of the whole class to which it belongs.*
Had these facts been sufficiently attended to, the component parts of precious stones had probably been better understood, and the different figures of these substances might have been shewn to have proceeded from one constant and permanent law of crystallization.

But, be this as it may, the principles already in our possession are sufficient to support a rational theory, not only of the formation of precious stones, but also of those substances known by the name of pebbles. Many substances which, under proper circumstances, shoot into crystals of the most regular form, concrete into disorderly masses, when the process is carried on with too much precipitation. Have we not reason therefore to conjecture, that pebbles, agates, and even common flint are the products of some such irregular crystallization? This may be exemplified in the pebbles found among the rocks of Arthur's seat near Edinburgh, which are a vitrifiable matter, mixed with different heterogeneous substances, from which a variety of colours and irregular shapes is produced; and the rocks,

* The topaz seems to be an exact rock crystal with a yellow colour, probably from the calx of some metal; it is a prism of six irregular sides. I have seen some of them of a very large size; many are found in the mountains of Scotland, and, sometimes, at the foot of mountains, buried in the earth, having been washed down by the rains.

where the pebbles are found, seem to have derived their origin from lava or volcanic matter.*

That the effects of volcanos are more extensive than philosophers, till of late, have been aware of, will, I am persuaded, be readily acknowledged; and by the help of many observations lately made, we are enabled to account for various phenomena, which otherwise, must have remained for ever unintelligible to the human species. Of these, however, we shall only take notice of those columnar pillars called Basaltes, or Giant's causeways. If we carefully attend to all the phenomena, observable in these productions of nature, we shall find reason to conclude, that they are nothing more than crystallizations of lava or matter, brought into a state of fusion by the heat of subterraneous fires.

If ever it could be said, that nature seemed to imitate art, it is in the formation of the Giant's causeways in the north of Ireland, where every pillar appears to have been hewn by an artist, and placed so close to each other, as scarce to admit a pin betwixt them. Their general figures are pentagons, hexagons and heptagons. Pillars with more sides are to be met with; their sides, however, are by no means equal. Each pillar, according to its number of sides, must be surrounded

---

* Quere, what is the reason why flint is generally found among chalk or calcareous earths?

by a like number of pillars, which differ from each other both in shape and in size, as not any two of them have been found alike in every respect. These pillars are moreover divided into joints, at unequal distances, which, by the assistance of a crow of iron, may be forced asunder; and, what is very remarkable, a pillar, separated at those joints, always shews one end convex, and the other concave; the convexity being sometimes turned from, and, sometimes, towards the horizon; but, in any single pillar, the direction is always the same.

Have we not every reason to conclude, that the island of Staffa, and the Giant's causeways have been productions of volcanic matter, made liquid by some subterraneous fire, and, as soon as it cooled by slow degrees, crystallized into that form which they now exhibit? Had the separation of these pillars been owing to accident, they would have appeared like cracks in the earth, formed during a very dry season, without order, beauty or regularity; whereas the reverse is very conspicuous.

By attending to the facts and observations already related, it will, I am persuaded, appear, that the setting of metals is, in reality, a species of crystallization. This idea is strongly confirmed, by the laminated texture which all the semimetals discover, when broken in any direction. The needle-like crystals, so conspicuous in crude antimony, clearly shew, that this substance, during its formation, has been acted upon by some cause, either the same, or some other, very analogous to that, by which the precious stones, basaltes, &c. are made to crystallize.* The same thing is true with respect to bismuth; and even pure silver, during its passage from a fluid to a solid state, discovers a tendency to form on its surface a number of striæ, which no doubt proceed from a disposition of the metal to crystallize, or arrange its particles in a particular order.

The expansion of water, during its freezing, is now universally allowed to be occasioned by the crystallization of its parts. And, to me, it seems probable, that the expansion of bismuth and iron, in similar circumstances, proceeds from the same cause.†

Lead ore, when tolerably pure, is generally found in masses of a cubic form; though, sometimes, in shape of prisms. Perhaps this variety is

---

* I observed at Warrington (where copper ore is smelted) the dross and flux which swim on the top of the metal in the furnace in a liquid state, are cast into moulds in shape of a double cube; these masses, when cold, very much resemble lava or volcanic matter, and, when broken, evidently shew a crystalline appearance in many parts, especially about the corners.

† Figures cast from melted iron are always very sharp, because that metal expands as it cools, by which means the whole dye or mould is completely filled.

owing to the proportion of silver contained in the ores.

Some writers affirm, that native gold has been found in a crystallized state, and the form it assumes is that of a prism of eight sides.

With these observations I shall conclude this paper, which has been extended to an unreasonable length, for which, I hope, the importance of the subject will plead my excuse.

On the PRESERVATION *of* SEA WATER *from* PUTREFACTION *by Means of* QUICKLIME. *By* THOMAS HENRY, F.R.S. *to which is added, an Account of a newly invented Machine for* IMPREGNATING WATER *or other* FLUIDS *with* FIXED AIR, &c. *communicated to Mr. Henry by* I. HAYGARTH, M.B. F.R.S. *Read November* 21, 1781.

IT has been frequently remarked by chemical and philosophical writers, that a new experiment is seldom made in vain. Though the operator may even fail of attaining the immediate object of his pursuit, he may yet, fortuitously, acquire the knowledge of some new fact, which may be productive of improvement and advantage to science.

About the time I published my Method of preserving water, at sea, from putrefaction, &c.* a Gentleman, who had obtained a quantity of sea water, for the purpose of bathing a child, complained to me that it soon became putrid, and requested that I would think of some expedient to preserve it.

The principal salts contained in sea water are, 1st. common marine or culinary salt, compounded of fossil alkali and marine acid; 2dly. a salt formed by the union of the same acid with magnesian earth; and lastly, a small quantity of selenite. The quantity of saline matter contained in a pint of sea water, in the British seas, is according to Neuman, about one ounce in each pint.† When this water is slowly evaporated, the common salt first crystallizes, and the marine magnesian salt is left in, what is called, the bittern, from which,

---

* An account of a method of preserving water, at sea, from putrefaction, and of restoring to the water its original purity and pleasantness, by a cheap and easy process, &c. London, 1781.

† In Sir Torbern Bergman's analysis of sea water taken up, in the beginning of June 1776, about the latitude of the Canaries, from the depth of sixty fathoms, the solid contents of a pint of the water were

	Grs.			Grs.
Of common salt	$253\frac{6}{11}$	ℨ.	℈.	
Salited magnesia	$69\frac{1}{11}$	or 3		
Gypsum	$8\frac{2}{11}$	5	1	$10\frac{9}{11}$
Total	$330\frac{9}{11}$			

by a subsequent process, the purging bitter salt, commonly named Epsom salt, is obtained. By this separation, the sea or bay salt is rendered much better adapted for the preservation of animal substances, than the salt of the rocks and springs in Cheshire and Worcestershire, where, from what I apprehend, to be a mistaken notion, that this bittern does not exist in the brine, the liquor is so hastily evaporated, that the crystals of common salt retain much of the magnesian salt among them. For the magnesian salt is highly septic, and greatly impairs the properties of the other.*

The two methods which occurred to me, as likely to answer the wishes of my friend, were, 1st. the addition of quicklime, and 2dly. that of common salt. To the trial of the former I was induced by its known antiseptic effects on common water; and, it is ascertained, that a small portion of common salt promotes, whereas a larger retards, putrefaction.

EXPERIMENT I.

To one quart of sea water were added two scruples of fresh quicklime; to another, half an

---

* At some of the works at Northwich, the evaporation is carried on, in so gentle a manner, that large cubical crystals are formed; and the salt thus prepared is said to be equal in strength to bay salt.

ounce

ounce of common culinary salt; and a third was kept as a standard, without any addition. The mouths of the bottles being loosely covered with paper, they were exposed to the action of the sun, in some of the hottest weather of the last summer.

In about a week, the standard became very offensive; and the water, with the additional quantity of salt, did not continue sweet many hours longer; whereas, that with lime, continued many months, without ever exhibiting the least marks of putridity.

It seemed probable, that all, or some, of three changes had been effected by this process. It was suspected, that quicklime might decompose the marine salt, with alkaline basis; a power which it has lately been supposed to possess, under certain circumstances: or that its antiseptic powers might depend on the formation of a lime water; by either of which, a material, and, perhaps, unfavourable, alteration might be produced: or lastly, that the precipitation of the earthy basis of the magnesian salt, by the quicklime, might contribute to the preservation of the sea water.

EXPERIMENTS II. & III.

On submitting the water to which the lime had been added, to the common trials for detecting a disengaged alkali, no signs of such a salt were discovered. And upon blowing into it a long
continued

continued stream of air from the lungs, no precipitation nor cloudiness ensued, as in the case of lime water.

It remained to see, whether the precipitation of the magnesian earth, from its acid, had been effected. Under some circumstances, it has been proved, by the very ingenious Dr. Black, that magnesia will precipitate calcareous earth from acids. As, for instance, if mild magnesia be thrown into a solution of calcareous earth, in marine or nitrous acid, the calcareous earth will be precipitated; the sum of the attraction between this earth and fixed air, and between the magnesia and the acid, being greater than those which subsisted between the magnesia and the air, and between the calcareous earth and the acid. But, if caustic calcareous earth be added to a solution of magnesia in those acids, its affinity to the acid is, in this state, increased, no fixed air attracts it, and it precipitates the magnesia.

EXPERIMENT IV.

To some of the sea water, which had been kept as a standard, some lime water was added, and a turbidness immediately took place, succeeded by a copious precipitation. This, at first, convinced an ingenious Member of this Society, Dr. Eason, who happened to be present, and myself, that we had discovered the manner in which the lime acted, and the reason why no lime water was produced. But, on adding lime water also to some of the sea water which had been preserved by the lime, a cloudiness and precipitation resembling the former took place, and staggered us in our theory; for we imagined, that the portion of quicklime had been sufficient to have precipitated the whole of the magnesia which the water might have contained, and we now suspected, that the solution of the lime, was, therefore, probably prevented by the sea salt.

Other avocations prevented my pursuing the inquiry at that time, but I have since resumed it, and been able to elucidate the whole matter.

EXPERIMENT V.

Into a strong solution of the common Cheshire salt, some lime water was poured. The mixture became turbid, and a white earth was separated, which did not sink to the bottom of the glass, but was suspended, partly, on the surface, and, partly, in the midst of the liquor.

But from whence did this precipitate proceed? Was it the lime thrown down by the salt; or did the lime separate something from the common salt?

EXPERIMENT VI.

To a portion of the same solution, instead of lime water, some drops of a solution of fossil alkali

alkali were added, and the same appearances occurred.

EXPERIMENT VII.

Each of these precipitates were rapidly and wholly dissolved, the greatest part of the water being first poured off, on the addition of a few drops of dilute vitriolic acid. A proof that the precipitated earth was magnesia.

EXPERIMENT VIII.

To determine whether the addition of a portion of bitter purging salt, to a solution of common salt, would prevent the forming of lime water, with an equal quantity of lime to that which had preserved the sea water, I mixed twenty grains of quicklime, seven drachms of common salt, and one drachm of bitter purging salt with a pint of rain water; but no lime water was produced. Whereas, a lime water was formed, by an equal quantity of lime with a pint of rain water, and also with a solution of common salt, from which the earthy matter it contained had been previously precipitated by fossil alkali, and the alkali neutralised by marine acid.

The next question that presented itself to my investigation, was, whether the common Cheshire salt was so impregnated with magnesian salt, as to prevent the forming lime water, with a like quantity of lime, when used in the proportion of an ounce of salt to a pint of water.

EXPERIMENT IX.

These proportions of Cheshire salt, quicklime, and rain water, being mixed, and suffered to stand a sufficient time, the filtered liquor exhibited no signs of being impregnated with unneutralised lime: but, on adding a few drops of lixivium tartari, it instantly became very turbid, and deposited a sediment, which, instead of disappearing on the addition of vitriolic acid, formed a selenite with it, and again settled at the bottom of the glass.

EXPERIMENT X.

Five grains of quicklime, being added to the mixture of the ninth experiment, and the liquor, after due time, being filtered, and subjected to the usual test, exhibited evident marks of having become a lime water.

I now began to suspect, that the portion of quicklime, added to the sea water, in the first experiment, had not been sufficient to precipitate the whole of the magnesia from its acid, and having some of the mixture of that experiment still by me, I again turned my attention to it.

EXPERIMENT XI.

The remaining part of the sea water, to which the quicklime had been added, was about a pint and half. Lime water, being added to a small

part

part of it, the same turbid appearance took place as formerly.

EXPERIMENT XII.

On the addition of another drachm of lime, the water, when filtered, no longer became turbid, on the mixture of lime water to it; but it did not yet exhibit any signs of being itself a lime water. But,

EXPERIMENT XIII.

When I added another drachm of lime, a lime water was formed. For the water now became very turbid, on blowing air into it from the lungs.

These experiments, therefore, not only prove that sea water may be preserved for the purposes of bathing, by means of quicklime, without forming a lime water, but they point out the rationale of this phenomenon; and also instruct us what portion of lime may be used, without a lime water being produced.

It appears that quicklime, dissolved in water, precipitates the magnesian earth from the marine acid, with which it is united in the sea water, and, uniting with that acid, is retained in the water, under the form of a marine selenite. What the water loses, therefore, of one salt, it gains of another. At the same time, the magnesia, being precipitated by a *caustic* calcareous earth, falls in a state similar to that to which it is reduced by calcination, viz. void of fixed air. In this state, I have formerly proved, by a train of experiments, that it is strongly antiseptic.* Being insoluble, the water is preserved without forming any combination with it; and the only alteration that is made in the component parts of the sea water, is, that the earthy marine salt changes its basis of magnesia for one that is calcareous.

We also see, that there are limits to the addition of quicklime, beyond which, we cannot proceed, without forming lime water. The quantity of two scruples, to a quart of sea water, though not sufficient to decompose the whole of the magnesian salt, was yet adequate to the preservation of the water. One drachm more quicklime separated the whole of the magnesia, and, when a further addition was made, a lime water was immediately formed.†

The properties of common salt, as an antiseptic, are greatly weakened by the portion of marine

---

* From these experiments, it appeared, that magnesia alba, while possessed of its fixed air, is highly septic to animal flesh, but antiseptic to bile; whereas, when calcined, and deprived of its fixed air, it is strongly antiseptic both to flesh and bile.
See Henry's Experiments and Observations, p. 58. & seq.

† These proportions may vary, according to the strength of the quicklime employed.

magnesian salt, mixed with it. It is probable, that the marine selenite may be less septic, and less soluble in water, so as to separate, during the evaporation of the brine. If so, the addition of quicklime may be useful, previous to that process at the salt works. But we are so little acquainted with the properties of calcareous salts, that, at present, we cannot determine what might be the effects of such a practice. I propose, however, at some future opportunity, to try, whether the calcareous marine salt will thus separate; and whether it be, in itself, septic, or antiseptic.

Dr. Haygarth of Chester, who is not more distinguished for his extensive knowledge, than for his friendly and benevolent disposition, has lately, in the most obliging manner communicated to me, a description of an apparatus, which he has invented to mix air with liquids. The Doctor apprehended, that this method might facilitate my design of precipitating the lime from water, to which it might have been added on ship board; and, with his usual candour, and generosity, delivered up his invention to my service. The plan is truly ingenious, but I fear, and all my friends, whom I have consulted, agree with me in the apprehension, that the machine would be much two complex to admit of being used at sea. It is capable, however, of being applied to so many useful purposes, that, I trust, the Society will think the communication of this valuable improvement well worthy of their attention.

Description of an Apparatus to mix Air with Liquids.

In the figure, plate 1. an effervescing vessel is represented (at E) in which fixed air is detached from a mixture of calcareous earth, and vitriolic acid, conveyed through the tubes (T *t*) into the air vessel (A). The fixed air, being of greater specific gravity, will fall to the bottom, and expel the common air at the top through the orifice (at O). It may be known when the vessel is full of fixed air, by smelling; or extinguishing a candle at this orifice; or by computing the quantity of vitriolic acid and calcareous earth that will generate a certain quantity of air. A pair of common bellows (at B) with a pipe, a few inches longer than usual and bent, is placed with the vent so as to receive the air pipe (P), and the bellows pipe at (B) is inserted into the top of the water vessel (W). The bellows being worked, the fixed air rises, from the bottom of the air vessel, through the pipe (P *p*) into the vacuum within the bellows, and is impelled, with force, through the bellows pipe (*b*) into the body of the water vessel, filled with lime water, or any other kind of liquid. The air, which is not absorbed by the liquid, rises to the surface in bubbles

bubbles occasioning considerable agitation; and returns into the air vessel through the communication *(cc)*. That portion of fixed air, which is incapable of absorption by lime water, &c. being specifically lighter than the rest, will escape through the orifice (at O) as the fixed air is supplied by the effervescing mixture, but the pure fixed air, thus returned into the air vessel, is again inhaled by the bellows, and blown into the lime water. The air and water vessels, in the model I have had made, are of tin, containing about four gallons a-piece. The orifices (at T, *t*, O, *b*,) are made air-tight, with perforated corks. The tubes (P, *p* and *t*) run down the sides of the air vessels. The tube *(b)* which is a continuation of the bellows pipe, runs down the middle of the water vessel. This pipe might be immersed twelve or thirteen inches into the body of the water, as I have found, that a pair of common bellows, will force air through water, to this depth, with moderate exertion.

In my model, the bellows, contrary to my direction, are of a large size, and there was difficulty in working them, as might be expected, when all the orifices are shut. To obviate this inconvenience, I tied a bladder, full of fixed air, upon the orifice (at O) and opening into the air vessel. By this device, the bellows work with as much ease as in the open air; and the bladder fills and empties exactly like the lungs in respiration.

tion. The tube P, *p* should be of the same diameter as the vent of the bellows, and the communication (C C) should not be of a less size, otherwise the water will rise into the bellows when they are worked.

After this description, it would be superfluous to explain, that, in this process, there would be no loss of fixed air or of time; or to observe, that from the known attraction between fixed air and quicklime, a sufficient quantity of lime water might be freed from lime in a short time, so as to supply a ship's company with little trouble or expence.

On the Nature and essential Characters of POETRY, *as distinguished from* PROSE. *By* THOMAS BARNES, D.D. *Read December* 5, 1781.

TO settle with precision the limits which divide *poetic* from *prosaic* composition, may perhaps appear, at first sight, to be neither very difficult, nor very interesting. As, however, one great object of this society is, the enjoyment of free and friendly conversation upon subjects connected with science, it is probable, that topics, which are not in themselves of the greatest importance, may sometimes open a wider field, than others of more intrinsic excellence. Where much may be said in support of different hypotheses, we may hope for that collision of friendly argument, which may strike out some sparks, both of amusement and information. Thus, a comparatively trifling subject may eventually contribute to the noblest uses, to the exercise of the mental faculties, and to the diffusion of candour, and intelligence. Our time will not be quite mispent, if we can only glean from the topic before us, a single hour's agreeable and literary entertainment.

"Wherein consists the *essence* of POETRY," is a question, which it will not be so easy to answer, as may at first be imagined. Different authors have given very different definitions. Some have denominated it, "The art of expressing our thoughts by fiction." Others have imagined its essence to lie, in "The power of imitation":— and others again, in "The art of giving pleasure." But it is evident, that *fiction*, *imitation*, and *pleasure*, are not the properties of poetry *alone*. Prosaic composition may contain the most ingenious *fables*. It may present the most striking *resemblances*. It may inspire the most sensible *delight*.

Poetry has been generally denominated an ART. HORACE, if he himself gave the title to his own celebrated and admirable poem, has characterized it under that name. The *term* itself (Ποιησις) would naturally lead to the same idea;

idea; for it seems to imply, that labour and ingenuity, the neceſſary companions of *art*, muſt be employed in poetic compoſition. But certainly, it has the neareſt affinity to *ſcience* of any other art; for all its excellence conſiſts, in its preſenting ſcience in a peculiar and engaging dreſs. An *art*, by which ſcience is aſſiſted, and ſentiment exalted; by which the imagination is elevated, the heart delighted, and the nobleſt paſſions of the human ſoul expreſſed, improved, and heightened, will appear important enough, to have its boundaries exactly drawn, and the limits aſcertained, which divide it from its humble neighbour. Or, if this be not poſſible, to have its *general* and *larger* characteriſtics clearly repreſented.

What is it, then, which conſtitutes the poetic eſſence, and diſtinguiſhes it from proſe? Is it METRE?—Or is it ſomething entirely different; ſublimity of SENTIMENT, boldneſs of FIGURE, grandeur of DESCRIPTION, or embelliſhment of IMAGINATION? Let us attend to the arguments, which may be offered on behalf of both theſe hypotheſes.

" *The characteriſtic nature of poetry*, it may be ſaid, *conſiſts, in* ELEVATION OF THOUGHT, *in* IMAGERY, in ORNAMENT."

" For, have there not been real poems formed, without the ſhackle of regular verſe? Poems, which none, but a faſtidious critic, would ſcruple a moment a moment to honour with that name? Is not TELEMACHUS a noble epic poem? For who would dare to degrade it to a lower character? Who would refuse the appellation to, the *Death of* ABEL, which those, who understand the German language, speak of with so much rapture? Or to the *Incas* of MARMONTEL, which the French celebrate, with equal enthusiasm of praise!

"Does not elevation of sentiment of itself produce *modulation* of language? The soul, inspired with great ideas, naturally treads with a lofty step. There is a dignity in all her movements. She declaims, with a measured, solemn, majestic utterance. Her stile is sonorous, and swelling. These attributes indicate; these *constitute* the poet. They give strength and feeling to his compositions. Where *these* are found, who would look for any *higher* claims, before he would confer the palm of poetic honours? Where these are *wanting*, what *other* properties could give, even the shadow of a title? Who would refuse the title of BARD, to the great Master of *Hebrew song*? For what can be more truly sublime, or poetical, than many of the *Psalms* of DAVID? And yet, after the ingenious labours of the learned Dr. LOWTH, the *metre* or *rhythm* has not been exactly ascertained; and probably will not, because it does not exist. The harmony of numbers, of which every ear must be sensible, arises purely from the *native impulse* of a soul, foul, infpired with fentiments, which it could not poffibly exprefs in any language, but what was fervid and poetical.

"By this theory, it may be faid, we account for the common remark, that the *original* language of mankind was poetical: becaufe, in the infancy of the world, every thing would naturally excite admiration, and vehement paffion. Their rude and imperfect fpeech would bear infcribed upon it, the ftamp of ftrong and animated feeling. It would refemble the harangues of Indian orators, at this day, whofe fpeeches are accompanied with tones and geftures, which, to a cultivated European, appear extravagantly pompous. Their lives were full of danger and variety. New fcenes were continually opening upon them. Growing arts and fciences were prefenting new objects of curiofity. Hence, their *feelings* were amazingly intenfe. And hence, their *language* was bold, and poetically fublime. Longinus, in the fragment of a treatife, which is unhappily loft, has this fentiment. "Meafure belongs properly to poetry, as it perfonates the paffions, and their language; it ufes fiction and fable, which *naturally produce* numbers and harmony."

It may be added, in fupport of this definition, "That our own inimitable poet, than whom none feems more to have enjoyed the infpiration of the Mufe, defcribes the poet, as chiefly diftinguifhed by the fervour of Imagination. He does not,
indeed,

indeed, assign him the most honourable company; but he makes ample amends, by a description of poetic fancy, wonderfully brilliant and captivating.

> "The LUNATIC, the LOVER, and the POET,
> Are of *imagination* all compact.
> One sees more devils than vast hell can hold,
> That is the MADMAN: the LOVER, all as frantic,
> Sees Helen's beauty on a brow of Egypt:
> The POET's *eye*, in a fine frenzy rolling,
> Doth glance from heaven to earth, from earth to heaven;
> And, as imagination bodies forth
> The forms of things unknown, the poet's *pen*
> Turns them to shapes, and gives to airy nothing
> A local habitation and a name." SHAKESPEARE.

Who can forbear applying to the *poet*, what has been so justly applied to the great *critic*, lately quoted,

"He is HIMSELF the GREAT SUBLIME he draws!"

"HORACE, likewise, seems to rank himself on this side of the question, in the fourth Satire of his first book, where he endeavours to settle the point of Poetic Characters. He, first, excepts himself from the number of those, to whom he would allow the name of *Poet*; because compositions like his own, "*sermoni propiora,*" do not give a just claim to the appellation. He, then, describes the REAL BARD;

INGENIUM cui sit; cui MENS DIVINIOR, atque os
MAGNA SONATURUM, des nominis hujus honorem.

With respect to himself, and to Lucilius, he tells us, that if you take away the *order* and the *measure*, their verses would become " sermo merus," *mere prose*. Not so, if you take in pieces that line of Ennius,

" Postquam discordia tetra
Belli ferratos postes, portasque refregit."

For then, he exclaims,

" Invenias etiam DISJECTI membra POETÆ!"

The true poetic essence, then, consists in ELEVATION, IMAGERY, and GRANDEUR; to which, *modulation* is no more than an adjunct; necessary indeed, because it, in some degree, necessarily accompanies animated and poetic *sentiment*."

To these arguments, it may be replied:

" That the modesty of HORACE, in excepting himself from the rank and honours of poetic character, will not be admitted, even with respect to those verses, as to which *alone*, he made the exception. For, who has not in every age classed the *Epistles* and *Satires* of HORACE, in the number of *poetic compositions*, though, as he says, his stile only

" Pede certo
Differt sermoni: sermo merus."

" If we adhere rigorously to this definition, shall we not exclude *many* candidates, from whom we should be sorry to pluck the well-earned wreath of poetic fame? All verses, where the subject is *low* or *ridiculous*, as the HUDIBRAS OF BUTLER.

Butler; where it is *simple* and *narrative*, as the Fables of Gay; or even, where it is *plaintive* and *melancholy*, as the Church Yard of Gray, must be banished from the region of the Muse. Parnassus must be, ' all cliff,' without a single *vale* in all its circuit. None must then be deemed a poet, who cannot soar to its loftiest summit, on *Epic*, or *Heroic* wing. If we should form an *index expurgatorius* upon this principle, what havock should we make among the *minor poets*? How many should we exclude, whom every lover of the Muse ranks, with grateful veneration, in the number of her inspired votaries?

"Elevation of sentiment, imagery, and creative fancy, are not to be found in poetry alone. They often belong as much to the *Orator*. For where will you find nobler flights of imagination, loftier sentiments, bolder addresses to the passions, or more animated, we might say, *modulated* language, than in the *Orations* of Cicero; not to mention those of our modern orators, whose eloquence, however, we would not scruple to compare with that of the most admired antients?

"If we might argue from the *name*, poetry, we should naturally conclude, that the antients themselves understood by the term, not those *irregular* modulations, which *naturally* arose from the impulse of strong and impassioned feelings, from grandeur of sentiment, from beauty, or boldness of imagery; but, something more

artificial

artificial and *elaborate*; something, which demanded more effort and ingenuity to *form*, than merely arose from the effusions of a glowing heart?

"Is not, then, the proper and peculiar characteristic of poetry, that METRE or RHYTHM, which the ear so easily distinguishes, and with which it is so unspeakably delighted? Is not this the *great distinction* between the modulation of poetry and prose; that the one, is *regular*, determined by certain *laws*, and returning upon the ear at stated *periods*; whilst the other, has no standard but the *general sense* of harmony, and is infinitely *irregular* and *various*? The imagery or sentiment is a mere *circumstance*, which does not *constitute*, however it may *adorn*, poetic composition. We can suppose nonsense in prose. Can we not equally suppose nonsense in poetry? And yet, shall there not be an *essential difference*, between poetic and prosaic jargon? If so, something else, besides the *sentiment* or *sense*, is the boundary between them. And what is this, but that METRE or MELODY, without which, the language which conveys the loftiest sentiments may be indeed *poetical*, but can never be, POETRY ITSELF."

I shall not pretend to decide, absolutely, upon the strength or weakness of the foregoing arguments. I shall be happy to hear them fully discussed

discussed in the ensuing conversation, from which I promise myself, both instruction and entertainment.

At present, I find myself disposed to rest in some such general conclusion, as the following.

To FINISHED AND PERFECT POETRY, or rather to the HIGHEST ORDER of poetic compositions, are necessary, elevation of *sentiment*, fire of *imagination*, and regularity of *metre*. This is the *summit* of PARNASSUS. But, from this sublimest point, there are gradual declinations, till you come to the region of prose. The *last line* of separation is, that of *regular metre*. And, in common language, not having settled with precision the nature or boundaries of either, we often apply the poetic character with great latitude, to compositions, which have more or less of the preceding qualities, but which are formed into uniform and regular *verse*. Often, the name is given to works, which have nothing to distinguish them, but *mere number*. What *has not* this metrical modulation, we call *poetical*; and what *has* it, we call *prosaic*, solely upon account of the *sentiment*. For poetry and prose, like two colours, easily distinguishable from each other in their pure, unmixed state, melt into one another by almost imperceptible shades, till the distinction is entirely lost. Their *general characters* are widely different. Their *approximations* admit of the nearest resemblances.

With respect to *mere number*, the difficulty is not great, in the present cultivated state of language, for any person, of a tolerable ear, to tag together lines, the music of which shall be flowing and agreeable. Hence, the multitudes of *indifferent poets*, who abound amongst us! But it has been justly observed, that a state of cultivated society is not favourable to those bolder exertions of poetic fancy, which elevate, astonish, and delight the mind.

It has been often said, as we have before remarked, that the *original* stile, both of history and conversation, was poetical. The friends of this hypothesis must mean no more, than that, in early ages, their language was, in general, bold and florid. And we have already observed, that strong conceptions naturally clothe themselves in figurative, and modulated expressions. From *strong*, to *regular*, the transition is not difficult; and the advantage would be great. Uniform metre would give more delight to the *ear*, by rendering the music more perfect; and it would be more easily retained by the *memory*.

We may account for the formation of *regular verse*, on another principle. The same animated feeling, which prompted men to *dance* and *sing*, would also prompt them, to express themselves with energy of *tone*, of *stile*, of *sentiment*. It would lead them to endeavour to adapt their *language* to their *song*. But, in order to this union, it must

muſt become meaſured, and exact. Hence, the early formation of *verſe*, which, when once adopted, would, for the reaſons before mentioned, be immediately employed, to convey their laws, and hiſtories, to future ages. It differed but little from the common ſtile of their orations. At leaſt, the difference was not to be compared with that, which is found in the more advanced periods of ſociety, and of language.

We have already obſerved, that, in the early ages of mankind, when their lives were filled with toils and dangers, and when new and intereſting events were continually opening upon them, their paſſions would correſpond to their ſituation, and would be various, vehement, and active. Civilization and ſcience have, as it were, minced into finer portions, the feelings of the heart. By this means, we enjoy a far *greater number* of pleaſurable ſenſations, and, upon the whole, I doubt not, a much *larger ſum* of happineſs. The life of an Indian conſiſts, either of glare, or of darkneſs. He is either tranſported with paſſion, or ſunk into ſtupor. Theſe larger maſſes have been broken, by the hand of culture, into ſmaller pieces, which are in perpetual currency, and which maintain, among us, a more equal and conſtant enjoyment.

But, from hence it will follow, that the *ſtrong poetic character* may be expected to decline, as TASTE improves. We may, perhaps, hope to excel, in softness, delicacy, and refinement. But these are *feeble* graces. The mind soon tires, with the perpetual chime of smooth versification, and with the unvaried flow of gentle and unimpassioned sentiment. The bursts of honest nature, the glow of animated feeling, the imagery, the enthusiasm—*These* are the charming properties, which will for ever exalt the poems, in which they are found, to the *first order* of poetic excellence. For *these*, no appendages of art can be deemed an adequate compensation.

A writer, whom I cannot mention without great respect, notwithstanding our difference of opinion upon some interesting subjects, seems not to have settled accurately his own idea of poetic essence. Dr. Johnson, *many* of whose criticisms upon the English Poets indicate the strength of judgment, and *some*, the elegance of taste, says, in his life of Milton, " Poetry is the art of uniting pleasure with truth, by calling imagination to the aid of reason." He then mentions the different sciences, of which the Poet should be a master ; history, morality, policy, the knowledge of the passions, physiology. " To put these materials to poetical use, is required, an imagination capable of painting nature, and realizing fiction. Nor can he yet be a Poet, till he has obtained the whole expansion of his language, distinguished all the delicacies of phrase, and all the colours of words, and learned to adjust all these different sounds, to all the variety of metrical modulation." In these last words, *metrical modulation* is supposed to be a necessary adjunct to knowledge, and imagination. In another place, he says, " It is by the music of metre, that poetry has been discriminated, in all languages." And yet he had just before said, " That, perhaps, of poetry, as a mental operation, *metre* or *music* is no necessary adjunct." I am unwilling to draw any other inference from these passages, than this, that, such is the difficulty of settling with precision the poetic essence, even Dr. JOHNSON is inaccurate, and inconsistent.

If, in order to avoid this charge, it be said, that a distinction is made, between poetry, as a *mental operation*, and poetry, as an actual expression of the thoughts in *language*; then it will follow, that a person may be a *mental Poet*, without being a *practical* one; because he may possess imagination, feeling, &c. without being able to express these mental operations, in a proper manner. He may have poetical *ideas*, but not poetical *stile*. And, exactly in the same sense, a man might be an *orator*, or a *painter*, without being able to *speak* in public, or to use the *pencil*.

I beg leave to finish the subject, by a few observations on modulation of language, which have suggested themselves, in the course of the foregoing speculations.

Different languages vary, exceeding widely, in their capability of modulation; and, from this cause, will vary as much, in the *mode* and *character* of their *rhythm*, or musical composition. Every good and rounded stile, in prose, as well as in poetry, has a *metre*, or *music*, which the ear, when at all refined by classical taste, can immediately *feel*, and *enjoy*. There is, in finished composition, as much of melody and sweetness, in the arrangement of *prosaic* syllables, as in the most *poetical*. The ear as nicely discriminates the soft, the plaintive, the bold, the nervous, the elegant, by the flow of *musical expression*, as in the most exact and perfect poem. From this circumstance alone, we are able, at once, to distinguish the stile, of ADDISON, and SHERLOCK, of TILLOTSON and WATTS, and YOUNG. We distinguish them, as easily, as a connoisseur in *music*, who *feels*, at once, the compositions of HANDEL, and those of CORELLI.

It is probable, the ears of the antient ROMANS and GRECIANS were more nicely tuned, to discern the melody of arrangement, and of cadence, than ours. Or, probably, we have lost that "*tune*," or mode of pronunciation, in which their languages were spoken; for a modern ear cannot feel that richness and harmony of numbers, which appears to have been, to them, so inexpressibly delightful. "Cicero tells us, that he was himself a witness of its influence, as Carbo was once haranguing the people. When that Orator pronounced the following sentence; 'Patris dictum sapiens temeritas filii comprobavit,' it was astonishing, says he, to observe the general applause, which followed that *harmonious close*. And he tells us, that, if the final measure had been changed, and the words placed in a different order, their whole effect would have been absolutely destroyed."

This musicalness, and flow of numerous composition, which charms the ear of every judicious reader, is certainly felt most strongly, when it is *read aloud*, with taste and expression. But when *read with the eye only*, without the accompaniment of the voice, there is a *fainter association of the sound*, the *shadow of the music*, as it were, connected with the words; so that, we can judge as exactly of the composition, as if were audible to the ear. This habit, of associating *sound* with *vision*, is formed gradually by habit; for common people, who are not much accustomed to books, hardly understand any thing they read, unless it be accompanied with the *voice*. And some Gentlemen are said to have acquired this art of mental combination so perfectly, as to *read*, even the *notes* of a musical composition, with considerable pleasure.

The difference of modulation in languages, must give a different character and expression to their poetic compositions. The Grecian and

Roman tongues were so happily constructed, that their *verse* easily distinguished itself by its *arrangement*, and therefore needed no secondary or artificial aid. It has been thought, that our English tongue is not equally happy; and that, therefore, *rhyme* is, in general, necessary to make the discrimination perfect, and to give that *chime* or *music* to the ear, which the succession of long and short syllables alone, could not effect. The fact adduced in support of this observation, by Dr. Johnson,* is certainly true; " that very few poems, in blank verse, have long maintained a character among us. Thomson, and above all, Milton, are *great exceptions*, but their stile is singular. They formed themselves upon no model; and are ORIGINALS which we may admire, but ought not to attempt to *copy*."

This remark, though, perhaps, in some degree just, is, however, degrading. And, if the *tag of rhyme* be, in general, necessary to our English poetry, it will be an additional argument in favour of that hypothesis, which supposes METRE to be the grand *criterion* of POETIC DICTION.

Yet, methinks, the Doctor is too severe, when he says, " The variety of pauses, so much boasted of by the lovers of blank verse, changes the measures of an English *Poet*, into the periods of a *declaimer*." To me, there appears a very essential difference,

* Life of Milton.

between

between the pauses of *verse*, and those of mere *declamation*. The poetry of MILTON has been celebrated by the best judges, as inimitably beautiful and harmonious, from the amazing variety, and judicious changes, of the pause. These are so admirably disposed, that the ear hardly ever tires. There is none of that perpetual sameness, and recurrence of sound, which, in common blank verse, is so insufferably disgusting. Surely, the verse of Milton is not, "*verse only to the eye.*" I cannot, therefore, subscribe to Dr. Johnson's sentiment, "that all the power of Milton's poetry consists, in the sublimity of his sentiment, or the peculiar (he elsewhere calls it 'perverse and pedantic') arrangement of his stile." His sentiments are, indeed, lofty and noble. But his *metre* also is inexpressibly rich, mellow, and harmonious. Whichever hypothesis, therefore, we adopt, as to the constituent character of POETRY, that of MILTON will have *every praise*,—of SENTIMENT,—of IMAGERY,—of MODULATION.

On the Affinity *subsisting between the* Arts, *with a* Plan *for promoting and extending* Manufactures, *by* encouraging those Arts, *on which* Manufactures *principally depend. By* Thomas Barnes, D. D. *Read January* 9, 1782.

" Omnes Artes, quæ ad Humanitatem pertinent, habent quoddam commune vinculum, et quasi cognatione quâdam inter se continentur.
Cicero pro Archiâ Poetâ

IT is a question, not only of speculation, but of real importance, " How far is it desirable, that a man of learning shall devote himself to one particular object?" Or, to put it in a different form, " Will not the interests of science be best promoted, by a *more general* and extended application to *different* studies?"

In the life of Dr. Isaac Barrow, we are told, that great man " entered upon studies of different kinds, whereby he could not totally devote himself to one, which would have been more for the public benefit, according to his own opinion, which was; that *general scholars* did more please *themselves*; but that they, who prosecuted *particular* subjects, did more please *others.*"

Whatever

Whatever truth there may appear to be in this sentiment, in some uncommon instances, I persuade myself, it will not, in general, accord with experience. Though every man should have some ONE OBJECT continually in view, to which he should refer all his knowledge, and by which he should direct all his studies; yet, with this aim, let him rove abroad, through the various walks of literature. He will, probably, meet with many things, which he will now apply, with great advantage, to his main subject, and by which he may illustrate, embellish, or extend it. General Science, with this particular application, collects the scattered rays, reflected from a thousand objects, into one focus, and blends all the variegated colours of the rainbow, into one white, and luminous point. Whatever praise may, in particular cases, have been given to the man, who has travelled only in *one* path of Science, his ideas must necessarily be very confined, and he will, probably, fall under the charge of pedantry, and affectation. The Sciences are sisters, *affectionate* sisters! and, as the Roman Orator, in our motto, has beautifully expressed it, " Quasi cognatione quâdam inter se continentur." To be in the good graces of any *one* of them, you must pay some respectful attention to the *rest*.

General knowledge, like the general motion of the various limbs of the body, gives an agility
and

and vigour to every part of the mental frame. The continual, solitary play of one particular limb, may give strength and dexterity to the muscles connected with that limb; but the probable consequence will be, awkwardness and imbecility in all those, which are not brought into action. The mere mathematician, the mere grammarian, or the *mere any thing*, may, perhaps, with microscopic eye, see *one little object* very distinctly. But, if not accustomed to look around him to a wider range of vision, his view will be narrow, and, when he turns from that lucid point, he will be enveloped with darkness. It is, indeed, impossible for the man, whose mind has not been expanded by some love of general knowledge, to appreciate the several sciences, according to their just value, and to assign to each their proportionable share of esteem and consequence. If Monsieur Vestris comprise all human excellence in dancing: if another man look down, with supreme contempt, upon every person, who has not plunged into the depths of mathematical, or metaphysical mysteries, what is the cause? Is it not, the want of some acquaintance with other sciences? This would have enabled him, to range the different branches of knowledge in their proper order, and to apportion to each, their proper share of attention and regard.

But

But we may advance a step further. The MAN OF ONE BOOK, is not likely to *understand* that one book, so well, as the man of more extended study. There is a general analogy and affinity, among all the sciences. In all those which require cultivated imagination, or improved taste, general knowledge is absolutely necessary. To form elegance of mind, there must be, a comparison of ideas, a combination of images, an extension of soul. Hence arise, the sense symmetry, elevation of sentiment, and a capacity to relish the beautiful, and the sublime.

The more abstruse sciences may seem to require *less*, of foreign and adventitious aid. The metaphysician may, like a mole, work under ground, blindfold. Buried, ten thousand fathoms deep, beneath the surface, he may need little the taper of the other sciences. And yet, the fact has often been, and experience confirms it, in many instances, at this day, that those, who have excelled most, even in the *abstruser* parts of literature, have been men of a large acquaintance with knowledge. And, in general, those who have shone with uncommon splendor, in some *one* professional, or favourite science, have been distinguished by an attachment to knowledge, in *all* its branches. NEWTON was not the *mere* astronomer, or calculator; BOYLE was not, merely, the natural philosopher; nor was LOCKE,
the

the mere metaphysician. They had occasionally wandered into the other walks of science, and had brought from thence treasures, to enrich their favourite stores. To these, how many names might be added? Barrow, Haller, Watts—and ONE, whose name I cannot mention, without strong and grateful sensations—the late Dr. AIKIN, than whom few have had mental treasures, more various, or more valuable.*

It is in general said, that the knowledge, which, like the broad stream, flows over a wider surface, must be proportionably shallow; whilst that which runs in the narrow channel, must be deep. But we are deceived by an image. We argue from a fancied resemblance. The mind, long poring upon one object, grows tired, and feeble. It is necessary, sometimes, to change the object, in order to restore its tone and vigour. He, who can thus diversify his pursuits, keeps up the spring and energy of his powers, the

---

* John Aikin, D. D. was Tutor in Divinity at the Academy at Warrington for several years. Though not known to the world at large as an author, his modesty having unhappily prevented him from appearing in print, he was uncommonly revered by all that knew him, for the wonderful extent of his knowledge, for the mild dignity of his character, and for the various excellencies which adorned the Scholar, the Tutor, and the Man. He was the father of Mrs. Barbauld, and of John Aikin, M. D. both of whom are well known in the Republic of Letters.

ardour

ardour of his studies, the keenness of his research. He borrows ideas, images, illustrations, from kindred sciences. His mind widens with increasing knowledge. He sees every subject, as it were, in a larger field of vision. He views it round, in a greater variety of aspects. His soul is expanded, his judgment strengthened, and all his powers assisted, and improved.

But I meant, principally, to extend this sentiment to the ARTS. Though *they* too have a near affinity, yet it is not generally imagined, that, to excel in one art, it is proper a man should have any knowledge of others; especially of those, which appear more remote and unconnected. That a poet should be a painter, or a painter a poet, may seem desirable, from the similarity of taste, of genius, and of imagination, necessary to excellence in these kindred arts. But, in the lower, and mechanic employments, how seldom is it known, that a man, versed in one kind of ingenious labour, has the most distant knowledge of others, even of those, which seem most nearly connected with his own? How many watchmakers know very little of clock-making; though, *here*, the connection is as close as possible? How many machines are used at Birmingham, in the different branches of manufacture carried on there, of which a mechanic at Manchester, even in the *same line*, is entirely ignorant? There are, it is probable, in every *manufacture*, I had
almost

almoſt ſaid, in every *place,* ſome peculiar, and local improvement, which has never yet been extended, beyond the vicinity, where it was firſt invented? Of late, indeed, the ſpirit of enterprize has gone forth, and the inventions, made in *one* manufacture, have been ſometimes transferred to others. The machines for ſpinning cotton, have been applied to woollen, and with great advantage. And, probably, both have been under great obligations to thoſe curious machines, for twiſting and manufacturing ſilk, which have ſo long excited general curioſity, and admiration.

So great is the analogy between the ſeveral arts, that no man knows, to what extent the improvement of any ſingle art may affect others, even where the relation, at firſt ſight, appears moſt diſtant. Who would have imagined, that the diſcovery of the properties of the magnetic needle, would have had ſuch amazing, and almoſt infinite effects? That, by this property alone, navigation ſhould become ſo aſtoniſhingly extended, new continents be diſcovered, and a NEW ÆRA opened, in the hiſtory of the globe! I was, a few days ago, greatly pleaſed with tracing the progreſs of an invention, into ſeveral branches of art, with which, at firſt, it appeared, not to have the moſt remote affinity. I refer to the Cylinder, covered with wire-cloth, of different fineneſs, originally intended only for ſifting flour, meal, and bran,

immediately

immediately as they come from the mill-stone. For this ingenious invention, Mr. Mills got a patent, the term of which is now, probably, expired; for the person who shewed it me, informed me, that he had himself applied the Cylinder, with little variation, in sifting *gunpowder, snuff, tanners' bark*, and *sand*. So that, by this simple, but beautiful discovery, the dealers in all those various articles have reaped already considerable advantage: and how far the advantage *may still* be extended, is as yet unknown. The power of *Steam*, in producing effects, to which hardly any powers of mechanism are equal, has been long observed, in the *Fire-Engines*, in the construction and application of which, Philosophy has lent her aid to Art; and Science has become the tutor, and guide of Genius. But we have not heard, till lately, that this active and potent principle has been applied, in any other instances; though there are many, in which a principle so powerful, and, it is presumed, so manageable, would be of unspeakable advantage. The extension of it to machines, for *spinning cotton*, and for *grinding corn*, is now, I am informed, under the contemplation of different Artists; and, if circumstances favour the execution, will, probably, be accomplished.*

* A machine for spinning cotton has now been worked, for sometime, upon this principle, at Manchester. And the other, for grinding corn, is said to be in considerable forwardness, near Blackfryars bridge, London.

That our manufactures, at present, depend very much upon our machines: that the Cotton Manufacture, in particular, is, under Providence, *entirely* dependent upon them: and, that their *utmost* improvement, to the very highest point, to which it is possible for them to arrive, is, in the present circumstances of trade, very desirable, for the sake of every interest, and of every order of men, dependent upon our manufactures, I will not here attempt to prove. They are positions, denied by none, but the lowest and weakest of the vulgar; where alone such weakness is pardonable. Whatever, therefore, may tend to encourage and assist those arts, by which mechanism may be improved, and our manufactures extended, is a matter of common utility, and importance. The Clergyman, the Physician, the Gentleman, are, I had almost said, *equally* interested with the Tradesman, and the Merchant.

To answer, in some degree, this important end, and to serve, however feebly, this GENERAL INTEREST, I have *imagined* to myself a PLAN, which appeared to me, not impossible to be carried into execution, and important enough to be attempted. It may, possibly, appear to some Gentlemen, an *Utopian* scheme. Many objections may, at first sight, appear to rise against it. But I have all the confidence of a Projector, in saying, that I firmly believe, with proper attention, such as has been paid to other defigns of public utility, it *might* be executed; and, if executed, *muft* be of public advantage; an advantage, which no man can eftimate at prefent, and the full extent of which, perhaps, no man could conjecture.

Before I ftate this *plan*, I will beg leave to make two obfervations, in addition to what has been already faid, on the fubject of improvements in our manufactures. And, firft,

It is now *more* neceffary than *ever*, that our artifts and workmen, in the different branches, fhall be poffeffed of fome degree of *tafte*. And tafte is only to be acquired by that general and mifcellaneous knowledge, which it has been the object of this paper to recommend. Our manufactures muft now have, not merely, that *ftrength* of fabric, and that *durability* of texture, in which *once* confifted their higheft praife. They muft have elegance of *defign*, novelty of *pattern*, and beauty of *finifhing*. To effect thefe, all the aid of improved and refined art is effentially neceffary. The dull plodder, accuftomed to pace round and round, like a mill horfe, is not likely to ftrike out any thing new, and elegant. He may, indeed, adopt the improvements of others: but his will never be the praife, of ferving his fellow-creatures, by any *inventions*, of real importance, and utility.

I would further obferve, that, in the prefent ftate of the Arts, capital improvements are not to be, in general, expected from those, who would, at first sight, appear most likely to make them; I mean, the workmen in different branches of mechanism. Turn your eyes to any of our numerous manufactures. You find every division of mechanical labour, executed by a separate set of workmen. Dr. Smith, in his Wealth of Nations, tells us, "that a Pin goes through *eighteen* several distinct operations," each of which, probably, in a large concern, is performed by a different operator, who, it may be presumed, would feel himself very awkward and unready, if obliged to change employment with any other of his fellow workmen. How many hands concur, in the formation of a Watch, but very few of whom are so well acquainted with the *whole mechanism*, as to be able to put the Watch together, or to calculate the different wheels, of which it is composed.

I imagine it to be owing to this circumstance, that improvements, *upon a larger scale*, such as the invention of great and complicated machines, &c. have generally been made, by persons, *not*, originally *educated* to the profession of those arts, in which they have made such astonishing discoveries. Whilst the regular artists have had their attention fixed upon the little points, and ramifications of art, in which indeed they have become astonishingly perfect, the others, standing more at a distance, have had a wider field, a nobler

nobler object in their view, at once. Hence, their minds have been extended to a *complex whole*, the firſt faint outline of which, they have, by ſlow degrees of patient labour, finiſhed into form and beauty. Hence, almoſt all our late machines have been invented, in a part of the country, where the ſtate of the Arts is not greatly improved, and where original genius is not minced down, to the ſhreds and atoms of a long-eſtabliſhed, and widely-extended manufacture.

It is acknowledged, that mere random genius has made aſtoniſhing diſcoveries and improvements, without any aid, but that of native ſagacity. But, on the other hand, how many minds, capable, with aſſiſtance and encouragement, of producing the happieſt inventions, have, for want of them, pined in obſcurity, loſt to the world, and incapable of any great atchievement? And, we may aſk, what *might* ſuch genius have atchieved, if foſtered by ſcience, by liberality, and by honour!* What Brindley executed by

---

* But knowledge to their eye, her ample page,
  Rich with the ſpoils of time, did ne'er unroll;
  Chill penury repreſſed their noble rage,
  And froze the genial current of their ſoul.

  Full many a gem, of pureſt ray ſerene,
  The dark unfathomed caves of ocean bear;
  Full many a flower is born to bluſh, unſeen,
  And waſte its ſweetneſs on the deſart air.
                         Gray's Church Yard.

the mere dint of natural parts, is no exception to the rule. How much *more* might even HE have done, if affifted by a more entenfive knowledge, and a more liberal education! What, if to genius and application had been added, a larger field of obfervation, a more general acquaintance with the mechanical powers, and with what thofe powers have already done, in the various branches of Manufactures, and of Arts! How much *further* might he have advanced! That human ingenuity is not exhaufted; that machines are not yet carried to their higheft improvement; and that they ought to be encouraged to their very utmoft exertions, none here will queftion.

Let us now apply thefe obfervations. I have ventured to chalk out the *outlines* of a PLAN, the fole object and principle of which is, the improvement of our *Manufactures*, by the improvement of thofe *Arts*, on which they depend. Thofe arts are, CHEMISTRY and MECHANISM. In an excellent paper, read to this fociety fome time ago, it was lamented, "that fo few of our dyers are chemifts, and of our chemifts dyers." We may add, How few of our Mechanics underftand the principles of their own arts, and the difcoveries made in other collateral and kindred manufactures? At this day, I am informed, not a fingle weaver in the Norwich trade underftands the ufe of a *Fly-Shuttle*.

But to proceed to our *Plan*.

The first object of this scheme is—To provide a PUBLIC REPOSITORY among us for CHEMICAL and MECHANIC KNOWLEDGE.

"In order to this, I could wish MODELS to be procured, of all such *machines*, in the various arts, as seem to bear the most distant relation to our own manufactures. All the processes in those of *Silk*, of *Woollen*, of *Linen*, and of *Cotton* should be here delineated. These would make the most necessary, and important parts of this *collection*. But to these might, with great advantage, be added, the astonishing effects of Mechanic Genius in *other* branches, which have not so *apparent* an affinity with our own.

"In this REPOSITORY, let there be, likewise, provided, an assortment of the several *ingredients* used in DYING, PRINTING, &c. for the purpose of *experiments*.

"A SUPERINTENDANT will be necessary, to arrange, and to apply this *collection* to its proper use. He should be a man, well versed in chemical, and mechanic knowledge. And let his province be, at certain seasons, and under certain regulations, to give LECTURES, *advice*, and *assistance*, to those who wish to obtain a better knowledge of these arts.

"Lastly; let the EXPENCE, necessary to open, and to support the scheme, be defrayed by a *subscrip-*

tion: and let every subscriber have the power of nominating *one*, or *more*, to receive the advantages of this Institution."

I mean only to draw the *rudest outline* of the plan, and would leave it to the ensuing conversation to be filled up, with colouring, or shade. By this scheme, properly methodized and conducted, I should hope for *some* of the following advantages.

This MECHANIC SCHOOL would properly *finish* the education of a young Tradesman, or Manufacturer. It would succeed, in its natural order, to the school for *writing*, and *arithmetic*. It would serve as a proper step of transition, from thence to the warehouse; and, perhaps, it might become a regular part of a young Gentleman's preparation for business. How desirable a part it would be, I will not here say. Other Gentlemen present are much better qualified to decide upon the question.

But the *principal* advantage I should propose from this scheme, is this. Here would be a kind of GENERAL ORACLE, which those might consult, who were engaged in mechanical improvements, and who might *here*, at once, gain that information, which it might cost them months and years to obtain, by their own unassisted efforts.

It would be very easy to enlarge, in *theory*, upon the possible, and probable benefits of this Institution.

Institution. But I check myself, hoping to hear, from Gentlemen more conversant with manufactures, their sense of this, it may be, visionary scheme.

Objections will, perhaps, have already arisen, which may appear strong: I hope not unanswerable. That of the *expence*, I cannot allow to be of this number. Nor the difficulty of finding a proper *person*, to superintend the Institution. Nor the *regulations*, necessary to its internal management and conduct. If no objections, stronger than these, be found against it, I shall not deem it altogether Utopian.

Something similar to this has been done, by the SOCIETY OF ARTS. But the two plans are essentially different. THEY give *premiums*: but THEY have no LECTURES, or modes of Instruction. OUR plan would be desirable, in *every large town*, and particularly, in the *center* of *every* important manufacture.

Whilst I was engaged in thinking upon this plan, and, like the Artist, enamoured with its imaginary beauty, I met with the following passage in Sully's Memoirs. My feelings, in reading it, I will not attempt to describe.

He tells us, that, among the great designs of Henry IV. which were prevented from being carried into execution, by the untimely and tragical death of that Great Prince, was the following.

"There was to be, says he, a CABINET OF STATE, in the Louvre, destined to receive, whatever could tend to the knowledge of *Finance*, of *Science*, and of *Art*." After enumerating several of these, particularly relating to the army, such as *lists*, *plans*, *charts*, &c. &c. he adds, "I conceived a scheme, of appointing a large room, as a magazine of *models*, of whatever is most curious in machinery, relating to *war*, *arts*, *trade*, &c. and all sorts of exercises, noble, liberal, and mechanical; that all those, who aspired to perfection, might, without trouble, improve themselves in this silent school. The lower apartments, were to hold the heavy pieces of workmanship; and the higher, were to contain the lighter. An exact inventory of both, was to be one of the pieces of the great cabinet."*

What a pity is it, that this noble plan was not carried into execution! It would not have been the *least* of the imbellishments of the reign of Henry. It would have done honour to the Prince, and to the age.† I mean not to disparage the utility of our modern collections, of *fossils*, *shells*, *mosses*, and *insects*. They are the works of God; and,

---

* Sully's Memoirs, vol. IV.

† I have been informed, that this plan is since carried into execution, in the Palais Royal.

therefore,

therefore, worthy of our highest admiration. But I can easily conceive, that a scheme like this, upon a smaller scale, might possibly be applied to better use, than many of those collections actually serve. In a town like this, the opulence, and even the very existence of which, depends upon manufactures, and these again upon *arts, machinery,* and *invention,* a PUBLIC CABINET, devoted to this purpose, would be at once of general ornament, and utility.

REMARKS *on the different* SUCCESS, *with respect to* HEALTH, *of some* ATTEMPTS *to pass the* WINTER *in high* NORTHERN LATITUDES. *By* JOHN AIKIN, M.D. *Read January* 16, 1782.

THOUGH the *cure of diseases* may, perhaps, most safely be confined to the members of a profession devoted by education and habit to this sole object, yet the *preservation of health* must, in some measure, be committed to the care and judgment of every individual. The discussion, therefore, of any means to obtain this end, divested, as it may be, of technical language and abstruse speculation, cannot fail of being generally

rally interesting. The most remarkable and useful account of success in this important point, perhaps any where to be met with, has been afforded by that celebrated and much-regretted navigator Captain Cook; an account which was justly thought worthy of the most honourable approbation a Philosophical Society could bestow. From similar sources, relations of voyages and travels by plain, unprejudiced men, I have collected some other facts, probably at present forgotten or disregarded, which appear to me capable of suggesting several striking and important observations relative to the preservation of health in particular circumstances. These, with a brief commentary and some general reflections, I beg leave to submit to your consideration.

Towards the beginning of the last century, several voyages of discovery were made in the Northern Seas; and the Greenland whale-fishery began to be pursued with ardour by various European nations. These two circumstances have given rise to various instances of wintering in the dreary and desolate lands of high northern latitudes; and the surprizing difference of success attending these attempts must strike every reader.

The first remarkable relation of this kind that I have found, is that of the wintering of Captain Monck, a Dane, in Hudson's Bay, latitude

latitude 63°. 20'. He had been sent on a voyage of discovery with two ships, well provided with necessaries, the crews of which amounted to sixty-four persons. The ships being locked up in the ice, they landed, and erected huts for passing the winter, which they occupied in September, 1619. At the beginning of their abode here, they got abundance of wild-fowl, and some other fresh provision; but the cold soon became so intense, that nothing further was to be procured abroad, and they were obliged to take to their ship-stores. The severity of the cold may be conceived, from their seeing ice three hundred and sixty feet thick; and from their beer, wine, and brandy being all frozen to the very centre. The people soon began to be sickly, and their sickness increased with the cold. Some were affected by gripes and looseness, which continued till they died. At the approach of spring, they were all highly scorbutic, and their mouths were so extremely sore, that they were unable to eat any thing but bread soaked in water. At last, their bread was exhausted; and the few survivors chiefly subsisted on a kind of berry dug out from beneath the snow. When the spring was far advanced, no fresh vegetables could yet be found. In June, the Captain crawled out of his hut, and found the whole company reduced to *two men besides himself*. These melancholy relicts supported themselves in the

best

best manner they were able, and recovered their strength by feeding on a certain root they discovered, and some game caught in hunting. At length they embarked in the smaller ship, and after undergoing numberless dangers and hardships, returned home in safety.

In the same immense bay, but as far south as lat. 52, Captain James, an Englishman, wintered with his crew. His residence was on an island covered with wood; but the cold was, notwithstanding, most intense. In the depth of winter they were able to procure very little fresh provision by the chace, and all became grievously afflicted with the scurvy, except the Captain, Master, and Surgeon. Weak and sick as they were, however, it was necessary for them to labour hard out of doors during the greatest inclemency of the season; for, believing their ship so damaged, as to be incapable of carrying them home, they undertook the laborious task of building a pinnace from the timber growing on the island. At the return of spring, the young greens sprouted up much sooner and more plentifully here, than where Monck wintered; and it became very hot before they left the place. They lost only two men out of a crew of twenty-two.

In the year 1633 two trials were made by the Dutch of establishing wintering-places at their northern fisheries; the one at Spitzbergen, the other

other on the coast of Greenland, in latitudes about 77 or 78. Seven sailors were left at each, amply furnished with every article of clothing, provision, and utensils thought necessary or useful in such a situation. The journals of both companies are preserved.

That of the men in Greenland takes notice, that on September 18th the allowance of brandy began to be served out to each person. On October 9th they began to make a constant fire to sit by. About this time, it is remarked, that they experienced a considerable change in their bodies, with giddiness in their heads. They now and then killed a bear; but their common diet was salt meat. In March they were all very ill of the scurvy; and on April 16th the first man died, and all the rest were entirely disabled, but one person. This poor wretch continues the journal to the last day of April, when they were praying for a speedy release from their miseries. They were all found dead.

The journal of those who were left at Spitzbergen recites, that they sought in vain for green herbs, bears and foxes, in that desolate region; and killed no other game than one fox, the whole time. The scurvy appeared among them as early as November 24th; and the first man died January 14th. The journal ends February 26th; and these too were all found dead.

Not many years after these unfortunate attempts, an accident gave rise to an experiment, the event of which was so entirely the reverse of these, that it merits very particular notice. On the same side of Spitzbergen, between lat. 77 and 78, a boat's crew, belonging to a Greenland ship, consisting of eight Englishmen, who had been sent ashore to kill deer, were left behind, in consequence of some mistakes, and reduced to the deplorable necessity of wintering in that dreadful country, totally unprovided with every necessary. From their narrative, drawn up in that style of artless simplicity which affords the strongest presumption of veracity, I shall extract the most material circumstances.

At their wintering place was fortunately a large substantial wooden building, erected for the use of the coopers belonging to the fishery. Within this they built a smaller one, which they made very compact and warm. Here they constructed four cabins, with comfortable deer-skin beds; and they kept up a continual fire, which never went out for eight months. They were tolerably supplied with fuel from some old casks and boats which they broke up for the purpose. Thus provided with lodging, their principal care was about their subsistence. Before the cold weather set in, they killed a good number of deer, the greatest part of which they cut up, roasted, and stowed in barrels; reserving some raw for their Sunday's dinners. This, I imagine, muſt have been frozen; as it began to freeze ſharply before they were ſettled in their habitation. This veniſon, with a few ſea-horſes and bears which they killed from time to time, conſtituted their whole winter's proviſion, except a very unſavoury article they were obliged to make out with, which was *whale's fritters,* or the ſcraps of fat after the oil has been preſſed out. Theſe too, having been wetted and thrown in heaps, were mouldy. Their uſual courſe of diet, then, for the firſt three months, was one meal of veniſon every day in the week, except Wedneſdays and Fridays, when they kept faſt on whale's fritters. At the end of this period, on examining their ſtock, they found it would not hold out at this rate, and therefore for the enſuing three months they retrenched their veniſon meals to three days in the week, and appeaſed their hunger, as well as they could, on the other four days, upon the mouldy fritters. At the approach of ſpring they had the good fortune to kill ſeveral white bears, which proved excellent food; and, together with wild fowl and foxes which they caught, rendered it unneceſſary any longer to ſtint themſelves to ſo rigorous an allowance; ſo that they eat two or three meals of freſh meat daily, and ſoon improved in ſtrength and vigour. Their only drink during this whole time, was running water procured from beneath the ice on the beach, till January; and afterwards, snow-water melted by hot irons. The cold in the midst of winter was extreme. It raised blisters in the flesh; and when they went abroad, they became sore all over, as if beaten. Iron, on being touched, stuck to their fingers, like bird-lime. The melancholy of their situation was aggravated by the absence of the sun from the horizon, from October 14th, to February 3d, of which period, twenty days were passed in total darkness, except the light of lamps, which they continued to keep continually burning. With all this, it does not appear that any of them were affected with the scurvy, or any other disorder; and the degree of weakness, which seems implied by the mention of their recovering strength in the spring, may be sufficiently accounted for, merely from their short allowance of nutritious food. At the return of the ships on May 25th, they all appear to have been in health; and all of them returned in safety to their native country.

The last relation I shall adduce, is one of late date, considerably resembling the foregoing in several of its circumstances, but still more extraordinary.

In the year 1743, a Russian ship of East Spitzbergen, in lat. between 77 and 78, was so enclosed with ice, that the crew, apprehensive of being obliged to winter there, sent four of their men in a boat to seek for a hut, which they

they knew to have been erected near that coast. The hut was discovered; but the men, on returning to the shore, found all the ice cleared away, and the ship no longer to be seen; and indeed it was never more heard of. I pass over their first transports of grief and despair, and also their many ingenious contrivances to furnish themselves with the necessaries they stood most in need of. Their diet and way of life are the circumstances peculiarly connected with my subject. After fitting up their hut as comfortably as they could, and laying in drift wood, collected on the shore, for fuel, they turned their attention chiefly to the procuring of provision. Three species of animals, which they caught and killed by various devices, constituted their whole variety of food. These were, reindeer, white bears, and foxes. The flesh they eat almost raw, and without salt; using by way of bread to it, other flesh, dried hard in the smoke. Their drink was running water in the summer, and melted ice and snow in the winter. Their preservatives against the scurvy were, swallowing raw frozen meat broken into bits, drinking the warm blood of reindeer just killed, eating scurvy-grass, when they could meet with it, and using much exercise. By these means three of them remained entirely free from this disease during the whole of their abode. The fourth died of it, after lingering on to the sixth year. It is remarked, that this person was of an indolent disposition, and could not conquer his aversion to drinking the reindeer's blood. The three survivors, after remaining six years and three months on this desolate and solitary island, were happily rescued by a ship driven casually upon the coast, and returned home in safety. They were strong and healthy at their return, but by habit had contracted an inability of eating bread, or drinking spirituous liquors.

To the above relations, I shall add the following short quotations relative to the same subject.

In a note to the account of the four Russians, it is said, " Counsellor Müller says, the Russians about Archangel should be imitated; some of whom every year winter in Nova Zembla without ever contracting the scurvy. They follow the example of the Samoides, by frequently drinking the warm blood of reindeer just killed. The hunting of these animals requires continual exercise. None ever keep their huts during the day, unless the stormy weather, or too great quantity of snow, hinders them from taking their usual exercise."

In a manuscript French account of the islands lying between Kamtschatka and America, drawn up by that eminent naturalist and geographer, Mr. Pallas, I find it mentioned, that " the Russians, in their hunting voyages to these islands, (an expedition generally lasting three years) in order

order to save expence and room in purchasing and stowing vegetable provision, compose half their crews of natives of Kamtschatka, because these people are able to preserve themselves from the scurvy *with animal food only, by abstaining from the use of salt.*"

Lastly, in the excellent oration of Linnæus, *On the advantages of travelling in one's own country,* printed in the third volume of the *Amænitates Academicæ,* it is asserted, " that the Laplanders live without corn and wine, without salt and every kind of artificial liquor, on water and flesh alone, and food prepared from them; and yet are entirely free from the scurvy."*

Having thus stated the facts which have fallen in my way relative to this subject, I proceed to a comparison of their several circumstances, and some remarks on the general result.

The *scurvy* appears to be the disease peculiarly dreaded and fatal in all the above-related attempts to winter in extremely cold climates. Whether the circumstance of cold itself, or the want of proper food occasioned by it, principally conduces to the generation of this disease, is a point not clearly ascertained. From the preceding

---

* " In Lapplandiâ observabit homines absque Cerere & Baccho, absque sale & potu omni artificiali, aquâ tantum & carne, & quæ ab his præparantur, contentos vivere.

" Quare Norlandi, ut plurimum, scorbuto sint infecti; & cur Lappones, contra, hujus morbi prorsus expertes?"

narrations, however, no doubt can be entertained, that it is possible for persons to keep free from the scurvy, in countries and seasons the most intensely cold, provided their diet and manner of living be properly adapted to such situations; and this, without the aid of fresh vegetables, or any of those other preservatives, which have of late been proposed by ingenious writers.

When we compare the histories above recited, it is impossible not to be immediately struck with these leading circumstances, that those in whom the scurvy raged, fed upon *salt provisions*, and drank *spirituous liquors*; whereas those who escaped it, fed upon *fresh* animal food, or, at least, preserved *without salt*, and drank *water*.

It is well enough known among sea-faring people, that fresh animal food is serviceable to scorbutic persons; but whether the constant use of it alone would *prevent* the scurvy, they have no means of experiencing. As little can we learn from their experience, whether any other mode of preserving animal flesh than that of salting, will keep it in such a state as to be salubrious food. But the narrative of the eight Englishmen seems to determine both these important points; for their provision was all of the animal kind, and the greatest part of it was flesh killed several months before, and kept from decaying, either by the coldness of the climate alone, or by the cooking

cooking it had undergone. It is evident, too, that the sailors of Kamtschatka, who subsist during so long a voyage on animal food unsalted, must either preserve it by smoking, freezing, or other similar processes, or must use it in a putrid state. To this last, indeed, from the accounts we have of the usual diet of these people, they seem not at all averse; though we may find it difficult to conceive how the body can be kept in health by food absolutely putrefied. The Laplanders, also, who subsist so entirely on animal food without salt, must have other methods of preserving it for a considerable time; and, indeed, it seems to be the constant practice in Russia and other northern regions, for the inhabitants to freeze their meat in order to lay it up for their winter's stock.

These facts lead to the consideration of the question, whether salted meat be prejudicial on account of the quantity of salt it contains; or merely because the salt fails to preserve the juices of the flesh in such a state as to afford proper nutriment? The latter, I believe, is the more prevalent opinion; yet, I confess, I cannot but think, that sea-salt itself, when taken in large quantities, must prove unfriendly to the body. The septic quality of *small proportions* of salt mixed with animal matters (and small proportions only can be received into the juices of a living animal) has been proved by the well-known experiments of Sir John Pringle. But besides this, it may prove hurtful, by the acrimonious and corrosive property with which it may impregnate the fluids. It is universally allowed, that much salt, and salted meats, are very prejudicial in the disorders vulgarly called *scorbutic* amongst us; which, though in many respects different from the genuine sea-scurvy, yet resemble this disease in many leading symptoms, as lassitude, livid blotches, spungy gums, and disposition to hæmorrhage. And some of the symptoms of the sea-scurvy seem to indicate a *saline*, and not a simply *putrid* acrimony; such as that of the disjoining of bones formerly broken, in which case, the osseous matter of the callus is probably redissolved, by the saline principle contained in the animal fluids. On the other hand, it seems to be a fact, that several of the northern nations, whose diet is extremely putrid, (as before hinted with respect to the people of Kamtschatka) are able to preserve themselves from the scurvy; therefore, putrid aliments alone will not necessarily induce it.

On the whole, on an attentive consideration of the facts which have been recited, some of which are upon a pretty extensive scale, I cannot but adopt the opinion, that *the use of sea-salt is a very principal cause of the scurvy*; and that *a total abstinence from it, is one of the most important means for preventing this disease.*

A considerable article of the diet of the eight Englishmen, though necessity alone could have brought them to use it, was probably of considerable service in preventing the disorders to which their situation rendered them liable. This was, the *whale's fritters*, which, though deprived of great part of their oil, must still contain no small share of it. All voyagers agree, that the Samoides, Esquimaux, Greenlanders, and other inhabitants of the polar regions, make great use of the fat and oil of fish and marine animals in their diet, and indeed can scarcely subsist without them. In what precise manner these substances act, is not, perhaps, easily explained; but as the use of them would, doubtless, cause an accumulation of similar parts in the body, and as we find all animals destined to endure the severe cold of the arctic climates, are copiously furnished with fat, we may conclude, that it possesses some peculiar efficacy in defending from the impressions of cold.

With respect to the *warm reindeer's blood*, which the Russian sailors seem to have thought so salutary, and the use of which is confirmed in one of the quotations; if it has any particular effect in preventing the scurvy, beyond that of the juices extracted from recent animal flesh by cookery or digestion, it must probably reside in some unassimilated particles, derived from the vegetable food of the animal, and still retaining considerably of a vegetable nature. It is well known that the chyle does not immediately lose its peculiar properties, and mix undistinguishably with the blood; and that the milk, that secretion the most speedily and abundantly separated from the blood, possesses many properties in common with vegetable substances. As to their other preservative, *the swallowing of raw frozen meat*, I am at a loss to account for any salutary effects it may have, except as an aliment rendered easy of digestion, by the power of frost in making substances tender.

To proceed to the next important article, that of *drink*. It appears, that in all the unsuccessful instances, vinous and spirituous liquors were used, and probably in considerable quantities. Thus, in one of the Dutch journals, notice is taken, that an allowance of brandy began to be served to each man as soon as the middle of September. Writers on the scurvy seem almost unanimously to consider a portion of these liquors as an useful addition to the diet of persons exposed to the causes of this disease; and due deference ought certainly to be paid to their knowledge and experience: but, convinced as I am, that art never made so fatal a present to mankind as the invention of distilling spirituous liquors, and that they are seldom or never a necessary, but almost always a pernicious article in the diet of men in health, I cannot but look with peculiar

satisfaction

satisfaction on the confirmation this opinion receives by the events in these narratives.

Indeed, from reasoning alone, we might naturally be led to the same conclusion. A great degree of cold renders the fibres rigid; and by repelling the blood and nervous principle from the surface of the body, increases the vital energy of the internal organs. Hence, the heart contracts more forcibly, and the stomach has its warmth and muscular action augmented. In these circumstances, stimulants and astringents seem by no means indicated; but rather substances of an opposite nature. We have acquired by association the idea of opposing *actual* cold by matters *potentially* or *metaphorically* hot; but this is in great measure a fallacious notion. On the contrary, it is found that the effects of excessive heat are best resisted by warm and acrid substances, such as the spicy and aromatic vegetables which the hot climates most abundantly produce, and which are so much used in the diet of the inhabitants. And if it be admitted as a general law of nature, that every country yields the products best adapted to the health and sustenance of its inhabitants, we should conclude, that aromatic vegetables, and fermented liquors are peculiarly appropriated to the warmer climates; while bland, oily animal matters are rather designed for the use of the frigid regions. Spirits, as antiseptics, may, indeed, seem to be indicated

where

where there is a necessity of living upon corrupted putrescent flesh; but they cannot act in this way without, at the same time, rendering the food harder and more indigestible, and, consequently, lessening the quantity of nutriment to be derived from it. The temporary glow and elevation caused by spirituous liquors are, I imagine, very fallacious tokens of their good effects; as they are always succeeded by a greater reverse, and tend rather to consume and exhaust, than to feed and invigorate, the genuine principle of vital energy. Another extremely pernicious effect of these liquors, is, the indolence and stupidity they occasion, rendering men inattentive to their own preservation, and unwilling to use those exertions, which are so peculiarly necessary in situations like those described in the foregoing narratives. And this leads me to the consideration of a third important head, that of *exercise*.

The utility of regular and vigorous exercise to men exposed to the causes inducing scurvy, is abundantly confirmed by experience. Captain Cook seems to attribute his remarkable success in preserving the health of his crew, more to great attention to this point, than to any other circumstance. This opinion is greatly corroborated by the relations before us. Captain Monck's crew, wintering with their ships in safety before them, and well furnished with all kinds of sea stores, could have little occasion for labour. The two companies

companies of Dutchmen seem to have done little during their melancholy abode, but drink brandy, and smoke tobacco over their fires. On the other hand, Captain James's men were very sufficiently employed in the laborious task of building their pinnace, which, notwithstanding their weak and sickly state, they had nearly completed, before they found the work unnecessary. The three Russians on East Spitzbergen who survived, are expressly said, to have used much exercise by way of preservative; as also, according to Counsellor Müller, do those who winter on Nova Zembla. A difficulty, however, here occurs; which is, that we know it to be the custom of the inhabitants of the very northern regions, to spend their long winter night almost entirely under ground; seeming, in that respect, to imitate the animals of the country, which lie torpid in their holes and dens during the winter. From the journal of the eight Englishmen, too, I should judge, that they were inactive during the greatest part of the time that the sun was invisible. But it is to be remarked, that in these instances, what I consider as the most powerful cause of the scurvy, the use of salted provisions, did not exist; and therefore less powerful preservatives would be necessary. Further, the English crew had a very scanty allowance of provision of any kind; which would, doubtless, take off from the necessity of much exercise. Thus, the animals which sleep out the winter,

take

take in no nutriment whatsoever, and therefore are not injured by absolute rest.

Exercise is probably serviceable, both by promoting the discharge of effete and corrupted particles by excretion, and by augmenting the animal heat. As far as cold in itself can be supposed a cause of disease; its effects will be most directly opposed by increasing the internal or external heat. And this leads to the consideration of the further means for guarding against and tempering the intense severity of the wintry air in these climates.

It appears from the journals of the unfortunate sufferers in these attempts, that they endured great miseries from the cold; their fuel soon proving insufficient for their consumption, and their daily increasing weakness preventing them from searching for more, or keeping their fires properly supplied. On the other hand, the English and Russians had not only made their huts very substantial, but had secured plentiful supplies of fuel. And the nations who constantly inhabit the arctic regions, are represented as living in an actually warm atmosphere in their subterraneous dwellings, and guarded by impenetrable coverings when they venture abroad. The animals, too, which retire during the winter, are always found in close caverns or deep burrows, rolled up, and frequently heaped together in numbers, so as to preserve a considerable degree

of

of warmth. Of the several methods of procuring heat, there can be little doubt, that warm clothing, and the mutual contact of animal bodies, must be the most friendly, as being most equable, and not inviting such an influx of cold air, as is caused by the burning of an artificial fire. And the advantage of subterraneous lodgings is proved by the well-known fact of the unchanging temperature of the air at certain depths beneath the surface.

These are the most material observations that have occurred to me, on reflecting upon the remarkable histories and facts above related. I would flatter myself that they might assist in the framing of such rules and precautions, as would render the success of any future attempts of the like kind, less precarious. I shall be happy if they prove acceptable to the Society to whom I have the honour of addressing them; and still more, if they in any degree conduce to the welfare of mankind.

An Essay *on the* Pleasure *which the* Mind *receives from the Exercise of its Faculties, and that of* Taste *in particular. By* Charles de Polier, *Esq. Read February* 27, 1782.

"Denique fit quodvis simplex duntaxat et unum."
Hor. de Art. Poet.

THAT the exercise of the mind is no less necessary to the existence of man, than that of the body, appears incontrovertible. The senses of the brute part of the creation, are so much more perfect than ours, that thereby they are enabled to pursue whatever is favourable, and to avoid whatever is detrimental to them. In giving us the powers of the understanding, the Author of the universe hath abundantly supplied that defect. By them, we not only rise superior to the beasts in every means of providing for our support, our defence, and our welfare; but we have improved upon nature, and made the whole world subservient to our wants, and to our desires. It was not, however, the intention of Providence, that those advantages should be gained without any trouble on our side. The intellectual faculties, for the most part, lie dormant in us; to rouse them, strong exertions are necessary; and men naturally fond of ease,

and

and prone to indolence, would for ever, perhaps, remain in a state little superior to that of the brutes, if necessity, at first, and pleasure afterwards, did not call forth these latent powers.

Pleasure, the parent of joys and amusements, will be found alike the parent of Sciences, and of Arts; Nature, in her kindness to man, having annexed an agreeable and pleasing sensation to *whatever gives exercise to the mind without fatiguing it*. To this, we are *indebted* for the improvements made to arts, taught, at first, by necessity; and for the discovery of many more, either agreeable or useful. Nay, such is the charm of that exercise, that it has been known so to elevate the soul, as to detach her, as it were, from the body;* and freeing her from its shackles, set

---

* We read in *Aulus Gellius*, that *Socrates*, to exercise his patience, as he says, but perhaps to indulge, in all its extent, the pleasure we are here speaking of, used to stand for twenty-four hours together, in a steady posture, unmoveable, without even so much as winking his eyes, which he constantly kept fixed upon the same place, entirely absorbed in his own thoughts, and seeming, as if an actual secession had taken place between his soul and body.

It will be but doing justice to *Aulus Gellius*, though not a very elegant writer, to set down here his own words.

" Stare solitus Socrates dicitur pertinaci statu, per dies atque per noctes, à summo lucis ortu ad solem alterum orientem, inconnivens, immobilis, iisdem in vestigiis, et ore atque oculis eundem in locum directis, cogitabundus, tanquam quodam secessu animi facto à corpore."

Aul. Gell. Noct. Attic. Lib. II. Cap. 1.

her in that state, so beautifully described by *Akenside*, when he says, in his Pleasures of Imagination,

> - - - - - - - - - - - - - "The high born soul
> Disdains to rest her heav'n aspiring wing
> Beneath its native quarry. Tir'd of earth
> And this diurnal scene, she springs aloft,
> Through fields of air; pursues the flying storm,
> Rides on the vollied light'ning through the heav'ns;
> Or, yok'd with whirlwinds and the northern blast,
> Sweeps the long tract of day."

I omit the rest of that noble passage, too long to be here inserted; but written *with all the enthusiasm of poetic genius, joined to all the sweetness and harmony of numbers.*

Vide AKENSIDE's Pleas. of Imag. B. I. Ver. 183.

The history of *Archimedes*, the famous *Sicilian* Philosopher, is well known. Neither the sense of decency on one occasion, nor the sense of danger on another, could divert his thoughts from the object they had in view, and from the pleasure they afforded him. If the truth of these surprizing anecdotes may be doubted, let us at least acknowledge the possibility of them, from what we may observe every day among us. Would not one imagine, on seeing a Chess-player, for instance, so entirely wrapt up in himself, as to appear insensible to every thing around him, that he is taken up with the care of his own fortune, the preservation of the state, or some such

such great and important subject? And yet, all this intenseness of thought is produced by the position of a small piece of ivory, which gives exercise to his mind, and procures him that pleasure, in which he seems so totally absorbed. Other instances might be adduced. The entertainment we receive from *riddles*, *charades*, and such other *Jeux d'Esprit*, proceeds from the same source. Every reader, of acute understanding and refined taste, delights to meet in authors with such *delicate* thoughts, as not being immediately obvious, are just concealed enough to give him the pleasure of finding them out, and as such, may be compared to *Virgil's Galatea*,

"Et fugit ad Salices, et se cupit ante videri."
Virg. Buc. Ecl. 3.

There have been some men who have thought, that the exercise of the mind was only agreeable, by anticipating the reputation which it might give. But, however strongly the motive of fame may operate on the minds of some, yet the proposition, when attempted to be made general, is confuted by daily experience. How often do we employ whole hours in reading and meditation, without the least view to futurity, and merely to gratify the present moment? Does not this prove, that, independent of any other incentive, there is a pleasure inherent in whatever exercises the mind without fatiguing it?

This principle does not hold good of the *mind* only, but is equally applicable to every other component part of our being. There is an agreeable sensation annexed to whatever exercises the organs of the *body* without weakening them; and in the sentiments or emotions of the *heart*, whatever keeps clear of the tumult of the passions, is attended with a degree of pleasure. Proofs of these positions might be brought innumerable, but would probably be unnecessary. Most of the ancient philosophers have laid them down, as the foundation of their ideas of human perfection: and there are few persons, I believe, of any reflection and experience, who have not felt the truth of them in themselves, or observed it in others. Illustrations might, perhaps, be more agreeable than proofs; but in a subject of such an extent, and which embraces no less than the whole circle of physiology, ethics, and *Belles Lettres*, it is necessary to confine oneself, and I shall therefore do no more at present, than offer to the Society some few imperfect remarks, on such works of art, as give exercise to the mind, and come, chiefly, under the province of that faculty of the understanding, known by the name of *Taste*. This choice is not altogether arbitrary. Mere intellectual pleasures, however agreeable in themselves, by overstraining the mind, become at length painful. Organic enjoyments last only as long as we are in vigour. But the pleasures

pleasures of the eye and the ear, as Lord *Kaims* ingeniously observes, in his *Elements of Criticism*, holding the middle way between these two, are particularly fitted to occupy the mind without exhausting it. They relax it after intense study, and restore it to its proper tone, after the satiety and disgust, caused by the mere pleasures of the senses: they tend, therefore, most essentially to prove the principle I mean to illustrate.

We shall find, accordingly, that the agreeable sensations we receive from the productions of the fine arts, are, in a great measure, owing to the order and symmetry, which enable the mind to take in, without labour, all the different parts of them. It is by this, that *rhyme* becomes agreeable in poetry. Some have contended indeed, that this return of the same sounds, invented in the Gothic ages, ought to be classed among the Acrostics, Anagrams, and such other frivolous productions, whose only merit lies in their difficulty. They instance the Greeks and the Romans, whose poetry, far more harmonious than ours, charms the sense, and delights the ear, without the help of rhyme. But they do not seem to have attended sufficiently to the use of poetry, and the nature of the ancient languages. Verses are made to be sung, or to be rehearsed. From the mouth of the actor, the musician, or the reader, whoever he may be, they are supposed to pass into the minds of a whole people; and their compofition is the more perfect, the more readily they prefent themfelves to the memory.

The Greek and Latin tongues, by means of their long and fhort fyllables, and the various meafures into which they may be reduced, form a kind of *chaunt, melody,* or *noted air,* which the memory can eafily lay hold of, and therefore, the return of the fame founds, becoming ufelefs, would caufe nothing but a difagreeable repetition.

Our modern languages have not the fame advantage, or poffefs it, at leaft, in a much lefs degree. The blank verfe of the Englifh, German, and Italian, except in very few fhining exceptions, feems (as was quoted fome time ago, in a very ingenious paper prefented to this Society) *to be verfe only to the eye,* or depends at leaft fo much on the fkilfulnefs of the reader, as not to obtain the effect above-mentioned, with by far the greateft part of thofe who read them. Poems, where it is ufed, are not popular: the ideas they convey, the fentiments they mean to inculcate, however forcibly exprefled, do not eafily recur to the memory: and, I dare fay, that for one perfon, who remembers a paffage from *Milton, Young,* or *Akenfide,* there are twenty who will quote fome from *Pope, Dryden,* or *Prior.*

This controverfy has long been decided in *France,* where, notwithftanding the ftrenuous efforts of one of its greateft poets (Monfieur de la Motte) rhyme has kept in poetry the dominion, which the nature of the French language inconteſtably gave it.

In *England*, where a *Shakeſpeare* and a *Milton* have written, the matter ſeems yet to be *ſub Judice*. It would ill become me, as a young man, and a foreigner, to be that judge; but I may be indulged in ſupporting what I have alledged here in favour of rhyme, by the opinion of the beſt critic now living in this nation, Dr. *Johnſon*; who, admiring the powers of *Milton*, and the amazing dignity given to his ſentiments, by a verſification which he otherwiſe rather diſapproves, adds, " He that thinks himſelf capable of aſtoniſhing, may write blank verſe: but thoſe that hope only to pleaſe, muſt condeſcend to rhyme."*

Another general objection has been brought againſt rhyme. " How comes it, ſays Monſieur de la Motte, that this monotony, which you affirm to be, by its nature, ſo agreeable in poetry, is almoſt conſtantly ſo unpleaſant in a ſiſter-art, in muſic?" To this might be anſwered, that the chief object of the muſician being to delight by the ſounds, he cannot ſucceed better, than by varying them judiciouſly: whereas, a Poet is not ſatisfied with charming the ears of his audience; he wiſhes to impreſs on their

---

* Dr. *Johnſon's* Life of *Milton*.

memory a series of ideas, of sentiments, of expressions; and there are none of his verses which he would not be glad to engrave, with indelible characters, on the hearts of all mankind. He avails himself, therefore, of the rhyme which modern languages offer him, as the most favourable help towards the attaining of his purpose.

But to return to our subject, from which I must beg pardon for having wandered so far. Imitation, which is the principle of all the fine arts, is another species of symmetry, whether it acts by means of colour, of sounds, of gestures, or of words. The objects it presents, easily take hold of our imagination, by the comparison we make of them with objects already known to us.

Aristotle and his followers have maintained, that the pleasure produced in the mind, by the representation of any object, was owing to its acquiring, by that means, a new degree of knowledge. This opinion seems wrong, because it allows no difference between a just, and an unfair representation; nor any gradation of pleasure, from the different degrees of execution. The mind every way makes a new acquisition of knowledge, and must, therefore, receive agreeable sensations alike, from the *Iliad of Homer*, and the *Thebaid* of *Statius*; the pictures of *Raphael*, and those of a sign-painter; the music of *Handel*, and the uncouth notes of an Irish piper.

Other

Other philosophers have asserted, that the representation of an object pleases, only by its interesting the passions. And so far it is true, that the soul cannot be moved, or strongly affected, without it. But does not even the least interesting object make a slight impression of pleasure, at least on the surface of the soul, if it is well represented, and if an exact symmetry is to be seen between the picture and the original? Every body must have felt it; and it proceeds from this principal law in the nature of our sensations—that any object becomes agreeable, whose parts are so formed, and so disposed, as to present the mind with an easy, clear, and distinct idea of the whole.

What is called *Contrast* in painting, poetry, and eloquence, is another sort of symmetry, which, by bringing contrary objects near to each other, sets off the features of the one, by the comparison we make of them with the features of the other. This relation has been taken from nature, in whose works it seldom fails of having a pleasing effect. It is from it, that the views in *Switzerland*, and in other mountainous countries, are so particularly agreeable. The dissimilitude of the objects, which the eye embraces, renders them all more striking, and helps the mind to get a clearer idea of the whole. Thus, when skilfully applied to the productions of art, contrast is generally attended with great success. We accordingly read, that the ancient sculptors,

sculptors, in order to set off the beauty of a *Venus*, a *Grace*, or an *Apollo*, used to place them in a niche formed in the statue of a *Fawn*, or a *Satyr*; and *Virgil*, in order to paint more strongly the agitation of *Dido*'s heart, places the scene of her agonies in the night, when *Morpheus* spread his peaceful influence over all the rest of mankind.

There are, besides symmetry, certain *relations* or *proportions*, which the mind easily conceives, and which therefore become agreeable. Thus, in architecture, for instance, the height of the porticos, in regular buildings, is double the breadth: the height of the entablature, is a fourth, and that of the pedestal, a third of the height of the column. All eminent architects, among the different proportions adapted to their design, have always made choice of those, which the mind could comprehend without any difficulty. The same may be observed in music. Of all concords, the *unison* and the *octave* should be the most agreeable, because they excite more vibrations in the fibres of the ear: but the pleasure we receive from this enchanting art, depends more on the mind, than on the organ adapted to convey it. The *fifth* is the most agreeable of all concords, because it presents to the mind a proportion, the finding out of which, gives it a degree of exercise, that causes no weariness, consequently no disgust.

Some compositions there are in music, which please only profound musicians, and strike, perhaps,

haps, the rest of the hearers, as harsh and discordant. May not this be owing to the very fine taste of the former, by which they are enabled, in the midst of seeming dissonances, to find out relations, which do not affect ears less exercised than theirs?

The analogy which we find in all the works of nature, allows us to conjecture, that the same law, which determines the agreeableness of sounds, has also an influence upon other objects of our senses. Some colours, for instance, set together, give an agreeable sensation to the eye, and more so, than if they appeared single. The same principle may, perhaps, be extended to smells, and to savours, with some restrictions, however; for, though it may be generally asserted, that those which are salubrious are agreeable; yet it must be owned, that their agreeableness does not always seem to depend on their salubrity.

But it is not just proportion and symmetrical relation alone, that renders the works of the fine arts agreeable. They are chiefly made so, by one principal object, or common end, to which all their different parts are adapted, and which enables the mind the more easily to comprehend, and to retain them.

Wisdom, in morality, has been defined—The having one good purpose in view, and using the best means to attain that purpose. So *beauty*, in the imitative arts, might be said to consist, in the

choice

choice of a good object, and in making every thing tend to the expression of it, as to one common end. Certain it is, that this correspondence of the parts with the whole, is to be considered, as the first and principal cause of agreeable sensations. It is alone sufficient to give beauty to the most simple objects; and, if other embellishments are wanted, it becomes the standard of their propriety, and the rule by which we can determine, whether they are real beauties, or only shining blemishes. But to give the mind an easier and more agreeable perception of the object, art has still gone farther. Among all these parts, which are made to refer to one common end, a principal one is chosen, to which all others are subordinate, and which becomes like a center of re-union for them. Architecture can illustrate this. Unacquainted with the real beauties of their art, the Gothic architects never failed to place, on both sides of the body of their buildings, such enormous wings, or rather masses of stone, as almost totally eclipsed it, and kept the sight divided and undetermined. *Bromante*, *Palladio*, and after them most of the modern architects, taught, perhaps, by *Vitruvius*, but certainly more acquainted than their predecessors with what would strike the eyes agreeably, have placed, in the middle of their buildings, a principal part, which, eminent above the rest, gives the sight a fixed point, from which it can glance

glance over all the rest, and so enable the mind to get, at once, a clear and distinct idea of the whole.

All sculptors, in those works, where the eye might be divided by the number of figures, such as, *groups, entaglios, basso-relievos,* shew great attention to this rule, and always chuse a principal object, to fix the sight of the beholders. The three *Rhodian* artists, whose joint work, according to the elder *Pliny,* * has produced the famous group of *Laocoon,* which now stands in the *Belvidere* at *Rome,* seem to have had that principle strongly in view, in the disposition of their figures. The Society, I trust, will forgive me, if, by way of illustration, I here join a description of that celebrated monument of human powers, which *Michael Angelo,* himself a wonder of modern times, used to call, a miracle of art. This description I shall, for the most part, take from a *French* book, which deserves to be better known in this country, from whence so many annually go to visit the classical ground of *Italy,* and so many in vain, from the want of proper guides. I mean, *Le Description historique et critique de l'Italie, par Monf. l'Abbé Richard,* 6 vol. 12mo. Paris 1769. In English,

* " Sicut in Laocoonte, qui est in Titi domo, opus omnibus, et picturæ et statuariæ artis, anteferendum, ex uno lapide, cum et liberos, draconum mirabiles nexus, de Consilii sententiâ fecere, summi Artifices, *Agriander, Polidorus,* et *Athenedorus,* Rhodii."
PLIN. Hist. Nat. Lib. XXXVI. cap. 5.

An historical and critical Description of Italy. By Abbé Richard. Six vols. 12mo.

The group of *Laocoon* was found in the *Thermes*, or *Baths* of *Titus*, about the year 1506, under the pontificate of *Julius* II. who immediately bought it from the possessor of the field, where it had been dug out. The figures are higher than nature, and of so beautiful white marble, that the sight of it alone charms the eye. The workmanship is exquisite, of such a noble style, and such a correctness of execution, as bespeak it a work of the best *Grecian* age. It is not the *Laocoon* described by *Virgil*, as rending the sky with his shrieks, struggling hard for his life, and roaring, like a bull flying from the altar where he has been wounded.

"Clamores simul horridos ad sidera tollit,
Quales mugitus, fugit cùm saucius aras
Taurus."
VIRG. Æneid. II.

"His roaring fills the flitting air around.
Thus, when an ox receives a glancing wound,
He breaks his bands, the fatal altar flies,
And, with loud bellowings, breaks the yielding skies."
DRYDEN.

It is not that man, execrated by a whole people, for having discharged a spear against the horse consecrated to *Minerva*, and whom the vengeance of the Gods pursues.

- - "Scelus

    ——————"Scelus expendisse merentem
Laocoonta ferunt, sacrum, qui cuspide robur
Læserit."
              Virg. Ibid.
—————————"The general cry
Proclaims *Laocoon* justly doom'd to die,
Whose hand the will of *Pallas* had withstood,
And dar'd to violate the sacred wood."
              Dryden.

It is a wretched parent, who feels his strength exhausted, and is ready to sink under the accumulated weight, of exquisite pain, and deep felt affliction. His mouth half opened, and his eyes lifted up to heaven, seem to call for assistance from the Gods, though despair at the same instant overwhelms him at the sight of his own fate, and that of his unfortunate sons, half smothered and devoured by the monsters, who crush them all three. The expression of that group is admirable: but the sculptors have distinguished a principal object in it: for, although the sons are equally well executed, and the one to the left in particular claims our sympathy, by the horrid state of pain in which he is represented, (one of the serpents beginning to tear open his side) yet the father attracts the chief notice. He is that principal part of the whole, to which all others are referred; and it is by that judicious subordination and reference, that the artists have found means to impress the spectator with all the sentiments they meant to convey, and which, without labour to the mind, give it all the pleasure such a representation is able to produce.

The pleasure we receive from a good painting, is also chiefly owing to this subordination of parts, and reference of them to the principal object. Painters call it *composition*; and those masters have obtained the first rank among them, who have been most attentive to it. It was *Raphael*'s, and *Ruben*'s forte; and, being the happy result of great genius, combined with a well cultivated taste, is always sure of causing the most agreeable sensations to the mind, that contemplates the effects of it.

In poetry, but particularly in epic and dramatic performances, the observation or neglect of this rule becomes, likewise, the test of the pleasure they afford to a person of taste. The different actors that appear in the narration, or on the scene, must all concur in their different stations to set off the main object, and keep the attention fixed upon it, or else, the mind, distracted with a multiplicity of objects, that seem to lay an equal claim to its notice, and perhaps to its feelings, grows weary, disgusted, and indifferent to them all. *Unity* of *action*, in painting and in poetry, is another consequence of the attention of artists to the principle I meant to illustrate. For nothing can be more satisfactory to the mind, than to take in, as it were, with a glance, a multitude of facts connected together,

by

by their mutual relation to some great and important action. One may introduce, indeed, in a poem, several *fables* or *plots*, and collect in it, as it were in a gallery of pictures, a series of portraits. It is what *Ovid, Statius, Ariosto, Shakespeare* in his historical plays, and several others, have done. But, many centuries before the oldest of them, the great genius of *Homer* had conceived, that it would be presenting a spectacle far more agreeable to the mind, if a multitude of persons were collected together in the same picture, and were made to contribute to one and the same action; and upon that idea he formed the plan of the epic poem.

Many years after him, *Æschylus*, the first who gave some order and some propriety to the drama, took from the epic poem, the plan of *tragedy*, which he made to be, the representation of an event unfolded in all its circumstances. That great Poet likewise understood, that this representation would far more please the mind, if all the scenes of it were connected by some principal action, which would help the memory to retain them easily.

He carried, moreover, this idea still farther, and to the *unity* of *action*, joined those of time and place. *Sophocles* and *Euripedes*, but especially the former, followed him pretty strictly, and *Aristotle* drew his rules from their practice. Swayed by the authority of great names, and, perhaps, led away too far by this principle, that there is a pleasure inherent in whatever enables the mind to get a clear and distinct perception of the object presented to it, the *French* critics defended, and the *French* dramatic poets wrote after, these rules. In *England,* the amazing genius of *Shakespeare,* probably unacquainted with *Aristotle* and his precepts, having early, and in general happily, soared above all restraints, gave, perhaps, a bias to the taste of the nation; or a sanction, at least, to future dramatic authors, for not attending scrupulously to the strict unities. These, however, were also defended by the *English* critics, and, in theory, admitted by the best poets: but the practice did not correspond; and there is not at present a theatre in *Europe,* in which these rules are less observed.

I do not mean this, as an absolute reproach. Convinced, as I am, that the pleasures of the heart are much superior to those of the mind, I think, that rules invented to give ease and pleasure to the latter, may often be sacrificed to a multitude of interesting events and situations, that raise strong emotions in the former, and strike it forcibly. But at the same time, illusion being the charm of theatrical representations, care ought to be taken not to destroy it, nor diminish the concern and sympathy of the spectators, by too great a deviation from probability. If, on the stage, an old man were to play the part of a young a young one, if, the scene being in a palace, the sceneries were to present trees and landscapes to our view, if the dresses did not correspond, in some degree, to the dignity of the persons represented, all these discordances would offend us.

The same is applicable to the deviation from the three unities. If, in a drama, the principal actions are multiplied, if, in the space of a few hours, many centuries are made to elapse, if the spectator is transported in an instant, from one part of the world to another, all these absurdities become so many warnings against the falsity of the spectacle; and a voice seems to issue out of them, which bids us, not to give sincere tears to feigned misfortunes.

Such are the arguments of the critics, who follow the rules of *Aristotle*. Lord *Kaims*, on the other side, proves, from the different nature of the Grecian, and the modern drama, that the unities of time and place are, by no means, so necessary with us, as they were with the ancients.

The interruption of the representation, on our theatre, between the different acts, gives the mind a facility of supposing any length of time, or change of place; and it becomes not more difficult for the spectator, at the beginning of an act, to imagine a new place, or a different time, than it was at first, to imagine himself at *Athens*, or in a period of time two thousand years back.

But the same freedom cannot be taken with the unity of action. The pleasure, which the mind, as we observed above, receives from a chain of facts connected together, and tending to one common end, renders this unity essential, alike in epic and dramatic compositions. Every thing, however beautiful in itself, that breaks this chain, or interrupts this relation, looks like an excrescence, and becomes unpleasant. An epic poem, with two principal actions, like a play, with two main plots, would soon confuse and tire the reader and the spectator; and so far do the rules of *Aristotle* agree with nature. An *episode* and an *under-plot* may be allowed for the sake of variety; but they must be connected with the principal action, or else they become great blemishes. *Milton*, in this respect, as indeed in many others, has the advantage over *Homer* and *Virgil*. His episode, of the battle of angels, and the creation of the world, is more intimately connected with his subject, than the description of *Achilles*' shield, or even the descent of *Æneas* into hell. Far from breaking the unity of action, it rather strengthens it, by making us acquainted with the cause of what we have read, and of what is to follow. It is, therefore, productive of great mental enjoyment, as there is no relation that pleases the mind more, than that of cause and effect.

This great rule, of the unity of action, is an insuperable objection to tragi-comedy; and inattention to it shocks persons of taste in some of our best plays. In the *Provoked Husband*, for instance, all the scenes relating to the family of the *Wrongheads*, however laughable, and characteristic in themselves, are certainly to be accounted blemishes, because they stop the tide of sentiment raised by the interesting scenes, between a sensible, loving, and justly incensed husband, and a giddy, extravagant, though good-natured wife.

This dissertation on the unities, will also be looked upon, I fear, as an excrescence to this paper, already too long; but I indulged myself in it with the thought, that it might, probably, give room to some interesting conversation—the avowed purpose of the essays presented to this society—and in that light, I beg, and I hope for, your indulgence.

From what has been read, it will appear, that *regularity* and *contrast*, *proportion* and *congruity*, *uniformity*, *variety*, and *simplicity*, in the objects presented to the mind, give it an exercise, which is attended with neither trouble nor fatigue, and which is therefore agreeable.

That these sources of pleasure exist in our nature, seems evident, from their being uniform and universal; and that they were given us for wise and good purposes, is what no one can dispute,

dispute, who considers, with what care the great Author of our being has provided us with all means of happiness. They evidently contribute to it, by adding beauty to the objects that surround us, and by procuring us enjoyments far superior to those of the senses. In this view only, it would be incumbent upon us to cultivate the natural relish we have for them: but *Cicero*, in his admirable work *de Officiis*, shews us a still nobler use, for which they may have been intended. After having enumerated the qualities which man has in common with other animals, and some of the advantages that distinguish him, he proceeds to say,

------ " Necverò illa parva vis Naturæ est, rationisque, quod unum hoc animal sentit quid sit ordo; quid sit, quod deceat; in factis dictisque qui modus. Itaque eorum ipsorum quæ aspectu sentiuntur, nullum aliud animal, pulchritudinem, venustatem, convenientiam partium sentit. Quam similitudinem Natura, ratioque ab oculis ad animum transferens, multo etiam magis pulchritudinem, constantiam, ordinem in consiliis, factisque conservandum putat: cavetque, ne quid indecorè, effæminat evè, faciat; tum in omnibus et opinionibus et factis, ne quid libidinosè aut faciat aut cogitet. Quibus ex rebus conflatur, et efficitur, id quod quærimus, Honestum."

Cicer. de Officiis. Lib. I.

" The

"The energy of nature and of human reason are strikingly displayed in this circumstance, that man is the only animal endued with the perception of order, decency, and propriety in words and in actions. He alone discerns, in visible objects, beauty, gracefulness, and symmetry. And, transferring the analogy, from the sight to the mind, he becomes sensible, that superior beauty, regularity, and order, should distinguish the intention and behaviour; and cautiously avoids whatever is unbecoming and unmanly, and particularly, every loose imagination and expression. An attention to these things forms and constitutes that *Honestum*, which is the subject of our enquiry."

Lord *Kaims*, whom every lover of genuine criticism must read with pleasure, and quote with gratitude, observes also, that, "The reasonings employed in the fine arts, are of the same kind with those, which regulate our conduct. Mathematical and metaphysical reasonings (says he) have no tendency to improve social intercourse, nor are they applicable to the common affairs of life: but a just taste of the fine arts, derived from rational principles, furnishes elegant subjects for conversation, and prepares us for acting in the social state, with dignity and propriety."*

---

* Introduction to Elements of Criticism.

Thus we find an analogy and a connection formed, between the pleasures of taste, and the sense of morality. The same principle of propriety, which leads us to the discovery of what is beautiful and pleasing to the mind, when applied to the heart, will help us to find, what is virtuous, what is honest, and what constitutes the true pleasure arising from its emotions. What I have attempted to illustrate, may then be carried farther, and we may pronounce, that, as there is a pleasure inherent in whatever exercises the mind, without fatiguing it, so there is a pleasing sensation annexed to every emotion of the heart, that is not poisoned by fear, hatred, envy, revenge, and such other irregular and disorderly passions.

On Œconomical Registers. By J. Wimpey.
Read March 13, 1782.

IN a country so justly respectable as Great Britain, for its proficiency in the Arts, in Manufacture, Trade, and Commerce, and in its literary acquisitions in every branch of Science, it is rather surprizing, that there should be so entire a deficiency in Œconomical History.

To the questions, What may be the amount of the circulating cash in the kingdom? What is the state of its population? Has it increased, or decreased, within the last fifty years? Have the many and great improvements in agriculture rendered the prices of provisions, &c. proportionably cheaper? And what is the increase of quantity, on an average, for half a century back, compared with preceding times?—To these questions, no satisfactory answers have been given.

These are interesting and important enquiries, concerning which, men of the best abilities have employed their thoughts with very little success, as nothing, with any degree of certainty, can be concluded from what they have written upon those subjects. Indeed, their opinions are so exceedingly wide of, and repugnant to, each other, that it clearly appears they have no certain data to calculate upon. This indeed is not so much a reflection on the present times, as on the past. But it will equally reflect on the present, when they, like the former, shall become the past, unless some means are adopted, to furnish our successors with those interesting facts, the want of which leaves us enveloped in the dark shades of ignorance.

Some years since, I was honoured with a letter from Monsieur Turgot, then high in the favour of his royal master, and at the head of one of the first departments in the kingdom of France. He requested I would inform him, What might be the proportion, which the produce in grain of the lands in England of one year bore to that of another, for a series of thirty or forty years. To this I could only answer, That we had no annual register, either public or private, that I knew of, which could answer his question; and that the only means we had of guessing, were, by the proportion which the price of one year bore to that of another.

This was not less astonishing to him, than it had been to several other sagacious foreigners, who have shrewdly remarked, "that, in England, so keen are individuals in the pursuit of their own private emolument, and so ignorant and remiss is its government, that they have frequently given a bounty of fifteen per cent. to export their corn, when all they had in stock was very far short of being sufficient to support their own people, till the next harvest." In this deplorable state of œconomical and commercial ignorance, we continue still, which I conceive might be remedied with little difficulty, trouble, or expence. But, for government to give a bounty for the exportation of grain, to the amount of from fifteen to thirty per cent. as it hath sometimes done, without knowing, either the average quantity grown, or the quantity

its

its people consume; and consequently, without knowing, if the stock remaining on hand would feed its people till the next crop be harvested; and whether it must not of necessity be forced to purchase again at double the price, as it has also sometimes done, is surely one of the most absurd measures, that a thoughtless, inconsiderate class of men ever adopted. It has been frequently observed, that our legislators have been very fruitful in the invention of penal laws; but in the measures of prevention, which are infinitely more salutary, they are either very inattentive, or very barren.

The question of population, whether it increaseth, or is upon the decline, is not to be ascertained with any tolerable degree of exactness, without an actual enumeration of all the people in the island. This may be thought a work of too great extent and trouble, to be attempted. So it would, indeed, if it were to be effected by one, or a few persons. But how very easy would it be, if performed by the parish officers? They, by the duty of their office, are obliged to have a complete list of all those, who are rated towards the relief of the poor; and another, of all those who are the objects of such relief. A list of those who are not in either of those classes, would cost the officers of any parish very little trouble. Consequently, the number in each class, and the sum total of the whole,

might

might be obtained with as little trouble, as the numbers in each class, and the sum total, could be obtained by the officers of any respective parish.

If such lists were correctly taken every two, three, four, or five years, the state of increase, or decrease, might be precisely known, with little or no expence to any body. Of such lists, might be formed a kind of General Directory; containing the names, addition, number, ages, and sex, of all the families in Great Britain. Thus, in Manchester,

N. R. Hatter, $\frac{12}{4}, \frac{3}{12}$ 3 males, 4 females.

that is, four under twelve, and three above; three of them males, four females. Let any one carry his ideas through the street he lives in, or is familiarly acquainted with, and he will see, with how much ease he may acquire a knowledge of all these particulars, respecting every family in it; and, by a similar practice, on a general plan, a precise knowledge may be obtained of every family in the nation.

Perhaps it would be too adventurous, to attempt to recommend a knowledge thus acquired to some practical uses, to which it seems capable of being applied, with a prospect of the most beneficial effects.

A very great part of those, who have no other means of subsistence, but the spoils and depredations committed upon the public, are, in their manner of living, a kind of citizens of the world, without character, or description, fixed habitation, residence or connection, by which they may be traced as to their mode of subsistence. And how desirable soever it may be to bring them into broad day light, that every man may have his eye upon them, yet in a country, where the blessing of liberty is deservedly in such high esteem, fears are awakened, suspicions alarmed, jealousies excited, lest any incroachment should be made on the liberty of the subject, under the specious, but deceitful appearance of public good.

Were this a proper place, I would endeavour to give the true idea of genuine liberty, in which that of the individual should perfectly accord, with the safety and happiness of the state. Like the base of a pyramid, it should be erected on a large extended bottom, its centre of gravity coinciding with its centre of magnitude, which nothing could shake or overturn, till its materials should be crumbled into one common ruin. At present, I think it seems to stand, like Fortune on the summit of a globe, whose descent on one side, is into the region of anarchy and licentious confusion; on the other, of tyranny and slavery, from both which I hope we shall ever escape.

I will beg leave, however, to throw out a few hints. They may suggest the means of preventing some, and of detecting others, in the pursuit

pursuit of practices, which are the bane of society, and a disgrace to humanity.

Let us suppose, then, that complete lists have been taken of every family in Great Britain, of men, women, children, servants, and lodgers. That every town and village were obliged to provide sufficient number of Medals made of copper, about an inch and half diameter, with the name of the town, country, and year, inscribed round the margin. That every person, above twelve years of age, should be obliged when they went above a certain number of miles from home, to wear it about them, that they might be able to prove satisfactorily, who they are, and from whence they come. Across the piece, should be engraved the name, the profession or address, and the age of the person, at the date of the impression. By this means, every person would have it in his power to confirm the account he might give of himself, by an incontestible voucher; and every suspicious person, wherever he might happen to appear, should be liable to be taken before the nearest civil officer, where he should produce his medal, and answer all proper questions, or be liable to be committed by any one of his Majesty's Justices of peace. The want of a medal should be deemed a suspicious circumstance, and the person should be retained in safe custody, till he could obtain sufficient proof of the place of his residence from the parish officers, or from some one of them.

If any labouring-man, handicraft-man, artificer, or workman of any sort, shall come as a stranger into any town, and ask employment, the person who employs him shall first demand a sight of his medal, take a copy of its inscription, and by the first post send a letter of advice to the officers of the parish he came from. And in neglect or contempt of such advice, he shall be liable to a penalty sufficient to compel its strict observance.

Upon this plan, should any servant, day-labourer, or workman of any sort, abscond from his place of abode for any misdemeanor, or trespass he had committed, he could not proceed many days unapprehended; for no person should be suffered to entertain a stranger above one night, without taking a copy of his medal, and sending advice to his parish. A man could not then run away, desert his family, and throw them as a burden on the parish, because detection would immediately pursue him, bring him back in disgrace, and inflict an adequate punishment upon him.

Were such a plan to be prosecuted with vigour, it would be a sufficient bar to every attempt of thievery and roguery, for impunity in which, the delinquent ultimately depended upon desertion. No man, in his senses, could depend upon a means for his security, in which he knew before-hand it would

would be impossible for him to succeed. Desertion is the dernier resort of every villain. When he finds himself suspected, he instantly runs his country, and endeavours to secrete himself at a distance, in places to which, as he imagines, suspicion is least likely to pursue him. But under this regulation, whither could he fly? Let it be whither you please, if he produces his medal, it betrays him; if he does not, it raises a suspicion which justifies his detention, till he is fairly cleared of all suspicion.

As this plan would operate beneficially, in the detection and prevention of villainy, it would sometimes prove no less useful to the honest, but unfortunate man. Innocent men have been sometimes apprehended for spies, for highwaymen, and other atrocious crimes, from a similarity of circumstances, which it was not in their power to avoid. A highwayman, well mounted on a grey horse, some years since, robbed in the neighbourhood of London. Soon after, a person from a distant county happened to pass the road on a good horse of the same colour. Some persons took the alarm, pursued him, and took him into custody. As he was innocent, he came to no harm, but that of being detained all night, and the trouble he was put to, of proving he was not the man suspected, which he could do no otherwise, than by proving who he was; which, in many cases, where a man is totally unknown,

known, might be attended with much trouble and vexation.

I by no means offer this, as a well digested plan competent to the accomplishment of the intended purpose; but as the outlines of a scheme, which I am well convinced, by a person of abilities, might be made perfectly adequate to every purpose proposed.

I will beg leave to make one observation more, before I have done.

In a fertile country like England, which grows more corn than its inhabitants can consume, and, of course, renders it a commercial article; it is of great importance to ascertain the following facts, for the regulation of the exportation of that article.

I. What is the annual average growth of corn in England for a series of years?

II. What is the annual average consumption for the same time?

These being known, it would appear, what is the annual surplus, and consequently, how much might be exported annually, consistently with the safety and well being of the people. This is a question of the greatest importance to this country; a question, the ignorance of which has cost this nation millions, and by which our sagacious neighbours, the Dutch, have profited millions. Though totally neglected, I conceive it might be ascertained with no great difficulty or

trouble

trouble to any body. But this is a matter of too much confequence and extent, to be explained in a curfory paper.

On the PLEASURE *which the* MIND *in many Cafes receives from* CONTEMPLATING SCENES *of* DISTRESS. *By* T. BARNES, D. D. *Read April 3,* 1782.

Suave mari magno, turbantibus æquora ventis,
E terrâ alterius magnum fpectare periclum.
Non quia vexari quenquam eft jucunda voluptas;
Sed quibus ipfe malis careas, quia cernere fuave eft.
LUCRETIUS.

THE pleafure defcribed by the Poet in this motto, and of which he has mentioned fo ftriking and appofite an inftance, may perhaps, at firft, feem of fo fingular and aftonifhing a nature, that fome may be difpofed to doubt of its exiftence. But that it does exift, in the cafe here referred to, and in many others, of a fimilar kind, is an undoubted fact: and it may not appear an ufelefs, or difagreeable entertainment, to trace its *fource* in the human breaft, together with the *final caufe*, for which it was implanted there by our benevolent Creator.

"Shall I, it may be faid, feel complacency in beholding a fcene, in which many of my fellow-creatures

creatures are agonizing with terror, whilst I can neither diminish their danger, nor, by my sympathy, divide their anguish? At the sight of another's woe, does not my bosom naturally feel pain? Do I not share in his sensations? And is not this strong and exquisite sensibility intended by my Maker, to urge me on to active, and immediate assistance? These sensations are indeed attended with a noble pleasure, when I can, by friendly attention, or by benevolent communication, sooth the sorrows of the poor mourner, snatch him from impending danger, or supply his pressing wants. But, in general, where my sympathy is of no avail to the wretched sufferer, I fly from the spectacle of his misery, unable, or unwilling to endure a pain, which is not allayed by the sweet satisfaction of doing good."

It will be incumbent on us, in answer to these objections, in the first place, to prove the *reality* of the feeling, the cause of which, in the human constitution, we here attempt to explore.

Mr. Addison, in his beautiful papers on the Pleasures of the Imagination,* has observed, "that objects or scenes, which, when *real*, gave disgust or pain, in *description*, often become beautiful and agreeable. Thus, even a dunghill may, by the charms of poetic imagery, excite pleasure and entertainment. Scenes of this nature, dignified

* Spectator, sixth volume, No. 418.

by apt and striking description, we regard with something of the same feelings, with which we look upon a dead monster.

- - - - - - - - - - - - - Informe cadaver
Protrahitur: nequeunt expleri corda tuendo
Terribiles oculos, vultum, villosaque setis
Pectora semiferi, atque extinctos faucibus ignes.

VIRGIL.

"This, he observes, is more particularly the case, where the description raises a *ferment* in the mind, and works with violence upon the passions. One would wonder, adds he, how it comes to pass, that passions, which are very *unpleasant* at all other times, are very *agreeable*, when excited by proper description; such as terror, dejection, grief, &c. This pleasure arises from the reflection we make upon ourselves, whilst reading it, that we are not in danger from them. When we read of wounds, death, &c. our pleasure does not rise so properly, from the *grief*, which these melancholy descriptions give us, as from the secret *comparison* we make of ourselves, with those who suffer. We should not feel the *same kind* of pleasure, if we *actually saw* a person lying under the tortures, that we meet with in a description."

And yet, upon the principle assigned by this amiable writer, we might feel the same, or even higher pleasure, from the *actual* view of distress,

than

than from any *description*; because the comparison of ourselves with the sufferer would be more vivid, and consequently, the feeling more intense. I would only observe, that the cause which he assigns for this pleasure, is the very same with that assigned by Lucretius, in our motto. Mr. Addison applies it to the *description*; the Poet, to the *actual contemplation*, of affecting scenes. In both, the pleasure is supposed to originate in *selfishness*. But, wherever the social passions are deeply interested, as they are here supposed to be, from the pathetic *description*, or the still *more* pathetic *survey*, of the sufferings of another, the sympathetic feelings will, of themselves, at once, and previous to all reflection, become a source of agreeable and tender emotions. They will thus dignify and enhance the satisfaction, if any such be felt, arising merely from the consideration of our own personal security. And the more entirely we enter into the scene, by losing all ideas of its being either past, or fabulous, the more perfectly we forget ourselves, and are absorbed in the feeling,—the more exquisite is the sensation.

But, as our subsequent speculations will chiefly turn upon the pleasure derived from *real* scenes of calamity, and not from those which are *imaginary*, it may be expected, that we adduce instances, in *proof*, that such pleasure is *felt*, by persons very different in their taste, and mental cultivation.

I will not mention the horrid joy, with which the favage feafts his eye upon the agonies and contortions of his expiring prifoner—expiring in all the pangs which artificial cruelty can inflict! Nor will I turn your eye to the almoft equally favage fons of antient Rome, when the majefty of the Roman people could rufh, with eagernefs and tranfport, to behold hundreds of *Gladiators* contending in fatal conflict, and, probably, more than half the number extended, weltering in blood, and writhing in agony, upon the plain. Nor will I mention the Spanifh Bull-Feafts; nor the fervent acclamations of an Englifh Mob around their fellow-creatures, when engaged in furious battle, in which it is poffible, that fome of the combatants may receive a mortal blow, and be hurried, dreadful thought! in this awful ftate, to the bar of his Judge.

Let us furvey the multitudes, which, in every part of the kingdom, always attend an *execution*. It may perhaps be faid, that, in all places, the vulgar have little of the fenfibility and tendernefs of more polifhed bofoms. But, in the laft-mentioned inftance, an execution, there is no exultation in the fufferings of the poor criminal. He is regarded by every eye, with the moft melting compaffion. The whole affembly fympathizes with him, in his unhappy fituation. An awful ftillnefs prevails, at the dreadful moment. Many are wrung with unutterable fenfations:

sensations: and prayer and silence declare, more loudly than any language could, the interest they feel in his distress. Should a reprieve come to rescue him from death, how great is the general triumph and congratulation! And, probably, in this multitude you will find, not the mere vulgar herd alone, but the man of superior knowledge, and of more refined sensibility; who, led by *some* strong principle, which we wish to explain, feels a pleasure greater than all the pain, great and exquisite as one should imagine it to be, from such a spectacle.

The man who condemns many of the scenes we have already mentioned, as barbarous and shocking, would, probably, run with the greatest eagerness to some high cliff, overhanging the ocean, to see it swelled into tempest, though a poor vessel, or even a fleet of vessels, were to appear as one part of the dreadful scenery, now lifted to the heavens on the foaming surge, now plunged deep into the fathomless abyss, and now dashed upon the rocks, where they are, in a moment, shivered into fragments, and, with all their mariners, entombed in the wave. Or, to vary the question a little; Who would not be forward to stand safe, on the top of some mountain or tower, adjoining to a field of battle, in which two armies meet in desperate conflict, though, probably, thousands may soon lie before him prostrate on the ground, and the whole field present the most horrid scenes of carnage and desolation?

That, in all these cases, pleasure predominates in the compounded feeling, is plain from hence, because you *continue* to survey the scene; whereas, when pain became the stronger sensation, you would certainly *retire*. I was lately in company with a Gentleman, who described to me, in very glowing and picturesque colours, an engagement between two privateers, of which he had been a spectator, from one of the cliffs on the eastern coast of England. Several lives were lost; and the contest was long, doubtful, and severe. Having this subject in my thoughts, I asked him, whether he felt *pleasure* from the spectacle. He answered with great energy, that he would not have missed the sight for a very considerable sum. His tone, and manner proved, that he spoke from his heart.

Cultivation may, indeed, have produced some minuter differences, in the taste and feelings of different minds. Those, whose sensibilities have not been refined by education or science, may feel the pleasure, in a more gross and brutal form. But do not the most polished natures feel a similar, a *kindred* pleasure, in the deep-wrought distresses of the well-imagined scene? Here the endeavour is, to introduce whatever is dreadful or pathetic, whatever can harrow up the feelings, or extort the tear. And the deeper, and more

tragical

tragical the scene becomes, the more it agitates the several passions of terror, grief, or pity— the more intensely it delights, even the most polished minds. They seem to enjoy the various and vivid emotions of contending passions. They love to have the tear trembling in the eye, and to feel the whole soul rapt in thrilling sensations. For that moment, they seem to forget the fiction; and *afterwards* commend that exhibition most, in which they most entirely lost sight of the author, and of their own situation, and were alive to all the unutterable vibrations of strong or melting sensibility.

Taking it, then, for granted, that in the contemplation of *many* scenes of distress, both imaginary and real, a gratification is felt, let us endeavour to account for it, by mentioning some of those principles, woven into the web of human nature, by its benevolent Creator, on which that gratification depends.

Dr. Akenside, with his accustomed strength and brilliancy of colouring, *describes*, and *accounts for* it, in the following manner. I will make no apology for the length of the quotation.

    - - - - - - - - - - " Behold the ways
Of heaven's eternal destiny to man!
For even just, benevolent, and wise!
That VIRTUE's awful steps, howe'er pursued
By vexing fortune, and intrusive pain,
Should never be divided from her chaste,
Her fair attendant, PLEASURE. Need I urge

Thy tardy thought, through all the various round
Of this existence, that thy softening soul
At length may learn, what *energy* the hand
Of VIRTUE mingles in the bitter tide
Of PASSION, swelling with distress and pain,
To mitigate the sharp, with gracious drops
Of cordial PLEASURE. Ask the faithful youth,
Why the cold urn of her, whom long he loved,
So often fills his arm? So often draws
His lonely footsteps, at the silent hour,
To pay the mournful tribute of his tears?
O! he will tell thee, that the wealth of worlds
Should ne'er seduce his bosom to forego
That sacred hour, when, stealing from the noise
Of care and envy, *sweet remembrance* sooths,
With virtue's kindest looks, his aching breast,
And turns his *tears* to *rapture*. Ask the croud,
Which flies impatient from the village-walk
To climb the neighbouring cliffs, when far below
The cruel winds have hurled upon the coast
Some helpless bark: whilst sacred pity melts
The general eye, or Terror's icy hand
Smites their distorted limbs, or horrent hair,
While every mother closer to her breast
Catches her child; and, pointing where the waves
Foam through the shattered vessel, shrieks aloud,
As one poor wretch, that spreads his piteous arms
For succour, swallowed by the roaring surge,
As now another, dashed against the rock,
Drops lifeless down. O deemest thou indeed
NO KIND ENDEARMENT HERE, by nature given,
To mutual *terror*, and compassion's *tears?*
No sweetly melting softness, which attracts
O'er all that edge of pain, the social powers,
To this their proper action, and their end?"

The Poet pursues the sentiment in the same animated imagery, describing the strong, but pleasurable sensations, which the soul feels, in reading the sufferings of heroes, who nobly died in the cause of liberty, and their country:

> ———————— "When the pious band
> Of youths, who fought for freedom, and their sires,
> Lie side by side in gore."

Or, in the strong movements of indignation and revenge against the tyrant, who invades that liberty, and enslaves that country.

> ———————— "When the patriot's tear
> Starts from thine eye, and thy extended arm
> In fancy hurls the thunderbolt of Jove,
> To fire the impious wreath on Philip's brow,
> Or dash Octavius from his trophied car;
> Say — Does thy secret soul *repine* to taste
> The big *distress?* Or, would'st thou then exchange
> Those *heart-ennobling sorrows* for the lot
> Of him, who sits amid the gaudy herd
> Of mute barbarians, bending to his nod,
> And bears aloft his gold-invested front,
> And says within himself," "I am a King,
> And wherefore should the clamorous voice of woe
> Intrude upon mine ear?"

The sentiment of this charming and moral poet is, that sympathetic feelings are *virtuous*, and therefore *pleasant*. And from the whole, he deduces this important conclusion; that every virtuous emotion must be agreeable, and that this is the *sanction*, and the *reward* of virtue. The thought

thought is amiable. The conclusion noble. But still the solution appears to me to be imperfect.

We have already said, that the pleasure arising from the contemplation of distressful scenes is a *compounded feeling*, arising from *several* distinct sources in the human breast. The *kind* and *degree* of the sensation must depend upon the various blendings of the several ingredients, which enter into the composition. The cause assigned by Mr. Addison, the sense of our own security, may be supposed to have *some* share in the mass of feelings. That of Dr. Akenside may be allowed to have a still *larger* proportion.—Let us attempt to trace some of the rest.

There are few principles in human nature of more general and important influence, than that of SYMPATHY. A late ingenious writer, led by the fashionable idea of simplifying all the springs of human nature into *one* source, has, in his beautiful Theory of Moral Sentiments, endeavoured to analyse a very large number of the feelings of the heart into sympathetic vibration. Though it appears to me most probable, that the human mind, like the human body, possesses *various* and *distinct* springs, of action and of happiness, yet he has shewn, in an amazing diversity of instances, the operation and importance of this principle of human nature. Let us apply it to our present subject.

We

We naturally sympathize with the passions of others. But, if the passions they appear to feel be not those of *mere distress alone*; if, amidst scenes of calamity, they display fortitude, generosity, and forgiveness; if, " rising superior to the cloud of ills which covers them," they nobly stand firm, collected, and patient; here, a still higher source of pleasure opens upon us, from complacence, admiration, and that unutterable sympathy, which the heart feels with virtuous and heroic minds. By the operation of this principle, we place ourselves in their situation; we feel, as it were, some share of that conscious integrity and peace, which they must enjoy. Hence, as before observed, the pleasure will vary, both as to its *nature*, and *degree*, according to the *scene* and *characters* before us. The shock of contending armies in the field,—the ocean wrought to tempest, and covered with the wreck of shattered vessels,—and a worthy family silently, yet nobly bearing up, against a multitude of surrounding sorrows, will excite very *different* emotions, because the component parts of the pleasurable sensation consist of very different materials. They all excite admiration; but admiration, how diversified, both as to its *degree*, and its *cause!* These several ingredients may, doubtless, be so blended together, that the pleasure shall make but a very small part of the mixed sensation. The more agreeable *tints* may bear

little

little proportion to the terrifying *red*, or the gloomy *black*.

In many of the instances which have been mentioned, the pleasure must arise chiefly, if not solely, from the *circumstances*, or *accompanyments* of the scene. The sublime feelings, excited by the view of an agitated ocean, relieve and soften those occasioned by the shipwreck. And the awe, excited by the presence of thousands of men, acting as with one soul, and displaying magnanimity and firmness, in the most solemn trial, tempers those sensations of horror and of pain, which would arise from the field of battle.

The gratification we are attempting to account for, depends, also, in a very considerable degree, upon a principle of human nature, implanted in it for the wisest ends; the EXERCISE which it gives to the mind, by rousing it to energy, and feeling. Nothing is so insupportable, as that languor and *ennui*, for the full expression of which, our language does not afford a term. How agreeable it is, to have the soul called forth to exertion and sensibility, let the Gamester witness, who, unable to endure the lassitude and sameness of unanimated luxury, runs with eagerness to the place, where, probably, await him all the irritation and agony of tumultuous passions.

Again; It is a law of our nature, That *opposite passions*, when felt in *succession*, and, above all,

all, when felt at the *same moment*, heighten and increase each other. Ease succeeding pain, certainty after suspense, friendship after aversion, are unspeakably stronger, than if they had not been thus contrasted. In this *conflict* of feelings, the mind rises from *passive* to *active* energy. It is roused to intense sensation; and it enjoys that peculiar, exquisite, and complex feeling, in which, as in many articles of our table, the acid and the sweet, the pleasurable and painful pungencies are so happily mixed together, as to render the united sensation amazingly more strong and delightful.

We have not yet mentioned the principle of CURIOSITY, that busy and active power, which appears so *early*, continues almost unimpaired so *long*, and to which, for the wisest ends, is annexed so great a sense of enjoyment. To this principle, rather than to a love of cruelty, would I ascribe that pleasure, which children sometimes seem to feel, from torturing flies, and lesser animals. They have not yet formed an idea of the pain they inflict. It is, indeed, of unspeakable consequence, that this practice be checked, as soon and as effectually as possible, because it is so important, that they learn to connect the ideas of pleasure and pain, with the motions and actions of the animal creation. And, to this principle may we also refer, no small share of that pleasure in the contemplation of distressful scenes,

scenes, the springs of which, in the human heart, we are now endeavouring to open.

To CURIOSITY, then—to SYMPATHY—to MENTAL EXERTION—to the idea of our own SECURITY—and to the STRONG FEELINGS occasioned by viewing the *actions* and *passions* of mankind in INTERESTING SITUATIONS, do we ascribe that *gratification*, which the mind feels from the survey of many scenes of sorrow. We have called it a PLEASURE; but it will approach towards, or recede from *pleasure*, according to the *nature*, and *proportion* of the ingredients, of which the sensation is composed. In *some* cases, pain will predominate. In OTHERS, there will be exquisite enjoyment.

The *final cause* of this constitution of the human mind is probably, that by means of this strong sensation, the soul may be preserved in continual and vigorous motion—that its feelings may be kept lively and tender—that it may learn, to practise the virtues it admires—and to assist those to whom its sympathy *can* reach—and that it may thus be led, by these social exercises of the heart, to soften with compassion—to expand with benevolence—and generously to assist in every case, in which assistance can be given. An end this sufficient,

- - - - - - " To assert eternal Providence,
And justify the ways of God to man."

OBSERVATIONS *on* BLINDNESS, *and on the Employment of the other Senses to supply the* LOSS OF SIGHT. *By Mr.* BEW. *Read April* 17, 1782.

> - - - - - - - - - tenebrasque necesse 'st
> Non radii solis, neque lucida tela diei
> Discutiant - - - -   LUCRET.

AMONGST the various accidents and calamities, to which the human species are subjected, there are none that excite compassion, or call forth our benevolent aid more powerfully, than blindness. The blind man, in all ages and countries, has ever been allowed an indisputable claim on the good offices of his fellow-creatures; his necessities have generally been supplied with sacred care; and his genius, if it approached to excellence, has been respected with a degree of reverence, superior to what is usually bestowed, on such as are possessed of the faculty of sight.

The faculty of sight, indeed, is justly considered as superior to any of the other senses. Hearing, tasting, and smelling, when compared with vision, appear very limited in their powers and determinations; and though the sense of touch may possess the most general, and accurate power of conveying the ideas of the various modifications of matter to the mind; yet the comprehensiveness, together with the instantaneous celerity, with which vision displays to us the wonders of Nature, or the varieties of Art, far transcend any of the perceptions, that the touch, or the other senses, are able to furnish us with. It is, perhaps, on this account, that we figuratively employ the term, *seeing*, in acknowledging the conscious evidence of reason and truth; and even extend the application, as the most expressive, to one of the distinguishing attributes of Almighty perfection.

In no part of the human fabric, or even throughout the whole of nature, with which we are acquainted, are there more evident marks of exquisite perfection and wisdom, than in what relates to the sense of seeing; whether we direct our attention to the wonderful regularity, order, minuteness, and velocity of the rays of light, which minister to this sense, or to the structure and formation of the little organ, in which this faculty is destined to reside. " With a ball and
" socket, (as a learned and elegant Philosopher,*
" beautifully observes) of an inch diameter, we
" are enabled, in an instant of time, without
" changing our place, to perceive the disposition
" of an army, the figure of a palace, and the
" variety of a landscape;" and not only, as he farther remarks, to " find our way through the

* Dr. Reid, p. 121.

" pathless

"pathless ocean, traverse the globe of the earth,
"determine its figure and dimensions, and deli-
"neate every region of it:" But,

– – – – – – "Breaking hence, take our ardent flight
"Thro' the blue infinite,"

ascertain the order, revolutions and distances of the planetary orbs, and even form probable conjectures on

– – – – – – – – – – – – – "Every star
"Which the clear concave of a winter's night
"Pours on the eye, or astronomic tube,
"Far stretching, snatches from the dark abyss."

THOMSON.

In contemplating, therefore, the extensive and almost unlimited properties of vision, we not only find our gratitude warmed and elevated to piety and devotion, but are, likewise, conscious of an involuntary impulse, that urges us to exert our endeavours, towards the assistance of such as are unfortunately deprived of this noble faculty, whenever they are presented to our notice.

And here, again, we have every motive to inspire us with admiration of the providential wisdom and benevolence, displayed by the divine Author of our existence. For, notwithstanding the great and comprehensive powers of sight, there is little of the actual knowledge acquired by this faculty, that may not, by attentive and patient perseverance, be communicated to the man who has been doomed to darkness from his birth. The bigot, or the enthusiast, who condemns the researches of philosophy, and erroneously pronounces them to be incompatible with religion; perceives, with astonishment, the blind enabled to expatiate on light or colours; on reflection, refraction, and on the various subjects, from which we might naturally suppose they would be excluded, by the deprivation of sight; and satisfies himself with abruptly referring the whole to the immediate dispensation of the Deity. The philosopher, on the other hand, though, with willing submission, he ultimately attributes the effects to Omnipotence; is, nevertheless, desirous to avoid the censure passed on the servant, "*who buried his talent in a napkin*;" and ventures to exert the abilities with which he may be endowed in endeavouring to investigate the means by which the effects are ordained to be accomplished, to the end, that the interests of humanity may be served with greater certainty.

The powerful influence of exercise and habit upon the intellectual, as well as upon the corporeal faculties, are too well known and acknowledged, to require much illustration. The muscles, of any part of the body, acquire peculiar vigour and fullness by habitual exercise;

cife; and the fame is remarkable, though in a ſtill higher degree, with reſpect to the effects of exerciſe and habit, on the faculties of the mind. From this wiſe regulation, in the œconomy of nature, reſults a train of reſources, which the blind are found capable of deriving, from the exerciſe of the other ſenſes; and which may be ſo far perfected, as to compenſate, in a great meaſure, for the loſs of the darling ſenſe of ſight. The delicacy and preciſion, with which ſome eminent blind people have employed the other ſenſes, particularly, *hearing* and *touch*, would, indeed, exceed the bounds of credibility, were we not aſſured of the facts, as well from actual experience, as from undoubted authorities.

Dr. Saunderſon loſt his ſight, by the ſmall-pox, ſo early in his infancy, that he did not remember to have ever ſeen. He had no more ideas of light, than if he had been born blind. Notwithſtanding this misfortune, he acquired ſuch profound and perfect knowledge in the ſcience of mathematics, that, by the influence of his merit only, he was appointed to the profeſſorſhip in the Univerſity of Cambridge. The addreſs of this celebrated philoſopher, was no ways inferior to the knowledge he poſſeſſed; a circumſtance, which we do not always meet with in thoſe who have the full powers of ſight. His lectures on the different branches of mathematics, natural philoſophy, aſtronomy, and optics, were remarkably clear and intelligible. Fully aware of the difficulties young minds have to contend with, from the abstruseness in which the subjects of natural philosophy are usually involved, his endeavours were successfully directed to obviate and remove these obstructions; and to furnish a method, at the same time, comprehensive, natural, and easy to be understood.

Dr. Saunderson's sensation of touch, as is usual with blind people, was very exquisite; and it was by means of this sense, that he acquired many of his principal ideas. He distinguished, with astonishing nicety, the peculiar properties of bodies, that depended on the roughness or smoothness of their surfaces. A remarkable instance is given of his nice accuracy in this respect. A series of Roman medals, some of which were true, and others false, were presented to his touch. Dr. Saunderson, by running his fingers over them, was soon able to distinguish the genuine antiques, from those that were counterfeited; though the latter had been executed, with such exactness of imitation, as to deceive a connoisseur, who only judged by the eye. But, says the professor, "I, who had not that sense "to trust to, could easily feel a roughness in "the new cast, sufficient to distinguish them by."

The impression made by the approach of bodies nearer to him, or their being removed farther

farther off; and the different states of the atmosphere, were distinguishable to him by the same delicate sense of touch; and his sense of hearing was refined to a similar degree of perfection. He could readily ascertain the fifth part of a note of music. He not only distinguished and remembered the different people he conversed with, by the peculiar sounds of their voices, but, in some measure, places also. Judging by the sounds of the pavements, of the courts and piazzas, and the reflection of these sounds from the walls, he remembered the different variations, so as to be able to recollect the places, pretty exactly, when conducted to them afterwards.

We might produce a great variety of instances, both antient and modern, where blind persons have excelled in different departments of science; and particularly, in the several branches of mathematics.* But the attachment, which these unfortunate

---

* Diodotus, the preceptor of Cicero, is represented as attaching himself, with greater assiduity to the Science of Mathematics after he became blind.

"Diodotus Stoicus, cæcus multos annos, nostræ domi
"vixit: is vero, quod credibile vix esset, cum in Philo-
"sophia multò etiam magis assiduè quam antea versaretur
"tum quod sine occulis fieri possit. Geometriæ munus tueba-
"tur, præcipiens discentibus, unde, quo, quamque lineam
"scriberent." Cic. Tusc. disp. L. V. 39.

unfortunate people display, for the pleasing pursuits of music and poetry, is still more general. The powerful influence of verbal expression, when communicated to the blind, in the form of poetry, and the congenial ideas it inspires, are really astonishing. Of this we have a recent proof in Dr. Blacklock of Edinburgh. This amiable gentleman was, I believe, either born blind, or became so very soon after his birth: yet, we find no defects, in those beautiful poems he has exhibited to the world, that can be attributed to his want of sight; on the contrary, we meet with descriptions of visual scenes and objects, as beautiful, expressive, and just, as if he had actually been possessed of the faculty of seeing; and had drawn his descriptions, from an enraptured survey of the variegated prospects of nature. Whereas, we must be convinced, when we accurately consider the matter, that the poetic enthusiasm, which inspired him, and excited these imitative powers, could only be produced by the various combination of sounds, which were conveyed, by words, to his imagination.

The influence of music is still more generally to be observed than that of poetry. Music, almost

---

Didymus of Alexandria, is celebrated by St. Jerom and the historian Cassiodorus, as a prodigy in logic and mathematics, though blind from his infancy. The latter writer, likewise speaks of one Eusebius, an Asiatic, who, though blind, distinguished himself highly in all kinds of learning.

without exception, appears to be the favourite amusement of the blind. There is no other employment of the mind, religious contemplation excepted, that seems so well adapted to sooth the soul, and dissipate the melancholy ideas, which, it may naturally be expected, will sometimes pervade the dispositions of those who are utterly bereft of sight. This, together with the beneficial influence that results from the practice of this delightful art, by quickening and perfecting the sense of hearing, is a matter that deserves the most serious attention. The celebrated Professor, just now mentioned, excelled in performing on the flute, in his youth; and the refinement of his ear, has been very justly attributed to his early attention to music. It is not, therefore, surprizing that so many blind people have distinguished themselves in this science. Stanley and Parry were deprived of their sight in early infancy; yet both these Gentlemen have displayed extraordinary proofs of their abilities, not only as composers and performers of music, but, likewise, in matters that, at a first view, we might be apt to consider as peculiar to those who are fully possessed of the faculty of vision. Their separate reputations, as musicians, are sufficiently known and acknowledged. The stile of Stanley is truly his own; and his execution on the organ, equal, if not superior to any of his cotemporary performers on that grand instrument. Parry may be revered as the British bard of modern times. The halls of the Cambrian Chief resound with the melodious vibrations of his harp, and he has united the refinements of taste and elegance to the rude, but expressive modulations of antiquity.

I pass over a number of instances, that might be offered to your notice, and proceed to give some account of Dr. Henry Moyes, the elegant reader on philosophical chemistry; whose lectures, the greatest part of this society had the satisfaction of attending; and whose personal acquaintance several of us have enjoyed.

This intelligent philosopher, like the celebrated professor of Cambridge before-mentioned, lost his sight, by the small-pox, in his early infancy. He never recollected to have seen: "but the first traces of memory I have," says he, "are in some confused ideas of the solar system." He had the good fortune to be born in a country where learning of every kind is highly cultivated, and to be brought up in a family devoted to learning.

Possessed of native genius, and ardent in his application, he made rapid advances in various departments of erudition; and not only acquired the fundamental principles of mechanics, music, and the languages; but, likewise, entered deeply into the investigation of the profounder sciences; and displayed an accute

and

and general knowledge of geometry, optics, algebra; of aftronomy, chemiftry; and, in fhort, of moft of the branches of the Newtonian philofophy.

Mechanical exercifes were the favourite employments of his infant years. At a very early age, he made himfelf acquainted with the ufe of edged tools; fo perfectly, that, notwithftanding his intire blindnefs, he was able to make little wind-mills; and, he even conftructed a loom, with his own hands, which ftill fhew the cicatrices of wounds, he received in the execution of thefe juvenile exploits.

By a moft agreeable intimacy, and frequent intercourfe, which I enjoyed, with this accomplifhed blind Gentleman, whilft he refided in Manchefter; I had an opportunity of repeatedly obferving the peculiar manner, in which he arranged his ideas, and acquired his information. Whenever he was introduced into company, I remarked, that he continued fome time filent. The found directed him to judge of the dimenfions of the room, and the different voices, of the number of perfons that were prefent. His diftinction, in thefe refpects, was very accurate; and his memory fo retentive, that he feldom was miftaken. I have known him inftantly recognize a perfon, on firft hearing him fpeak, though more than two years had elapfed fince the time of their laft meeting. He determined, pretty nearly, the

ftature

stature of those he was speaking with, by the direction of their voices; and he made tolerable conjectures, respecting their tempers and dispositions, by the manner in which they conducted their conversation.

It must be observed, that this Gentleman's eyes were not totally insensible to intense light. The rays refracted through a prism, when sufficiently vivid, produced certain distinguishable effects on them. The red gave him a disagreeable sensation, which he compared to the touch of a saw. As the colours declined in violence, the harshness lessened, until the green afforded a sensation that was highly pleasing to him; and which he described, as conveying an idea similar to what he felt, in running his hand over smooth polished surfaces. Polished surfaces, meandering streams, and gentle declivities, were the figures, by which he expressed his ideas of beauty. Rugged rocks, irregular points, and boisterous elements, furnished him with expressions for terror and disgust. He excelled in the charms of conversation; was happy in his allusions to visual objects; and discoursed on the nature, composition, and beauty of colours, with pertinence and precision.

Doctor Moyes was a striking instance of the power, the human soul possesses, of finding resources of satisfaction, even under the most rigorous calamities. Though involved "in ever during darkness,

darkness," and excluded from the charming views of silent or animated nature; though dependent on an undertaking for the means of his subsistence, the success of which was very precarious; in short, though destitute of other support than his genius, and under the mercenary protection of a person, whose integrity he suspected—still Dr. Moyes was generally chearful, and apparently happy. Indeed it must afford much pleasure to the feeling heart, to observe this hilarity of temper prevail, almost universally, with the blind. Though "cut off from the ways of men, and the contemplation of the human face divine;" they have this consolation; they are exempt from the discernment, and contagious influence, of those painful emotions of the soul, that are visible on the countenance, and which hypocrify itself can scarcely conceal. This disposition, likewise, may be considered, as an internal evidence of the native worth of the human mind; that thus supports its dignity and chearfulness under one of the severest misfortunes that can possibly befall us. Nor is this chearful resignation peculiar to those who have been blind from their birth; we find it, also, generally prevail with such as have lost their sight, even at a more advanced age; and who must, undoubtedly, feel the misfortune with the utmost anguish. The distressing recollection, which memory must present, of former enjoyments, we find, however, soon subsides. Gentler and more pleasing reflections succeed. Contemplation takes her residence in her proper province, the human mind; and the blind, submissively and chearfully resign themselves to the will of Heaven, and the benevolent protection of the less unfortunate of their fellow-creatures. And hard, indeed, is the heart of him, who will not stretch out his hand to succour the blind; or who, by injustice, illiberality, or unkindness, adds a sting to the conscious dependence, to which, whilst they live, they must ever be subjected.

The blind people I have hitherto selected to speak of, it may be remarked, were such as had their native faculties excited and matured by early and attentive education. But we shall find, even where education has been wanting, and the blind left, in a great measure, to the simple exertions of nature; that the natural faculties themselves make surprizing efforts towards supplying the deficiency of sight. I shall bring forwards to your notice a person, well known in this neighbourhood, of which he is a native. This is one John Metcalf, who, like the Gentlemen already mentioned, became blind at a very early age, so as to be intirely unconscious of light and its various effects. This man passed the younger part of his life as a waggoner; and, occasionally, as a guide in intricate roads during the night, or when the tracks were covered with snow. Strange

as

as this may appear to those who can see, the employment he has since undertaken is still more extraordinary: it is one of the last to which we could suppose a blind man would ever turn his attention. His present occupation is that of a projector and surveyor of highways in difficult and mountainous parts. With the assistance only of a long staff, I have several times met this man traversing the roads, ascending precipices, exploring valleys, and investigating their several extents, forms, and situations, so as to answer his designs in the best manner. The plans which he designs, and the estimates he makes, are done in a method peculiar to himself; and which he cannot well convey the meaning of to others. His abilities, in this respect, are, nevertheless, so great, that he finds constant employment. Most of the roads over the Peak in Derbyshire, have been altered by his directions; particularly those in the vicinity of Buxton: and he is, at this time, constructing a new one, betwixt Wilmslow and Congleton, with a view to open a communication to the great London road, without being obliged to pass over the mountains.*

The

---

* Since this paper was written, and had the honour of being delivered to the Society, I have met this blind projector of the roads, who was alone as usual; and amongst other conversation, I made some inquiries respecting this new road. It was really astonishing to hear with what accuracy he described the courses, and the nature of the

different

These instances will, I am perfuaded, be fufficient to prove, how effectually, by proper exercife, the other fenfes may be refined and perfected, fo as, in many refpects, to fupply the lofs of fight. The fenfations of fmell and tafte, indeed, are fo very limited, that they do not feem capable of yielding many peculiar advantages to blind people: but the perceptions of hearing and touch, as we have feen, may be applied to purpofes wonderfully extenfive.

By the nice diftinction of touch and found, the blind man not only acquires knowledge with refpect to perfons and fituations; is not only warned from danger, and excited to pleafure; but by means of thefe delicate faculties, he is enabled to conceive many of the vifual qualities of bodies, and to diftinguifh them with certain precifion. I do not mean to infer, that a blind man annexes the fame ideas to vifual qualities, as are excited in the minds of thofe who are poffeffed of the perfect faculty of fight. I only wifh to obferve, that he forms a general conception of their characters, by the analogy which he finds they bear to qualities he is ac-

---

different foils, through which it was conducted. Having mentioned to him a boggy piece of ground it paffed through, he obferved, that " that was the only place he had doubts " concerning; and that he was apprehenfive they had, " contrary to his directions, been too fparing of their " materials."

quainted

quainted with, by means of his other senses. Thus, for example, if we present a violet to him, and demand of him what ideas he has of its qualities; he will be able to answer with great precision respecting its smell, &c. which, as well as the name of the violet are soft, sweet, and pleasing. But, with regard to the colour, he will be wholly unable to conceive any idea of it, except what takes place from very distant analogies: the plaintive melody of the flute, the soft smoothness of surfaces, &c. In like manner, by apposite associations, he may compare the intense colour of scarlet to the glow of a furnace, the noise of a trumpet, or the odour of aromatics; because they severally affect his senses with intense excitements.

But whatever amazing information, the senses of hearing and touch, may afford the blind; these powers would, nevertheless, be transient and ineffectual, were not the impressions and ideas they excite in the mind, preserved and matured by the assistance of the memory. It is chiefly by the assistance of the memory, that the blind acquire the exquisite advantages, derived from the other senses. In this respect, providential benevolence seems to have determined the greatest compensation, for the severe deprivation of the sense of sight. The soul of the blind man, undistracted by the never ceasing variety which is always present to the organs of vision, when

awake,

awake, pursues its internal perceptions and contemplations with unconfounded serenity. The blind unlettered projector of roads could reply to me, when I expressed myself surprized at the accuracy of his discriminations, "that there was "nothing surprizing in the matter; You, Sir," says he, " can have recourse to your eye sight "whenever you want to see or examine any "thing; whereas, I have only my memory to "trust to. There is one advantage, how-"ever," he remarked, that he possessed. " The "readiness with which you view an object at "pleasure, prevents the necessity of fixing "the ideas of it deeply in your mind, and the "impressions, in general, become quickly obli-"terated. On the contrary, the information I "possess, being acquired with greater difficulty, "is, on that very account, so firmly fixed on the "memory, as to be almost indelible." Such, indeed, is the wonderful influence, resulting from the union of exercise and habit, on the faculties of the blind, that the permanency of their knowledge, in a great measure, compensates for the labour required in its attainment!

The instantaneous facility, with which, by the aid of sight, we are able to ascertain the peculiarities of any place we survey, and the ease with which we review and recognize them, renders dependence on the memory, to us, less necessary. For instance, the dimensions of the
apartment

appartment I sit in; the furniture, &c. will, by the organs of vision, be immediately presented to the mind of any stranger who may call on me, so that he will be able, in a moment, to recollect the whole whenever he repeats his visit, to the same place. This kind of information can only be acquired by the blind man, in consequence of the most patient attention. He is to be led round the several parts of the room, his finger conducted to the surfaces of the furniture, pictures, &c. before he can possibly form any idea with respect to the place. But when, by means of the perceptions of touch, and a necessary degree of information, he conceives a regular train of distinguishing ideas, his mind associates them, with such tenacity, that he seldom has occasion to repeat his inquiries.

It is this accurate and retentive power of the memory, that enables the blind mathematician to make exact calculations and inferences; to work problems in algebra, and in infinite series; to conceive, with precision, the different effects that bodies must produce to the sight, by their being nearer or farther off; by their moving in a straight or in an oblique line; and, that directs his investigation with respect to the principles of projection, and the various rules of perspective.

It must here be remarked, that though the blind man may conceive the properties of figure and extension with certain accuracy; yet it does not follow that he would be able to distinguish them, with the same certainty, by vision, provided that faculty were, immediately, bestowed on him. On the contrary, the question started by Mr. Molineux,[*] was found to prove exactly as that philosopher expected, in the extraordinary case of a blind youth, whom Mr. Cheselden had the good fortune to bring to sight, by couching, at thirteen years of age. This young man, at his first feeling the impressions of objects on the organs of vision, imagined every thing he saw touched his eyes; nor was he able to discriminate one object from another, however different their forms. When things that were before known to him, by touching, were presented to him, he considered them attentively, in order to recognize them; but, on a sudden, he felt himself confused, from the multitude of objects that crowded for admission, and the whole was involved in obscurity. It appears, therefore, from the above fact, as well as from a due examination of the subject, that those who make use of their eyes, for the first time, see only surfaces and colours; and have no conception of the visible effects of light and projection, until they learn it from experience. In fact, if we carefully attend to the operation of our own minds, we shall find, that the

[*] Lock on the Understanding, vol. I. p. 107.

visible appearances of objects are seldom accurately attended to, unless we are employed in delineating those objects. The visible appearance of things, is varied according to the direction of the light, the position, and the distance, with respect to the beholder: yet, as we are conscious from experience, of the identity, the real figure is conceived in its actual proportion, and the visible, or perspective, appearance is considered only as a sign or indication.

The accurate painter is well aware of this operation of the mind, and in delineating his objects, and relieving them with the distribution of light and shade, is carefully attentive to avoid forming conclusions, before he accurately considers the premises. The effect produced by a well managed picture, sufficiently evinces the actual appearance of bodies, according to their point of view; and the impressions they must make on the organs of sight, when employed previous to the influence of reason, and the correction of the judgment. The painter, who exerts the imitative powers of his art to deceive the eye, does not merely draw the out-line of his figure, and colour it with the exact uniform tinge it naturally displays: he surveys it in one certain point of view, and then proceeds to delineate and adapt his tints, as if the figure were, in reality, adhering to the canvas. It is no wonder, therefore, that the young Gentleman, just mentioned,

mentioned, was astonished to find, on examining the pictures, presented to him, with his finger, that they had not the same projection, with the objects they represented. This, as well as the art of diminishing a figure, and still preserving the resemblance, would evidently be as much an enigma, to a person just possessed of vision, as the circumstance of the Mirror, mentioned by *M. Diderot.**

It is more than probable, therefore, that the blind man, has no ideas of colour, except, as has been already remarked, what are derived from a kind of distant analogy, regulated by the associating powers of the mind, and preserved by the memory; and, indeed, most of the persons of this class I have conversed with, have frankly confessed themselves wholly ignorant of its qualities. Nor is this deficiency in the forming of ideas peculiar to the sense of sight. A deaf man would be just as much embarrassed, with respect to the qualities of sound; and the same may be observed with respect to the other senses.

In the course of my inquiries, however, on this subject, it occurred to me, that I might possibly derive some new matter for observation, from the recollection of the blind man's perceptions, whilst under the influence of his dreams. In the usual silent hours of repose, when the

* Vid les Œuvres de *M. Diderot*, tom. II. Art, Lettres sur les Aveugles, &c.

exercise of the memory is, in a great measure, suspended; and the unfettered imagination displays its powers, in a very peculiar manner; I conceived it might be possible for the blind to experience some transient impressions, relative to visual qualities. It is true Mr. Lock gives it as his opinion, "that the dreams of sleeping "men are made up of waking men's ideas; "though," he allows, "they are, for the most "part, oddly put together." The impressions of dreams, it must be acknowledged, are too fleeting to admit of much investigation; and our recollection of them is liable to the greatest uncertainty: yet, notwithstanding the opinion of this great philosopher, there are few, I am persuaded, who have not felt themselves sometimes affected, during their dreams, in a manner which they could by no means account for, or reconcile with any circumstance that had previously taken place in real life. And though I have not been able to gratify my curiosity to its full extent, yet I have gained sufficient information to convince me, that the blind feel impressions in dreaming, in some degree, similar to the visible appearances of bodies. A blind Gentleman, with whom I have lately conversed, clearly proves to me, that he is conscious of the figure, though he cannot distinguish the varieties of the human countenance: and from the confused efforts he makes to explain himself, it may be perceived, that he feels himself alarmed with new sensations, that bear a strong relation to our ideas of light and colour; but which he finds it impossible to describe, because he cannot fix on any comparative idea whereby to explain himself. These dreams, my intelligent friend informs me, are always painful, and, as may naturally be expected, the impressions are extremely transient and unsatisfactory.

But it is not the blind only, who are unable to trace the various effects produced by light and colour. There are persons, whose organs of vision are so imperfectly formed, that they cannot distinguish colours, though they see the objects perfectly. In the Philosophical Transactions we have an account of a man who knew no difference of colour whatever; and there is an ingenious person, within the circle of our acquaintance, whose knowledge in Perspective, as well as in the other branches of Natural Philosophy, is unquestionable; yet who finds himself deficient in discerning the difference of some colours, which he knows to exist, and which are distinguishable to perfect vision. In particular, I think I have heard him mention, that the sensation he felt, from the colours of brown and green, had no obvious difference, provided they were diffused with equal degrees of intenseness.

But these speculations, however curious and entertaining, were not the principal objects I had

had in view, when I sat down to consider the subject of blindness. It may be remarked, that in the sketches, relative to blind people, I have offered to your notice, I have purposely avoided speaking of such, as had ever possessed the faculty of vision, so as to recollect it with any degree of accuracy: and I have been the more particular in my account of Dr. Moyes, and the blind projector of roads, because I had an opportunity of availing myself of immediate information from them, with respect to such peculiarities, as it was not in my power to derive from the writings of the few authors, who have treated on this subject.* In tracing the progress, and marking the degrees of perfection, to which the most celebrated blind people have carried the exertions of the other senses, to supply the loss of sight; I was persuaded, that farther observations and discoveries might be made, which might be applied to advantage in the education of blind children; and also in rendering more perfect, the different inventions, that have already been devised, in order to facilitate their information, and the means of their improvement: and I

* Besides occasional hints which I have acquired from conversing with various blind people, whose names are not mentioned; I have particular acknowledgments to make to Mr. Cheese, the organist of the collegiate church in Manchester, for the satisfaction he has afforded me in many of my inquiries.

flattered myself, that these matters would be deemed sufficiently important, to engage the attention of the learned members of this Society. Instances too frequently occur, that most powerfully call for the generosity and compassion of mankind; and though our abilities rarely arrive at the divine perfection of *giving sight to the blind*, we shall always experience a conscious benevolent satisfaction, in ministering to their knowledge, their convenience and happiness.

A TREATISE ON SALTPETRE.

By JAMES MASSEY, Esq.

---------- si quid novisti rectius istis
Candidus Imperti, si non his utere mecum.

INTRODUCTORY OBSERVATIONS.

THE great importance of Saltpetre, since the invention of gun-powder, is too well known to be here expatiated upon, as well as the numerous rewards that have been offered to those who should give us the clearest and best accounts of it; a sure sign that, notwithstanding it has been

been long made in very confiderable quantities in almoft every part of Europe, our knowledge of this falt is ftill very imperfect.

This induced the author of the following pages, many years ago, to turn his attention to this fubject, and he flatters himfelf, that, by long obfervation, and a practice which, though not very extenfive, may have been fufficient for this purpofe, he has made fuch difcoveries, as may render the bufinefs of faltpetre-making no lefs eafy and familiar to his countrymen, than it has long been to our neighbours upon the continent.

He never, indeed, could be brought to believe, that it was owing to any defect in our climate, or to the want of materials, that we have fo often failed in our attempts this way, but merely to our inattention to fome particular points in the practical part, upon which our fuccefs, in a great meafure, depended. Thefe, therefore, he has principally laboured to explore, and to fet them in fo ftrong a light, that they can no longer efcape our obfervation.

It is the cuftom of the faltpetre-makers abroad, to wait till the earths they have procured, or prepared for this purpofe, are found fit to anfwer their end; a practice, which we have reafon to think has rarely been followed by our countrymen, who, finding the earths they have employed, imperfect upon the firft trial, have feldom afforded them a fecond, and thus have rejected

many

many that, in a due courfe of time, might have anfwered their moft fanguine expectations.

They have, likewife, not duly attended to the large quantities of earth, that our neighbours are obliged to elixiviate, in order to obtain a fmall portion of faltpetre; and finding their portion but trifling in the trials they have made, have too haftily concluded this bufinefs to be fcarcely worth following; when, had they reflected upon the great number of faltpetre-makers in France and Germany, they muft, certainly, have entertained a very different opinion.

But what has chiefly difcouraged us, we prefume, may have been, our ignorance of the true grounds and principles, upon which the practice of making faltpetre is founded; which, we may obferve, have never been clearly laid open. All that we are told is, that faltpetre is extracted from the rubbifh of old houfes, the bottoms of ftinking pits and ditches, and the like; which has induced many perfons to conclude, that this falt is generated in thefe earths: whereas, the truth is, that nothing is extracted from thefe earths but a peculiar acid, which, in conjunction with the fixt falt of wood-afhes, and not without, forms this neutral one which cryftallizes in the ley when boiled down as above-mentioned; which circumftances being omitted, it can be no wonder that we are led into very great errors.

Of this acid, the source from which it is derived, and the manner in which these and other earths become impregnated with it, we shall endeavour to give the most full, and satisfactory account, as well as of the practical methods of making saltpetre, all which might be comprized in a page or two, had we not a variety of chimeras to encounter, and this practice particularly to explain. By these means we hope to remove all that mystery and obscurity in which this subject has been so long involved; and to render the practice of making saltpetre as easy and familiar to the English, as it has long been to the French and Germans, so much to the advantage of those nations.

ON SALTPETRE.

The great use of saltpetre in the composition of gun-powder, has long rendered it an object of the first importance; upon which account, the learned have spared no pains to obtain the most perfect knowledge of it; but hitherto, as it seems, without success, as no clear and satisfactory account has yet been given of it. And though the methods of making it in France, Germany, and many other parts of the world,

world, have been minutely described, these descriptions, through some defect or other, have been of little service to us, if we may judge from the many fruitless attempts to make this salt in England.

The common accounts that are given us of nitre or saltpetre, are, indeed, so very vague and various, as rather to confuse and perplex, than give us any clear knowledge of it. Some will have it to be a production of *nature*, others entirely of *art*. Some tell us it is drawn from the air; others, that it is extracted from vegetables and animals. We are told too, that it is found upon the surface of the earth, and upon old walls in the form of hoar frost, and that whole provinces are sometimes covered over with it; all which is certainly very false and fallacious; if, by saltpetre, in this place, is meant that saline concrete, which is of so much use in the composition above-mentioned; which, though sometimes found in the walks of nature, is most assuredly, in general, a production of art.

Saltpetre, to give a just description of it, is a neutral saline concrete, evidently formed by a combination of a peculiar acid, with a fixt vegetable alkaline salt. This acid is found in certain earths, from which it is extracted, by elixiviating them along with wood-ashes, the fixt salt of which, uniting with the acid, forms this neutral

neutral one, which cryftallizes in the ley when boiled down to a due confiftence.

From this plain account of the formation of faltpetre, it muft be obvious, that it can no where be found, without the concurrence of thefe two principles; and, confequently, not in the air, or in vegetables or animals, becaufe, though this peculiar acid may, perhaps, be found in thefe fubjects, the fixt falt muft needs be wanting.

That it may be fometimes found in the earth, we fhall not deny, owing to the accidental introduction of wood-afhes to a foil impregnated with this acid. And that from hence it may pafs into the ftems and apices of fome plants, with the moifture that enters their roots, is far from being improbable. But that whole provinces can even be covered over with it, or that it can be generated in thefe organized bodies, as Lémeri and fome others have imagined, muft exceed all belief.

The accounts, which travellers generally give us of this falt, are, that it is extracted from the foil of the countries they have vifited, by elixiviating it with water, and evaporating the fluid; which we believe may be confiftent with truth; but here it fhould not be forgotten, that a certain portion of wood-afhes is always added to this foil before it is elixiviated, a circumftance which, either through ignorance or inattention they have too often omitted to mention. We are told, indeed

indeed, by Mr. Bowles, that in some parts of Spain, they have an earth that yields the crystals of this salt without any assistance of this kind; and this in such quantities, as might supply all Europe with this article. But till this fact is better authenticated, we have many reasons to doubt the truth of it.

Be this as it may, we shall here judge it of more use, to advert to those earths, that are well known, with the assistance of wood-ashes, to yield us the crystals of this salt, to point out their peculiar quality, and the source from which it is derived; together with the true reason why they are not always in a condition to yield us these crystals, even with the addition of a fixt salt; a circumstance that has much perplexed the most experienced saltpetre makers. After which, nothing we trust will remain, but to lay down the practical methods of making it, supported by the best authorities, as well as our own experience.

Of these earths, the most distinguished are, the rubbish of old houses, the ruins of old vaults and cellars, &c. which rarely fail to yield us the crystals of this salt, when elixiviated with wood-ashes. That these earths possess an acid quality, is not to be disputed; seeing, that upon reducing them to a coarse powder, and percolating a fixt alkaline solution through them, this solution will be neutralized, and no longer yield us an alkaline, but a neutral salt.

From what source this acid is derived, is at present unknown. The most general opinion is, that it is drawn from the air; but to this there are many objections. In the first place, the aerial or universal acid, is generally allowed to be not of the *nitrous*, but *vitriolic* kind. And secondly, there are many earths impregnated with this acid, which, in all appearance, have had no communication with the air, of which the soil at the bottoms of graves is a flagrant instance.

From the well known fact, that the rubbish of all such houses, as have been occupied by the filthiest inhabitants, and of such clay walls, as have stood in the neighbourhood of dunghills, or wherever putrid vapours more plentifully abound, is always most strongly impregnated with this acid, it is most natural to believe, that these vapours must confer it upon them, and consequently, that it must have its origin in putrid substances; but to this, there are likewise many objections. In the first place, the recent juices of vegetables and animals, some few of the former excepted, if we are not mistaken, contain no kind of acid whatever; and in a putrid state, every body knows they are of a volatile *alkaline* nature, which being the most powerful objection, we shall here principally endeavour to remove; and upon the whole, shall undertake to shew, that there is an original acid

acid in all vegetables and animals, which being rendered volatile by putrefaction, assumes the specific character of the nitrous. And that, since this acid constantly arises in vapour from putrid substances, hence it is, that the rubbish of old houses, and of old clay walls, become impregnated with it, as well as those earths that lie in conjunction with them.

That the recent juices of vegetables and animals, are, in general, perfectly neutral, we shall readily admit; but from hence, we think it does not follow, that they contain neither an *acid* nor *alkali*, as is commonly concluded; on the contrary, we apprehend, a more just inference is, that being *mixt*, they must necessarily contain *both*. It is certain, that if we throw a calcareous earth, or fixt salt into any of these juices, the earth or salt will be neutralized by it; which we take to be a proof, that it contains an acid, which quits the *weaker* to join with the *stronger* alkali, according to the law of affinities.

And the case will be the same, if these juices are putrefied. If we throw a fixt salt into any putrid liquor, it will be neutralized by it, and now, if we dip a piece of soft paper into this mixture and dry it, it will burn like a match, in the same manner as if dipped into a weak solution of saltpetre; which shows, that it not only contains an acid, but one of the *nitrous* sort; and provided this liquor were perfectly putrefied,

fied, and the marine salt, with which all nitrous leys greatly abound, carefully removed, we cannot help thinking that upon being boiled down to a due consistence it would yield the crystals of saltpetre. The author must acknowledge he has boiled down many of these mixtures without success; but it was at a time when he was ignorant of the necessity of attending to the above circumstances.

That all putrid substances, and consequently, their juices, are of a volatile alkaline nature, is not to be denied, owing to an union of their acid and oily parts with their earth, which is equally subtilized by the putrid process. But that the two former are safely separated from the latter, by adding a calcareous earth or fixt salt to them, the meanest chemist can tell us, the earthy or alkaline part flying off, and leaving the acid and oily ones combined with the earth or salt, with which they have a greater affinity. And that thus calcareous earths, by lying in conjunction with putrid matters, become possessed of a *volatile acid, oily mixt*, which is *Stahl's* precise description of the nitrous acid, must be clear to conviction.

But the strongest proof of the existence of an acid in putrid juices, if the earths of stables and cow-stalls do not afford an equal one, must be drawn from the soil at the bottoms of graves, which can certainly derive its nitrous acid quality from

from nothing, but the corrupt bodies with which it lies in contact; and this may satisfy us, in respect to the source, from which other absorbent earths may derive it.

Other earths, in common use among the saltpetre makers, are those of stables and cow-stalls, that have drank up much animal urine; the bottoms of stinking pits and ditches, and the like. These they take out, and lay in heaps, till, by repeated trials, they find them fit for their purpose. It is commonly supposed, that, during this period, they draw their nitrous quality from the air; but for this, there is certainly no just foundation, seeing they are brought to maturity as soon, in the closest vault or cellar, as in the most open exposure. The truth is, that all putrid juices contain many oily and mucilaginous parts, which, till they are duly attenuated by putrefaction, will not suffer any crystals to form in the leys that are drawn from these earths; and they are laid in these heaps, for this event to take place. Another end is answered by this manœuvre. By being thus laid apart, these earths are prevented from receiving any fresh supplies of *unputrid* matter, which might contaminate the juices, that were already far advanced in putrefaction.

The ingenious author of the Chemical Dictionary has told us, That the nitrous acid is no where

where found, but in such earths, as are impregnated with the juices of vegetables and animals, and where these juices *have sustained the whole putrefactive process.* But having assigned no reason for it, he seems to have been little regarded. The observation is, however, certainly a very just one, and had it been duly attended to, we imagine, might have prevented most of those disappointments, which our countrymen have met with, in their attempts to make saltpetre; as we have reason to think, they have been chiefly owing to their premature use of these earths.

The common soil, in some parts of India, is naturally nitrous, owing plainly to the fish and slime that is left upon it by the inundations of the river Ganges, which soon corrupt in that hot climate, and fill the earth with putrid juices; and here putrefaction, being carried on with the greatest rapidity, is, of course, soon completed, and the natives are, in a short time, furnished with a nitrous earth perfectly matured. But it must not be forgotten, that their strongest earths are found at the bottoms of their tanks or shallow ponds of water, which, in this country, are often of great extent, where, the water being evaporated by the heat of the sun, large quantities of fish are left to corrupt, which furnish a mud of the strongest nitrous quality.

In this manner, are nitrous earths naturally formed in these parts of the world, and might, doubtless, be formed in others, though not perhaps so expeditiously, by throwing into shallow ponds of water, natural or artificial, all sorts of dung and carrion, with other putrid and putrefiable matters; where the water, being evaporated by the heat of our summers, must certainly leave a mud of the same kind and quality.

Putrid juices and putrid vapours are dispersed through the earth and air, so that there are few earths, of an absorbent kind, that are not, in some degree, nitrous. But it is in those only that have been drenched in an extraordinary degree with these juices, or have been long exposed to these vapours, that this acid is found of any considerable strength. And, even here, we find it but very sparingly disseminated in them, if we may judge from the large quantities of earth that must be elixiviated, to obtain a small portion of saltpetre. *Cramer* has told us, that two ounces of saltpetre may sometimes be extracted from one pound of earth, which we have reason to think is an arrant fable; since, in the city of Paris, where, we may presume, those earths are selected with the best judgment, we shall find that one bushel of earth, with half that quantity of woodashes, will scarce produce one pound of this salt; and we are informed, that it requires eight cart loads,

loads, which are perhaps small ones, to make one hundred weight. There can be no doubt, that the trifling value of the materials, and the small labour that is required, alone enable the saltpetre makers to carry on this business, and that, under the same circumstances it may be carried on in other places.

From the nature and constitution of these earths, it must be evident, that they may be easily formed by methods of art, nothing more being necessary than to lay calcareous earths, in conjunction with putrid matters, or to drench them with their juices, and to wait, till we find them fit for our purpose. All this is well known; but not so, we apprehend, the process by which they are brought to maturity, which is the reason that our patience is often put to too severe a trial, in waiting for this event. It is a folly to deny, that it is yet a secret, that these earths derive their peculiar quality from the putrid matters with which they are connected, and that they are brought to maturity, entirely by putrefaction.

Glauber, who, from the observations he had made upon the fruits and effects of the bottoms of stinking ditches, seems to be the first that attempted to form artificial nitre beds, threw into pits, covered from the rain and sun, but exposed as much as possible to the air, all sorts of dung, with the cuttings of trees, refuse of gardens, and other putrid and putrefiable matters, to which he added wood-ashes; and, by this means, in a course of time, obtained, not a mere *nitrous*, but a *true saltpetre* earth, that afforded him the cryſtals of this ſalt, upon ſimple elixiviation and evaporation.

It does not appear, that this celebrated Chemiſt had the leaſt idea, that theſe putrid matters were of any other uſe, than to draw the nitre, as he called it, from the air, in which the fixt ſalt of the wood-aſhes might poſſibly aſſiſt. In this ſtate of ignorance, his followers, for the moſt part, ſeem ſtill to remain; having adopted, as far as we know, no other doctrine; and having varied from this practice, only in diſpoſing theſe materials above ground, inſtead of below, in order to expoſe them the more to this element.

It muſt not be paſſed over, that Glauber ſometimes filled large wooden veſſels with all kinds of dung, and, when they had completed their putrefaction, he percolated a ſtrong alkaline ſolution, through them, drawn from lime and wood-aſhes, which afforded him a ley of the ſame kind and quality, with that drawn from the earth of his other nitre beds.

A late writer has told us, that there are but three ways of obtaining nitrous earths. In *walls*, that is, by raiſing clay walls, and expoſing them to the air—In *pits*; by throwing all ſorts of

putrid

putrid and putrefiable substances into them—And in *hovels*; by laying these materials in heaps under them. The first he disapproves, because, as he tells us, though these walls are generally covered with straw, the nitre, or rather the nitrous earth that is formed upon them, is frequently washed away by the rain. But there is certainly another objection, and that is, the tedious time which these walls must commonly stand, except they are raised in the neighbourhood of dunghills, before they receive any considerable impregnation. In Prussia, where we are told these walls are raised, by order of the king, throughout the the country, for the use of the saltpetre makers, we are at the same time informed, they are often found but weakly impregnated, at the end of twenty years, though dung or litter is sometimes mixt up with the clay, of which they are composed.

He does not approve of disposing the materials in pits, because, as he observes, the air cannot be conveniently admitted to their interior parts. He, therefore, gives the preference to the disposal of them under hovels, where, by various contrivances that he lays down, the air may be freely admitted to them. And here we should certainly join him, could we be brought to believe that a current of air, for which he contends, was any great promoter of putrefaction. But we have been told, and have

good

good cause to believe, that a close, warm, moist air is the greatest promoter of this process; and, therefore, must have leave to think, that a vault, or a cellar, must be the most proper repository for these materials, where their putrefaction, being carried on with the greatest vigour, must, of course, be the sooner completed.

Or, in defect of these conveniences, that the same end might be answered by laying them, about a yard thick, upon a piece of ground, sunk a few inches below the level, and bedded with clay, where, through the rain that falls, in the space of a year or two, they must be completely putrefied; particularly, if they were now and then turned over, and no fresh additions were made to them; for, whilst we continue to heap fresh materials upon old dunghills, it is impossible that the whole mass should be equally putrefied.

It is observable, that the writer last mentioned says not a word of the use of putrefaction, nor of the expediency of promoting this process, by all the means that lie in our power, in order to accelerate the maturity of these earths; which we commonly attribute to his ignorance of this circumstance.

Nor does the practice of the saltpetre makers indicate any superior knowledge. Many of their nitre beds are raised ten or twelve feet high, whose putrefaction must advance very slowly, through the pressure of the *upper* parts upon the

lower,

lower, and the want of moisture, which cannot easily be introduced to such lofty heaps.

About thirty years ago, an ingenious Chemist, of our own nation, having visited many of the great works abroad, and made the observation, that to form a nitrous earth, nothing more appeared to be necessary, than to mix up calcareous earths with any kind of dung, and expose these materials to the air, returned home, fully persuaded that he was master of the secret, and had interest enough to prevail upon many of his friends to join him, in erecting a large saltpetre work, at Fulham, near London. Here, many hundred loads of lime were got together, and laid with strata of horse muck, in long high ridges, the more to be exposed to this element; the consequence of which was, that the rain running off, without penetrating the mass, no putrefaction ensued, and the lime, at the end of four or five years, was found to have received little or no impregnation; upon which the work was dropped, with great loss to the Proprietors.

Two errors were here committed. In the first place, the dung, which ought to have been, at least, in treble the proportion to the lime, made but about one fourth part of the heaps. And secondly, they were so disposed, that, for want of moisture, they could never enter into a putrid state: whereas, had the dung been in a due proportion, and the whole been spread about a yard

thick

thick, there can be no dispute, that, in the space of a year or two, they had been perfectly putrefied, and a nitrous earth had been formed that might have prevented this catastrophe; especially if the heap had been treated, as we have before hinted.

When the author saw these materials, some time after the work was dropped, the dung appeared to have been quite burnt up by the lime, and to have had no effect upon it; but his judgment was not then ripe enough, to point out the cause of this disaster.

This work, as we have been informed, was afterwards taken up by a foreigner, who formed his nitre beds in a very different manner; but they were raised so high, and consequently so long in arriving at maturity, as quite tired out the patience of those who were concerned with him.

There may have been other reasons for laying aside this work; and among the rest, its not answering the expectations of the Proprietors in respect to profit; which, in new undertakings, are apt to run pretty high, without considering, that the profits of every business depend upon the skill and knowledge with which it is conducted. We have before remarked, that Glauber generally added wood-ashes to the materials, of which he composed his nitre beds; by which means, in a course of time, he obtained not a mere

mere *nitrous*, but a true *faltpetre* earth, which required nothing but elixiviation with water, and a subsequent evaporation, to afford him the crystals of this salt; which practice is still followed by many of his successors; though, as it seems, without any clear conviction of their use; it being a point in dispute, whether they are of any use or not.

The author of the article *Nitre*, in the French Enclypedia, boldly affirms, that the juices or decoctions of all such plants, as yield much fixt salt by incineration, being putrefied and clarified with lime, according to Mr. Boldue's method, laid down in the Memoirs of the Academy of Sciences for the year 1734, will yield us the crystals of a true saltpetre, without the assistance of any fixt alkaline salt whatever; and that at Montpelier, and all over Languedoc, they make saltpetre without using the least particle of such salt. Upon which we can only observe, that, if this be a fact, it must be very surprizing, that it is not known in Paris, and that the Gentlemen of the Academy, who, some time ago, drew up and published by order of their monarch, an account of the several methods of making saltpetre in all parts of the world, so far as they could arrive at the knowledge of them, should not take the least notice of it; though they have thought proper to record one of a similar nature, Mr. Brown's method of making saltpetre in Virginia.

This

This Gentleman tells us, that if we sprinkle the clay floor of a tobacco house with *ambeer*, which we take to be a putrid infusion of tobacco, and cover it with the rotten leaves, in a fortnight's time, upon removing the leaves, we shall find the floor covered with saltpetre, in the form of hoar frost, *drawn from the air*, which being swept up, and elixiviated with warm water, will afford us a ley, that, being boiled down to the consistence of cream, will shoot into crystals of this salt. Now we can easily believe, that these sweepings, with the assistance of wood-ashes, would afford us such a ley, but not without; and therefore must conclude, that there is here some omission.

We must farther observe, that this Gentleman takes no notice of any marine salt that is formed in this ley, which, being found in all nitrous leys, must render this account very suspicious. And what may give us a more unfavourable opinion of this method, is, that, since the author obtained a reward of three hundred pounds from the British Parliament for this notable discovery, we have heard no more of it.

Whilst the several parts or principles of which this saline concrete is composed remained unknown, we might give credit to a number of tales respecting its origin and formation; which, at this time, without betraying the greatest weakness, nefs, we cannot give the leaft ear to—of its being drawn from the air—of its being generated in vegetables and animals—of its being found upon the furface of old walls—and, to conclude the whole, of its being formed without the affiftance of a fixt falt; all which muft be found equally repugnant to reafon and experience, which we may bring the ordinary practice of making faltpetre to confirm.

And here, we cannot help expreffing our furprize, that fo much time has been fpent by many ingenious perfons in the difcovery of *new* methods of making faltpetre, when it muft be obvious, that, in cafe they fucceeded, there is none that could be more plain, fimple, and lefs expenfive, than the *old* and approved one, of which we fhall now proceed to give a more particular account.

In large and populous towns, the faltpetre makers chiefly make ufe of the rubbifh of old houfes, the ruins of old vaults and cellars, &c. Thefe they collect, and, having reduced them to a coarfe powder, elixiviate with about one third the quantity of wood-afhes; in which ley, when boiled down to a due confiftence, the cryftals of faltpetre are found to fhoot. During the boiling, large quantities of marine falt are formed in this lixivium, which, cryftallizing whilft the liquor is hot, are taken out with perforated ladles.

The ley is then taken out, and set in a cool place for the saltpetre to crystallize.

In defect of these earths, they collect those of stables and cow-stalls, that have drank up much animal urine, the bottoms of stinking pits and ditches, especially of those, that have received the contents of slaughter and privy houses. These they take out, and lay in heaps, commonly mixt up with a little lime, till, by repeated trials, they find them fit for their purpose; which is known, in some measure, by their having totally lost their offensive odour, a sure sign that their putrefaction is completed.

Where these earths cannot be procured in sufficient quantities, they form, what are called, artifical nitre beds, by laying all sorts of putrid and putrefiable substances in conjunction with calcareous earths, keeping them in a moist state, and waiting, as the phrase is, till they are brought to maturity. If the wood-ashes are not added, when these materials are committed to putrefaction, they are added when they are elixiviated, but never, that we have heard omitted.

The common peasants in France and Germany, who are almost all saltpetre makes, scrape together the muck and offals of their farm yards, and, throwing them under open sheds, suffer them to lie, till they find they will answer their end. Though they know little of the use of putrefaction, they take care to promote this process, by by drenching them with urine or muck water, and frequently turning them over, by which means, they are brought to maturity much sooner than the larger nitre beds. These materials, with the wood-ashes that their hearths supply, if not added before, are thrown into a large tub, and water poured upon them, which runs out through a hole, stuffed with straw, at the bottom of the vessel. Thus simply do they procure their leys, in the boiling of which, their women and children are chiefly employed.

Where any article of commerce is composed of materials of little or no value, and which require small skill or ingenuity to manufacture, great numbers of poor persons will naturally take up this employment, whose distresses will oblige them to dispose of it, upon the most moderate terms; to which they will be farther urged by the policy of the government under which they live, which will restrain them from exporting it, till its own wants is supplied. To this we may fairly attribute the small price that saltpetre bears in France and Germany. But this can be no discouragement to the English, among whom it bears a much greater price, notwithstanding the importations of their India Company; and consequently, must afford the makers a much greater profit, should the government refuse, by a small bounty of one penny per

per pound, upon all the saltpetre made in England, to give them suitable encouragement.

The French are not insensible of the great advantages they derive, from making their own saltpetre; and, therefore, pay no small attention to it.

The saltpetre makers in Paris are incorporated, and have, besides, the privilege of carrying off the rubbish of all the old houses they shall think proper, without fee or reward; though this indeed is but a poor compensation for the extraordinary expence they are put to in firing, in a city where fuel is so dear.

In the year 1775, some defect being found in the saltpetre brought to market, owing more, perhaps, to their parsimonious methods of making it, than to any thing else, the King of France immediately ordered a committee, of the Gentlemen of the Academy, to draw up and publish an account of the several methods of making saltpetre, in all parts of the world, that all his subjects might be made equally acquainted with them; and, at the same time, offered a considerable reward, to whoever should discover the secret of nature in the formation of this salt, that they might equally avail themselves of it.

It has been shewn, that nitrous earths are not uncommon in the walks of nature, and that, by the addition of wood-ashes to them, they are converted into true saltpetre earths. Now it is only

only allowing that these ashes may sometimes be accidentally introduced to an earth of this kind, to shew us how a true saltpetre earth may naturally be formed; and if the streets of the city of Paris, or their dunghills upon which they throw their wood-ashes, sometimes exhibit a true saltpetre earth, it can be no great rarity.

It can scarcely be conceived that the English have been ignorant of the method of making saltpetre in France and Germany, where this business has been long carried on, in the most public and open manner. But that some points of no small importance may have escaped their observation, may easily be credited, from the ill success with which their attempts have always been attended; and none more likely than their custom of waiting till the materials, they lay together, for this purpose, are found fit to answer their end.

The author of this Essay once formed a nitre bed with great care and exactness; and, at the end of a year, expected to have reaped the fruits of his labour; but herein was totally disappointed. The leys, that he drew from these earths, afforded him no crystals of this salt; upon which they were thrown aside as useless; till, a year or two after, he took it into his head to make a second trial of them, and now found they answered his purpose extremely well; which he could only attribute to their being more perfectly putrefied, as they had been secluded from the air the whole time. This gave him the first idea of the use and necessity of putrefaction, which made too strong an impression upon his mind to be easily erased.

With earths, thus duly matured, we can scarcely fail of succeeding in this business as well as our neighbours. Yet there may be reasons for our declining it.

The large quantities of earth that must be elixiviated to obtain a small portion of saltpetre, it must be owned, affords no very tempting prospect. And the fears of not finding a sufficient quantity of wood-ashes in this country may have still greater weight.

The labour of collecting these earths, it is certain, cannot be small; yet may the value of this commodity fully pay the price of it, when brought to a good market, which it is likely to find in England.

In respect to wood-ashes, they may reasonably be judged to be less plentiful in this than in other countries where wood is the only fuel. But where pot-ash is made, in considerable quantities, as in many of our counties, there certainly can be no scarcity of them; and, if their place may be supplied by another commodity equally cheap, and easily procured, we can never find any real want of them. This is foreign pot-ash, which we find recommended in a small work, not long ago published

published, by order of the King of France, by some of the most eminent chemists, as far preferable to wood-ashes. Upon many accounts it has been before observed, that Glauber, sometimes, threw all sorts of dung into a large wooden vessel, and, when they had completed their putrefaction, percolated a fixt alkaline solution through them; which furnished him with a ley of the same kind and nature with that drawn from nitrous earths and wood-ashes. This, we may presume, gave occasion for these ingenious Gentlemen to make some experiments this way, the result of which they have given to the public. We tried this method many years ago, with some success; but found it depended upon the maturity of the materials; which, indeed, may be collected from Glauber. What the French writers have said upon this subject, we shall give in a postscript; in order to remove every objection against our attempting to make saltpetre in England, upon account of the scarcity of wood-ashes.

This difficulty being got over, we trust nothing will remain, but to give such an account of the practical method of making saltpetre as may be relied on, and be sufficiently explicit, to prevent our falling into any errors.

The saltpetre makers in Paris chiefly make use of the rubbish of old houses, the ruins of old vaults, and cellars, &c. This they reduce to a coarse powder, and having screened it, proceed as follows.

They provide a number of small open tubs, which they prefer to large ones, upon account of their being more easily moved, and emptied of the materials. These they place upon stillages, about two feet high, and in such a manner that one vessel may receive the ley, that runs from two of them. In each tub, near the bottom, is fixt a spiggot and fauset, and, to prevent the wood-ashes from choaking up the latter, a parcel of the round earth is thrown in first, and the ashes upon it. They then add the remainder of the earth in the proportion of two bushels of the latter to one of the former. They throw the earth in lightly, that the water may more readily pass through it, and they hollow it at the top, that it may more conveniently receive it.

They have different numbers of these tubs, but generally twenty four, which they place in three rows, eight in each; and into each tub they throw three bushels of wood-ashes, and six of earth. Ten demiqueus* of water being passed through the first row of eight tubs, is poured upon the second, and afterwards upon the third; and now the first row of eight tubs being emptied of the earth and ashes, is re-

* A demiqueu, as far as we can learn, contains about ninety gallons.

plenished

plenished with fresh materials, and the ley, which has passed through the three rows of eight tubs, is passed through this likewise.

Having thus passed through four rows of eight tubs, and been reduced to two demiqueus by the absorption of the materials, it is carried to the boiler under the name of *le Cuite*.

Such is the process when a new work is erected; in an old one, only six demiqueus of water are passed through the three rows of eight tubs, which are filled with fresh materials every day.

The lixivium is carefully scummed, during the boiling, and, when it is so far advanced, that a pellicle begins to appear upon the surface, a workman is constantly employed, with a perforated ladle, to take out the marine salt, which now begins to form and fall to the bottom of the boiler. This being thrown into a whisket, drains into the boiler again. When the lixivium is so far evaporated, that a drop of it will congeal upon a piece of cold iron, it is taken out, and thrown into a tub, for the remainder of the marine salt, and other dregs, to settle; and, after standing about half an hour, it is drawn off, whilst yet warm, into shallow copper pans, and set in a cool place for the saltpetre to crystallize.

The produce of this operation is generally about one hundred and thirty pounds of a brown sort of saltpetre, which is sold to government for three-pence halfpenny per pound, and carried to the arsenal to be refined.

The liquor remaining in the basons, when the saltpetre is crystallized, is called *Eau Mere*, or mother water, and is poured upon the earths in small quantities, when disposed in the tubs for elixiviation; though some makers think it best to dilute it with water, and percolate it through a fresh bed of wood-ashes. The earths, when discharged from the tubs, are thrown aside to dry under an hovel, and when dry, are spread, about a foot thick, to receive the scummings, *eau mere*, putrid urine, or any other putrid liquor, they can get to throw upon them, and in a few months, we are told, are fit for use, a second time, particularly, if now and then turned over.

To improve the colour of this saltpetre, and to cleanse it still more from the marine salt, two thousand weight is thrown into a large boiler, with one demiqueu of water, in which it dissolves, and, in the course of the boiling, another demiqueu is added by pailfuls, which, every time it is thrown in, raises a thick scum that is carefully removed. And now, the evaporation being pretty far advanced, and the marine salt taken out as before, a large pitcher of whites of eggs, or of a solution of isinglass or English glue, is poured in, and well stirred-up in it, which raises

a thick

a thick black scum, and is taken off with it. But, before the whites of eggs, &c. are thrown in, the boiling liquor is cooled, by adding a pailful of cold water. The lixivium being thus clarified, is treated as before.

The *eau mere* of this operation, being boiled again, yields a saltpetre of the same colour with the first; and some saltpetre goes through a third operation of the same kind to give it a greater degree of purity.

The basons in which the ley is set for the saltpetre to crystallize, are closely fitted with wooden covers, to prevent the too free entrance of the air, which, by cooling the liquor too soon, would not admit the crystals to form of so large a size.

The crystallization is generally completed in two or three days; and about one fourth part is supposed to be lost in refining.

Such is the method of making saltpetre in Paris, as transmitted to us by those whose knowledge and veracity cannot be called in question; in which we can find no mystery or difficulty, or any expence that can reasonably deter us from engaging in undertakings of this kind. The English will, in all probability, be obliged to employ other earths than the rubbish of old houses, which is the case with all our neighbours, that do not live in large and populous towns; of which earths, we flatter ourselves, we have given a full description. And here we cannot help observing one encouragement which an adventurer in this way will always have, viz. that whatever materials he may lay together, for this purpose, if they do not answer his end, as a saltpetre maker, will always find their value with the farmer.

Wood-ashes are certainly an article of great importance, but should they ever be found wanting, their deficiency may be supplied, as we have hinted above. Those who may engage in these undertakings, with the least risque or expence, are certainly the pot-ash makers in this kingdom, who, being provided with the necessary utensils, can only want a proper earth to begin their operations, which, in case they are unprovided, we have shown, may be easily procured in the space of a year or two, by mixing up their dunghills with fallen lime, and suffering them to lie till they are perfectly putrefied.

The author, some years ago, caused a trench to be dug in an open field, ten yards long, one yard wide, and one foot deep. This he half filled with good muck from a dunghill, and covering it up with the soil, mixt with one third the quantity of fallen lime, left it to take its fate. The weeds were plucked off, as they sprouted up, and it was twice turned over in the space of a year; at the end of which, this earth, being elixiviated with wood-ashes, afforded him fair crystals of saltpetre. In so easy a manner may a nitrous earth be prepared.

We shall add no more than that the crofter's ley, after it has performed its office of carrying off the foul oily parts of linen, or linen yarn, and which is generally suffered to run waste, may here be certainly used to good advantage: and that we would advise every one who is inclined to try experiments, in this way, not to make them with less than one bushel of earth, and half this quantity of wood-ashes, from which two gallons of ley may be drawn, which, being boiled down to about a pint, may indicate the success, if any is to be expected.

P. S. *Of the Use of Pot-ash in making of Salt-petre, translated from the French.*

Those who have attended to the former part of this work, will, doubtless, be sensible of the use of wood-ashes in the formation of saltpetre. That it is impossible to make this salt without them, or something of a similar nature. Remembering that saltpetre, properly speaking, is a composition of two substances, united and combined in the same proportion, which are the nitrous acid, and a fixt alkali.

That the saltpetre formed in some earths, for the most part contains only one of these two principles; the nitrous acid, which being combined with a calcareous earth, forms a nitre

with

with an earthy basis, from which the earth must be precipitated, and a fixt salt introduced in its stead, to convert it into a true saltpetre.

Wood-ashes, upon account of the fixt alkali they contain, are very proper for this purpose, and the saltpetre makers, by mixing these ashes with the earths they elixiviate, perform a complex operation in chemistry; they decompose one salt, and compose another.

But as it is the fixt alkali, in the wood-ashes, that alone acts upon the nitre with an earthy basis, it follows, that if we extract this alkali from them, by elixiviation and evaporation, it will be brought into a smaller compass, and supply the place of a large quantity of wood-ashes.

The fixt alkali, or salt extracted from wood-ashes, is known, in commerce, by the name of *Pot-ash*, and is made in large quantities in Sweden, Denmark, and in all the northern parts of Germany; nor is it hard to procure pot-ash of a good quality in France, so that we have always a simple, easy, and cheap method of supplying the place of wood-ashes in those provinces where they are scarce or dear, and the business of saltpetre-making contracted upon this account.

And we can assure the reader, that where wood-ashes are found in the greatest plenty, pot-ash will be found far preferable to them for the following reasons.

In

In the first place, because the wood-ashes used by the saltpetre makers, in large towns, are generally the refuse of other trades, and contain little or no fixt alkali. Those that are used by the saltpetre makers in Paris are of this sort, and often afford, upon elixiviation, only a little Glauber's salt, Tartar of vitriol, and above all, large quantities of marine salt, of which the tartar of vitriol alone contains any fixt vegetable alkali, that can furnish the basis of saltpetre, or be of any use in decomposing the nitre with an earthy basis.

Secondly, wood-ashes taking up one third of the room in the vessels, in which the lixivium is made, there is, of course, less room for the earth, and the saltpetre must consequently be less in proportion.

Thirdly, wood-ashes, being very porous, absorb a large quantity of water, which they obstinately retain, and this water holds a quantity of saltpetre in solution, which is a clear loss in proportion to the quantity of water they contain.

Fourthly, wood-ashes bear a very considerable price in most parts of France, and we are certain this price is superior to that of pot-ash, considering the portion of fixt alkali that they respectively contain.

Fifthly, these ashes are commonly impregnated with many gross parts, and much dirt and filth,

that

that is extracted from them, which must not only injure the saltpetre, but obstruct its crystallization.

All these things being considered, with the practice of the Swedes, and the success of our own experiments, we judge ourselves authorized to advise all those who are employed in making saltpetre, to place but a few wood-ashes at the bottom of their tubs, to serve by way of filter, and to supply their place with pot-ash in the following manner.

When the tubs are filled with earth, the quantity of pot-ash we mean to employ, is to be laid upon it, and we are to proceed to elixiviate it in the usual way. The water will immediately dissolve the pot-ash, which filtering through the earth, will decompose the nitre with an earthy basis, and convert it into saltpetre, and, if the pot-ash has been in a just proportion, none of the former will be left behind. It is not necessary to lay the pot-ash upon the earth, in all the tubs, but only upon those in the first row; because these earths being washed successively by three waters, the less pot-ash will remain in them.

Nothing can be said, precisely, of the quantity of pot-ash to be laid upon any given quantity of earth; this depending upon the condition of these earths, their richness, and the quantity of nitre, with an earthy basis that they contain; and, in short, upon many other circumstances which it is impossible to foresee. We can only, therefore, lay down such rules as may enable the saltpetre maker to judge, what quantity of pot-ash he ought to employ, according to the state in which he finds these earths.

For this purpose, let him dissolve one part of pot-ash in two parts of water, and either filter the liquor, or let it stand till it is clear, and set this solution aside.

Let him then elixiviate some very pure nitrous earth in three or four times its weight of water, and set this lixivium likewise aside; and if, upon dropping some of the solution of pot-ash into a glass of his ley, he finds the latter grows whitish or muddy, he may be assured that the precipitation of the earth is not completed, and consequently, that a sufficient quantity of pot-ash has not been employed. If, on the other hand, the ley remains untroubled, let him drop in some of the lixivium drawn from the nitrous earth, upon which, if the pot-ash is in too great a quantity, it will likewise turn muddy. Upon the whole, if, in neither of these cases, the liquor is disturbed, we may be assured the pot-ash has been employed in a just proportion.

In general it is better to use too little than too much pot-ash. When too little is employed, it is true, part of the nitre, with an earthy basis, will not be decomposed, but it will be found in the mother-water after crystallization; and

when

when a large quantity is collected it may be elixiviated separately.

Instead of using pot-ash in substance, it may be dissolved in a given quantity of water; for instance, one pound of pot-ash in two pounds of water, and three pounds of this liquor used in the room of one pound of pot-ash.

The French ministry are so desirous of bringing pot-ash into use, being sensible of the great advantages that must result from it, that they have ordered the *Registres des poudres*, to furnish the saltpetre makers, and others who may be inclined to take up this business with this article, and to take care that it is of the best quality. Thus far the authors, who have set their names to this little piece, who are no other than Messrs. Macquer, Lavoisier, D'Arcy, Cadet, and Sage.

It is certain, that by percolating a fixt alkaline solution through a nitrous earth, *duly matured*, the same kind of ley may be obtained with that in common use among the saltpetre makers; and that a solution of pot-ash, of some kinds, if not of all, may answer this end; but we cannot approve of using it in substance, as is here recommended. By dissolving it in water, and weighing it, we can know the exact quantity of fixt alkali we employ, and may with great ease increase or diminish it, as we see occasion.

The

The value of foreign pot-ash is no where better known than in England, there being, perhaps, no part of the world in which there is a greater consumption of it, nor which is supplied with it upon cheaper terms; which circumstance must strongly recommend its use.

An Attempt to shew, that a Taste *for the* Beauties *of* Nature *and the fine Arts, has no* Influence *favourable to* Morals. *By the Rev.* Samuel Hall, A. M. *Read May* 15, 1782.

Nullius addictus jurare in verba magistri.
Hor. Ep. I. Lib. I.

Scilicet uni æquus virtuti.
Hor. Sat. I. Lib. I.

THE Society, which I have now the honour to address, has lately been presented with several ingenious papers on TASTE. It may, therefore, be thought necessary to make an apology, for bringing forward a subject, which has been already so well investigated.

Were I to pursue the track of those who have gone before, it would be the highest presumption to suppose, that any observations I could make, would be deserving attention. It would be to offer the Society a few scanty gleanings, after the full harvest had been gathered in. But I have no design to invade the province of another. I shall neither examine the principles, on which taste is founded; nor enquire, whether it is more the child of nature, or of education, or the joint product of both. I shall confine my remarks to the EFFECTS which TASTE, however produced, may be supposed to have on the MORAL CHARACTER; and shall endeavour to shew, that its influence on the heart, is not favourable to virtue.

A distinguished Member of this Society, in whom the Scholar and the Gentleman are most happily united, has, in an elegant paper,* supported the reverse of this proposition; which, it must be owned, is no singular opinion. It is maintained by very high authorities in the literary world; particularly, by LORD KAIMS, in his *Elements of Criticism*; by GERARD, in his *Essay on Taste*; and indeed, by many others, who have professedly treated on this subject. It may, perhaps, be the prevailing and popular opinion of the present day. But are we thence to conclude, that it is founded in truth? Doctrines are sometimes fashioned " to the varying

---

* The Paper, here alluded to has been published, since it was read to the Society, in the volume of Moral Dissertations, by T. Percival, M. D. &c.

hour;"

hour;" and many popular opinions are governed by no better motive, than fancy or caprice.

To me, I own, it does not appear surprizing, that writers on taste have generally been led to suppose, that its influence must be friendly to virtue. When a subject has been long contemplated, the mind becomes, in some measure, enamoured of it, views it with complacency, and, from an over-weening fondness, bestows attributes and perfections, which are not naturally its own. How often has this been the case, with some new discovery in philosophy! Its ingenious advocate is seldom willing to confine its effects, to the rank it justly holds. He would have it considered, not only as a law of nature, operating in its proper sphere; but as a great and *universal* cause, to which all other causes must be subordinate; and will even attempt to solve all the phenomena of nature by its means. Thus, ELECTRICITY was lately a favourite theory, which, for a while, seemed to bid fair for universal empire in the philosophical world. And thus, some useful discoveries in medicine have been rashly exalted into panaceas, or universal remedies. The same species of enthusiasm *has, indeed,* at different periods, prevailed in every science. Hence, the vast variety of new theories, and systems, which have sprung up; and for awhile amused the world, and which have, at length, yielded their usurpation

usurpation to some new conqueror, which will probably be equally short-lived.

But to return from this digression. The advocates for the influence of Taste on the Moral Character, have generally confounded that faculty with the MORAL SENSE. They seem to be persuaded, that the same power, which discovers, and relishes the beauties of nature and of art, must equally discover, and relish the beauty, the order, the harmony of virtue. LORD SHAFTESBURY* has fully adopted this notion. His disciple HUTCHESON,† with some trifling distinctions, has embraced the same opinion. The very ingenious author of the *Elements of Criticism* tells us, that there is a strong and close affinity between taste, and the moral sense. " Taste, says he, in the fine arts, goes hand in hand with the moral sense, to which indeed it is nearly allied."‡

This natural connection, and close alliance, of taste with the moral sense, may, perhaps, be very justly disputed; as taste, I apprehend, must be the joint result of delicate, corporeal, and intellectual powers; whilst what is usually understood by a moral sense, must be of a nature altogether intellectual.

* Lord Shaftesbury's Characteristics passim.

† Hutcheson's Inquiry into the Orig. of our Ideas of Beauty, &c.

‡ Elem. Crit. Introduc. p. 7.

But

But let us, for a moment, suppose that such an union is really established; and that taste can take cognizance of the merit or demerit of actions, with the same ease and precision, that it pronounces on the abilities of the statuary, or of the painter. Will it necessarily follow, that such a taste must always be productive of a virtuous conduct? It will not be disputed,* that taste generally operates in some favourite direction. It does not embrace all the beauties of nature, or of art, with equal relish; nor explore every science, even of those esteemed elegant and refined, with the same keenness of discernment. The painter is not always possessed of an ear finely tuned to music; nor the musician always delighted with the elegance and vigour of poetical composition. Nature seldom produces an accomplished master, unless her efforts have been directed to one particular object. And in vain would be the attempt to rise to excellence, in any art or science, save that, which is congenial to the taste. Some men, indeed, seem to be possessed of, what may be termed, a general taste; and are capable of, at least, moderate attainments in every branch. But taste, like every other energy, perhaps is weaker, in proportion as it is diffused.

* Brown's Essays on the Characteristics, Sect. II. 8.

Upon this suppofition, it is evident, a man may have an exquifite tafte for fome particular art or fcience, and yet, no tafte for virtue. To this fpecies of beauty the faculty may be fo little fenfible, as to produce no effects. In fuch a cafe, virtue only fhares the fate of many other things, which are confeffedly objects of tafte, and which are rejected, becaufe the capacity adapted to them is fo weak, that it may be faid to be wanting.

But let us fuppofe, that tafte really exercifes fome of the privileges and powers of the moral fenfe. The advocates for its practical influence would not gain much, by this very ample conceffion. The mere fenfe of the beauty of virtue (and it is not pretended, that any thing further can be the object of tafte) abftracted from every other confideration, will fcarcely be thought fufficient to fupport her caufe. The theory appears more fpecious, than folid; more pleafing, than efficacious. When dreffed with the art, the ingenuity, and the eloquence of a Shaftefbury, it may entertain and amufe, the heart being fuppofed in a ftate of eafe, calm and indifferent. But its effects will not be fufficiently ftrong with the generality of mankind, to fpur them on to action. We furvey the lovely picture, are convinced that it is a fine one, yet turn afide to fome other object, that agitates our hopes and fears.

The doctrine may, probably, suit the retired temper of the philosopher, or the apathy of the stoic: but is ill calculated for " the busy haunts of men," and the tumults of social life. The man of taste admires the beauty and expression exhibited in the works of a Raphael, or a Michael Angelo, without feeling the slightest wish to become an artist, and to rival these great masters. May he not, in like manner, view the charms of virtue, and of a moral conduct, without making one single effort to become a moralist, or a virtuous man?

I should imagine it impossible for any person, possessed of the least sensibility, to read the character of Sir C. Grandison, drawn with so much delicacy by Richardson, and not admire and approve, the elegance of manners, and purity of morals, with which he has adorned his hero. But is it certain, that he will bestow more than his approbation? Will he entertain a single thought, of copying the amiable portrait? To admire and reverence virtue, is a tribute extorted even from vice. The most profligate, and wicked characters experience a secret consciousness, that every preference is due to virtue; and are not insensible to her superior loveliness. But does this sense operate on the mind, with sufficient tone, to influence, or to reclaim? *Video meliora proboque, deteriora sequor*, must be the language of every sinner, whose faculties are not utterly depraved.

"It is a remarkable circumstance, says Brown in his *Essay on the Characteristics*,* that, in the decline of both the Greek and Roman states, when religion had lost its credit and efficacy, this very taste, this species of philosophy, usurped its place, and became the common study and amusement both of the vile and vulgar." Quintilian, no doubt, had a view to this, in the following passage. *Nunc autem, quæ vel ut propria philosophiæ asseruntur, passim tractamus omnes. Quis enim modo de* justo, æquo, *ac* bono, *non et vir pessimus loquitur?*

The truth seems to be, that a mere sense of the beauty of virtue cannot operate, as a coercive power;† and, however the theory may please the reasoner in the shade, when the passions stagnate without impulse, and the appetites are secluded from their objects, it will be of little force, against the ardour of desire, or the vehemence of rage; amidst the pleasures, or conflicts of the world. To counteract the power of temptations, hope must be excited by the prospect of rewards, and fear, by the expectation of punishment. In a word, virtue may owe her panegyric to a Plato, or a Shaftesbury, but must derive her efficacy and authority, from religion.

From what has been advanced, it appears to me extremely evident, that, supposing taste were

---

* Essay II. Sect. 10.

† See the Preface to the Preceptor, by Dr. Johnson.

considered, not only as connected with, but even advanced to the rank of, the moral sense, its influence on the heart would be too faint and languid, to produce any moral effects. The charms of virtue* may be seen with the eye of speculation, without exciting in us a desire of becoming virtuous; just as an excellent picture, or fine prospect, may afford us very considerable pleasure, and yet produce not a single wish to dispossess the owners, and to make them ours. And though it may be supposed, that a sense of the charms of virtue must naturally give us a prejudice in her favour; yet, Will this prejudice be sufficient to keep us steady to her interests, when Vice steps forth, attired with every seductive ornament of taste, that can win the affections; and engages the strongest passions of the heart, as advocates in her favour?

But we are told, that "taste naturally sweetens and harmonizes the temper, and restrains the turbulence of passion, and violence of pursuit."† On this supposition, the beauty of virtue may have considerable effects on

---

* " Our sense of beauty from objects by which they are constituted good to us, is very distinct from the desire of them, when they are thus constituted."
Hutcheson's Inquiry, &c.

† Elements of Criticism. Introduct. page 11.
Percival on a Taste for the Beauties of Nature.

a mind, already disposed, by calmness and composure, to yield to the gentlest influence.

This reasoning will not easily be supported by experience, and matter of fact. The connection between *genius* and *taste* is so common, that they may almost be considered, as inseparable companions. Genius, without taste, would be no better than frenzy: and taste, without genius, would be distinguished for nothing, but a lifeless accuracy. But genius, it is generally agreed, is united to a warm and inflammable constitution. "If," says an eminent critic, "the imagination be lively, the passions will be strong; true genius seldom resides in a cold and phlegmatic constitution. The same temperament, and the same sensibility, that makes a poet or a painter, will be apt to make a man a lover, and a debauchee."* These propensities of nature may be restrained by the dictates of reason, and especially, by the awful sanctions of religion; and thus, genius and virtue may unite, and adorn the same person. But in vain shall we look for these important effects, from the influence of taste. In vain shall we expect to find, that men of genius and of taste will be always distinguished, for the sweetness of their tempers, and the purity of their morals. The irritability of

---

* Warton's Essay on the Writings and Genius of Pope. Vol. I. p. 105.

a POPE, and a GRAY; and the voluptuousness of a MONTAGUE, and a CHESTERFIELD, may be adduced as instances, amongst numberless others, of the truth of what has been advanced.

But we are further told, " that a taste for the beautiful scenes of nature, not only composes and harmonizes the temper, but disposes the mind to acts of piety and devotion, by raising our ideas from Nature, to Nature's God."* The thought is pleasing, and ingenious; but must not be admitted, without many exceptions. The impressions, made by the beauties of nature, will greatly depend on the passions, the habits, and the pursuits of the beholder. Let the musician take the " wildly devious walk," his notice will probably be attracted by the melody of the grove, as most nearly related to his favourite art. The eye of the Painter will be engaged, by the rich landscape that lies before him; and his thoughts will be naturally turned to the effect which might be produced, by a lively transcript on canvas, of so picturesque a scene. While the Poet, however struck by the granduer or elegance of surrounding objects, will only meditate, how they would " live in description, and look green in song." It is the calm contemplative mind alone, influenced by religious impressions, that surveys this fair heritage, with

---

* Percival on a Taste for the Beauties of Nature.

with pious and grateful sentiments towards the almighty Creator. A mind thus happily disposed, in the animated language of Shakespeare.

"Finds tongues in trees, books in the running brooks,
Sermons in stones, and good in every thing."

I shall now mention a few instances, where taste seems to be productive of misfortune, and immorality. We frequently see a man of real and acknowledge taste, run into all the folly, and extravagance of virtu. It is not sufficient for him, that he may be regaled with the productions of art and genius, in the possession of another. A man of this unhappy turn, feels a restless desire to call them his own. He is perpetually in quest of some new object; but his unfortunate passion grows more violent by indulgence; and, however a new acquisition may gratify for the moment; yet, in the end, it becomes the source of fresh disquiet. Thus, like Pope's Curio, who,

--------- " Restless by his fair one's side,
Sighs for an Otho, and neglects his bride :"

He is perpetually haunted by the demon of taste; his mind becomes fretful, peevish, and dissatisfied; equally incapable of giving, or receiving satisfaction. But, should his circumstances be contracted, the consequences are dreadful indeed! He involves his dearest connections in all the miseries of poverty.

" The

" The bailiffs come, rude men, profanely bold,
And bid him turn his Venus into gold.
No Sirs!" he cries, " I'll fooner rot in jail!
Shall Grecian arts be truck'd for English bail?
Such heads might make their very buftos laugh:
His daughter ftarves: but Cleopatra's fafe."*

Another is betrayed into a conduct equally ridiculous and fatal, by a tafte for the elegances of life, and domeftic refinements. Fancy is ever ready to fuggeft fome new plan to be executed, or improvement to be made. The houfe is capable of ftill higher embellifhments; and the garden may be laid out, in a manner more beautiful. He complies with the fuggeftions of his refined tafte—involves himfelf in difficulties—and is at length ruined.

The malady of a third is, an exceffive and fickly kind of delicacy. His feelings are fo nice, and his ideas fo refined, that he is irritated and vexed with every trifle. He is not only affected

---------------" with quick difguft,
From things deform'd, or difarranged, or grofs
In fpecies."†

Even thofe objects, which to others afford very confiderable pleafure, are feen by him, with a joylefs indifference. But, indeed, almoft every avenue to enjoyment is fhut up, by this unhappy

---

* Young's Satires.
† Akenfide's Pleafures of Imagination.

disease. Yet he nurses it with the greatest assiduity; fancies himself formed of nature's finest clay; and looks with contempt, on the coarse delights of his fellow-creatures. By degrees, he becomes unfit for the common duties of life, and is cut off from the blessings, and advantages of social intercourse.

But we need not appeal to a few instances of individuals. The prevailing manners of whole nations may be brought in proof, that taste has no influence favourable to virtue. It is scarcely necessary to remark, that Athens was once the seat of learning, taste, and refinement. The liberal arts were cultivated with the greatest care and attention, and rose to a pitch of perfection, which has been generally imitated, but never excelled. A taste for elegance was so universally diffused among all ranks of people, that even a herb-woman, we are told, could detect a very small deviation from propriety of speech.* Taste could not possibly have a fairer field, wherein to display its natural effects. But the history† of those times, and the moral lectures of Socrates, sufficiently evince, that the Athenians were a people, addicted to every kind of sensual pleasure: at once, refined and voluptuous, licentious and effeminate.

* Xenoph. Memorab. passim.
† Rollin's Antient History, vol. IV.

When a taste for the liberal arts was introduced among the Romans, with the rich spoils of Grecian elegance and ingenuity, can we discover in the history of that wonderful people, a consequent improvement in the habits of virtue? You will say, perhaps, their rugged tempers were softened, and their austere manners refined. But refinement is often remote from virtue; and external graces unconnected with internal beauties. It is true, they improved in all the elegances of life; but it is equally true, that their native vigour degenerated, into unmanly sloth; and the *Amor Patriæ*, which had carried the Roman name so high, was succeeded by a mean and abject selfishness.* Cato seems to have been well aware, that a taste for the enervating arts of Greece, would be productive of these mischievous effects;† and endeavoured by every means in his power, to ward off the threatened evil. But in vain was every remonstrance. A rage for the beautiful productions of genius universally prevailed, and bore down all opposition. And we find the latter Cato, in one of his speeches recorded by Sallust, reproaching his countrymen, in the following warm expressions. *Per Deos immortales, vos ego appello: qui semper Domos,*

---

* Græcia capta ferum victorem cepit.
                Hor. Epis. Lib. II.

† Liv. Lib. 34. C. 4.

*Villas, Signa, Tabulas vestras, pluris quam rempublicam fecistis.**

Let me now call your attention to a much later period of history, when taste revived, in the fifteenth century, after a long and gloomy night of Gothic ignorance and barbarity. Fostered by the favour and liberality of the princes of the MEDICI family, literature and the arts made a rapid progress. But it does not appear, that moral duties made equal advances, or were more generally cultivated. Observe, in what unfavourable colours, the characters of these Medici, the great patrons of genius and learning, are drawn by Lord ORRERY, in his *Letters from Italy*. "If," says he, "you take a view of the princes of the Medici, in a group, you will feel reverence and respect, at one part of the picture, and be struck with horror and amazement, at the remainder. To revere and honour them, you must consider their generosity, their benefactions to men of learning, their policy, and scientific institutions. To view them with horror and amazement, you need only listen to the undoubted outrages of their private lives; by which you will be convinced, that few or none of the whole race were endued with the softer passions of the human soul. I wish, that in many of their group, their love

* Sallust. Bell. Catilinar.

was not lust; their good nature, ostentation; their dignity, pride; and their sense, cunning."

From these, and numberless instances of refined depravity, which modern times will furnish, one might almost be tempted to conclude, that the effects of taste are so far from being favourable to virtue, that they have rather a pernicious tendency. But I mean not to bring such a heavy charge against a faculty, which, connected with reason and religion, will, doubtless, enlarge the sphere of our innocent enjoyments. I wish only to disprove the affirmative of the proposition, and shew, that taste cannot reasonably be considered as a moral principle of action: that, unassisted by reason and good sense, it becomes subservient to the purposes of folly and extravagance; and that, connected with a base and sensual heart, it unhappily serves to embellish guilt, and gloss over the deformity of vice.

Let taste, however, be cultivated, as the source of many elegant pleasures: but let it ever be cultivated, in subordination to sound morality. Taste can ill supply the want of moral discipline. Where there is no superior principle, to check the assaults of an alluring temptation, the heart must fall an easy prey. A truly virtuous character, set off by a just taste, is not only engaging, but even beneficial to mankind: while, on the contrary, a vicious character, however distinguished for taste and elegance, becomes only,

the

the more finished hypocrite, or the more exquisite voluptuary. In a word, let virtue form the base and the shaft of the column; and I have not the least objection, that taste should furnish the foliage, and ornament the capital.

Observations *on the* Use *of* Acids *in* bleaching *of* Linen. *By Dr.* Eason. *Read August* 7, 1782.

THE use of acids, in bleaching of linen, has been long known. Formerly milk was chiefly employed; but it had several inconveniences. The quantity requisite could scarcely be obtained; its effect was slow; and, containing animal matter, it was apt to rot and spoil the cloth.

About thirty years ago, it was discovered, that the fossil acids, when properly diluted with water, answered much better, and would do more in a few hours, than animal acids could do in a week, in facilitating the whitening of cloth.

At first, it was imagined, that the mineral acids would be apt to burn, or corrode linen substances, when immersed in them. But experience soon dispelled such fears, and convinced bleachers,

bleachers, that, by proper management, the danger was next to none.

According to the strength of the acids they must be mixed with water, sometimes, to seven hundred times their bulk.

The nitrous acid, being the most corrosive, and most expensive, has not been used.

The vitriolic acid is that which has universally been employed: not because it is preferable to the muriatic acid, but because it was to be bought in large quantities, and at a small expence.

The muriatic acid being now sold nearly as cheap as the vitriolic, and answering in a superior degree, will, in a short time, I am convinced, be generally adopted by bleachers.

As I must confess my ignorance in the art of bleaching, it may seem presumptuous in me to hazard a conjecture concerning the manner in which acids act in whitening cloth; but it seems probable, that alkaline salts, which are used in washing out the oil and glutinous parts of flax, on which the green colour depends, deposite an earth, in the pores of the cloth. As it is known that acids will also dissolve the earthy parts of vegetables, that acid should be preferred, which will keep earthy particles suspended in water. The vitriolic, therefore, is not so proper; because, with earthy substances, it forms immediately a selenite;

a substance

a substance only soluble, in a very large quantity of water. This selenitic matter, adhering to the threads of the cloth, will injure it, and make it feel hard to the touch, and probably is the reason, why some linens wear so badly.

When the muriatic acid is used, no selenite is formed. Whatever quantity of earthy matter is dissolved by it, is easily washed out by pure soft water, and the cloth having a soft silky feel seems to strengthen this conjecture.

As the muriatic acid is now sold at three-pence per pound, and the common vitriolic acid at four-pence halfpenny, and as the muriatic acid will, in proportion, acidulate a larger quantity of water than the vitriolic, besides the great probability of its answering better in whitening of cloth, the bleachers in this part of the world would do well to give it a fair trial.

Conjectural REMARKS *on the* SYMBOLS *or* CHARACTERS, *employed by* ASTRONOMERS, *to represent the several* PLANETS, *and by the* CHEMISTS, *to express the several* METALS, *in a* LETTER *to* THOMAS PERCIVAL, M.D. F.R.S. &c. *By* MARTIN WALL, M.D. *Prælector of Chemistry in the University of Oxford. Read October* 9, 1782.

SIR,

I AM extremely apprehensive, lest the following observations, as relating to a subject more speculative than useful, may be thought unworthy of the attention of your very respectable Society; yet, desirous to shew my just sense of the compliment, which you have paid me, by proposing me as an honorary member, I advance them with great deference, hoping you will suppress them entirely, if they should not meet the approbation of your correct judgment.

Whoever engages in the study of Chemistry, cannot but remark, with some degree of curiosity, how extensively the use of symbols or characters has prevailed in this science; and is naturally led to enquire, from whence this practice originated, and whether the characters used are merely arbitrary, or have any relation, real or imaginary,

imaginary, to the substances which they are employed to represent. That many of them are entirely arbitrary, is commonly supposed by those, whose knowledge of chemical authors is only slight and superficial; but the enthusiasm of a few, whose reading has been more extensive, suggests a different idea. Every character is, by these, conceived to convey an accurate description of the qualities of the substance, which it represents. It is hardly necessary to observe, that this opinion is not indirectly supported by *Boerhaave*, and his commentator *Shaw*:[*] and Dr. *Price*[†] in his account of his extraordinary experiments on mercury, silver and gold, asserts, that the ancient chemists either knew or believed, that the imperfect metals had a saline principle, which they denoted by a cross attached to their characters. It is impossible, perhaps, to advance very far in our enquiries into this subject; yet some little light may be thrown upon it, by a due attention to those characters, which are above alluded to, those by which the metals are represented. And first, it cannot but appear very striking, that the symbols employed to represent the seven metals, which alone were known in the earlier ages, are the same, as those which were applied by the first astronomers, to denote the seven planets. The chemists have, in gene-

---

[*] *Shaw's Boerhaave*, vol. I. p. 68.

[†] *Price's Experiments* on Mercury, &c. Preface, p. 11.

ral, arrogated to themselves the prior right to these characters, upon the pretence, that they point out most accurately the various qualities of the metals; whereas, to the planets they have no kind of relation. Yet, notwithstanding the plausibility of their arguments, I am inclined to entertain a contrary opinion, and to believe that the pretensions of the astronomers have a better foundation.

Astronomy was cultivated in all the oriental nations, particularly in Ægypt, Phœnicia and Chaldea, in the very earliest ages, of which we have any record. Not only the uniform appearances of the fixed stars, but even the more irregular movements and revolutions of the planets, and the peculiar circumstances of colour and splendour, by which they are distinguished from each other, were accurately marked and observed.

In the same period of time, the opinion of polytheism had been gradually disseminated: and it was extremely natural, that those splendid bodies rolling, apparently above the earth, in the immensity of space, by such determined laws, should be considered as the habitations of the immortal beings, by whose immediate influence and superintendence the affairs of the world were conducted.

Having premised this, let us now, for the farther investigation of this subject, pay a particular attention to the Mythology of Ægypt, which opens an important fund of information, with respect to the history of religion and science, in those early periods: but we must not expect to find the path free from obscurity and difficulty.

In that country, the hieroglyphic mode of writing was used in the greatest extent, and was connected not only with the sciences, but even with religion. By this learned people a circle was employed to denote perfection, and particularly the infinite perfection of the Supreme Being, their *Osiris*, whose residence they conceived to be in the great luminary of the day, from whence he distributed the blessings of light and heat, to animate the universe. Hence, by a very easy and obvious application, a circle came also to be employed, as the hieroglyphic of the sun.

The form of the crescent moon naturally pointed out the symbol, by which she has always been represented: nor was this planet destitute of a divine inhabitant; but was supposed to be the palace of the Queen of Heaven, the wife of Osiris, the common mother of mankind.*

---

* ---------- Imitataque Lunam
 Cornua fulserunt ----------
  Says Ovid of the Ægyptian Isis. Met. Lib. IX. 782.

That, the idea of the wife of the Supreme Being presiding over the moon, was afterward introduced into Greece, appears from a beautiful Medallion of the Samian Juno in Mr. Bryant, vol. II. Pl. 12.

To explain the remainder of the astronomical symbols, upon the same principle, it is necessary previously to remark, that polytheism, in its purest form, is nothing more than the deification of particular attributes of the Supreme Being, arising from the infirmity of human nature, unequal to the comprehension of one all perfect Being. Hence we are not surprized to find, that the two planets distinguished by a splendor, next to that of the sun and moon, were also supposed to be inhabited by, or at least consecrated to the service of the two chief Deities, under a different form and name.

One of these planets is known by the title of Jupiter, and probably derived both its appellation and its symbol, from that part of the Ægyptian mythology, which asserted, that when the gods, in the war with the giants, fled from the wrath of Typhor into Ægypt, they concealed themselves in the shapes of various beasts, under which they were afterwards worshipped, and particularly Jupiter under that of a ram, at the celebrated Libyan Temple of Jupiter Hammon. To this circumstance *Lucan* alludes, in his description of the march of Cato through the wilds of Africa;* and Ovid, more distinctly, in his ac-

---

* Ventum erat ad Templum, Libycis quod Gentibus unum
Inculti Garamantes habent: stat certior illic
Jupiter, ut memorant, sed non aut Fulmina vibrans,
Aut similis nostro, sed tortis Cornibus, Hammon.
Luc. Pharf. L. IX. 511

count of the wars of the Gods.* This image of Jupiter was not confined solely to the Libyan temple, as we find from some passages in Herodotus,† and many remains of Ægyptian superstition which are still preserved.‡ As Jupiter, therefore, was so frequently worshipped under the form of a ram, or a figure with a ram's head, or at least wearing the horns of a ram, it is not improbable, that the symbol of this planet was taken from these images. It might originally be the perfect head of a ram, or only one horn. The cross annexed to it *(see fig. 1. in the plate)* may be an imperfect remainder of the outline of the head of the ram, or with more probability we may imagine, that is was originally annexed

---

* Bella canit superûm: falsoque in Honore Gigantas
Ponit, et extenuat magnorum Facta Deorum,
Emissumque ima de sede Typhoëa terræ
Cælitibus fecisse metum, cunctosq dedisse
Terga fugæ: donec fessos Ægyptia tellus
Ceperit, & septem discretus in Ostia Nilus.
Huc quoque terrigenam venisse Typhoëa narrat,
Et se mentitis superos celasse figuris:
Duxque gregis, dixit, fit Jupiter; unde recurvis
Nunc quoque formatus Libys est cum Cornibus Hammon.
                                        Ovid. Met. V. 319.

† *Herod.* Euterp. 42.

‡ See a beautiful engraving from a Medallian, representing *Helius Serepis* in Mr. *Bryant's* Mythology, vol. II. Pl. 12. and six presentations of *Jupiter Hammon* in *Montfaucon's* Antiquities, Pl. 14. Tom. I.

to convey some particular information, and was afterwards retained in the figure, though the intention of its first application was forgotten.

The Ægyptians, we are told,* expressed the different stages of the inundation of the Nile, by exposing columns or poles, with one or more crosses upon them: and this cross was sometimes connected with other symbols, to denote some other circumstance, either of the season or situation of the planets, which concurred with the inundation. Hence, we see it annexed, not only to this symbol of Jupiter, but also to that of Venus, Saturn, and Mercury.

As Jupiter was represented under this form, it became common in after-times for great princes, who wished to be considered as his descendants, or whose ambition led them to aspire to deification, to assume the same mark of distinction in their medals and statues, as we see frequently in those of Alexander the Great, and his successors, particularly the Seleucidæ and the Ptolemies. Hence too it was adopted by Marc Anthony, when his extravagant attachment to the Ægyptian Queen prevailed upon him, to relinquish the Roman dress and manners, and to assume the habits and insignia of honour, used by the eastern nations.† As this practice pre-

* L'Histoire du Ciel par *l'Abbe Pluche*, Ch. I. §. 8.

† *Cooke*'s Medallic History of Imperial Rome, vol. I. Pl. 7. Fig. 11, 12, 16.

vailed very extensively in the east, may not those metaphorical expressions, relative to temporal greatness and dignity, so frequently occurring in the oriental languages, and in the Sacred Scriptures, have been derived from thence, viz. *Thou hast lifted up my* horn; *my horn shall be exalted,* &c. &c. &c. &c?

That brilliant planet, which we call *Venus,* was also considered by the Ægyptians, as sacred to the Queen of Heaven, who, by them, was known by the name of Isis, and in different countries by almost innumerable different appellations. It would lead me very far into the depths of mythology, to prove that the Goddess, intended by all these appellations, was the same, and that the Isis of the Ægyptians was the Venus of the Greeks and Romans.* To those who are conversant with studies of this nature, hardly any proof is necessary. Accordingly, it may be supposed, that the astronomers assumed, as the symbol of this planet, the *Sistrum* of Isis, which we are told by antiquarians,† was a small oblong circle of metal, crossed by iron rods, with a handle (as in fig. 2. of the plate) by which it might be held; and that it was used

* See *Montfaucon*'s Antiq. Part II. B. II. Ch. 2. and *L'Abbe Pluche* Hist. des Ciels. Ch. II. §. 3, 11, 12, 13, 14, 15.

† See *Montfaucon*'s Ant. Tom. II. p, 287. & *Abbe Pluche* Hist. des Ciels, &c. Ch. II. §. 3. & Pl. 17.

at feasts, to point out, by exact cadences, the movements of the songs and dances. There might be, therefore, a peculiar propriety in assuming this instrument, as the symbol of that planet, which was supposed to be peculiarly favoured by the residence of the Goddess of mirth and love; and so often appears in its greatest splendour and beauty, in those evening hours, when the heat, the hurry and labours of the day, give place to coolness, tranquillity and peace, or to mirth and joy, the song and the dance.*

The

---

* The Roman Poets have many beautiful allusions to the pleasures which attend the rising of the *evening star*.

          - Cum frigidus aera *Vesper*
Temperat, & Saltus reficit jam roscida Luna,
Littoraque; halcyonem resonant, & acanthida dumi.
                       Virg. G. III. 336.

Venerisque salubre Sidus. *Lucan Phars*. Lib. I. 661.

Vesper adest, Juvenes, consurgite; *Vesper* Olympo
Expectata diu vix tandem Lumina tollit;
Surgere jam tempus. *Catulli* Caren Nupt. I.

Hespere, qui Cælo lucet jucundior Ignis?
Qui desponsa tua firmes connubia flamma
Quæ pepigere Viri, pepigerunt ante Parentes,
Nec junxere prius, quam se tuus extulit ardor.
Quid datur a Divis felici optatius Hora. Id. V. 24.

It is well known that this planet is often a *morning* star. Virgil has given a charming description of her rising in this station, and has taken particular pains to point her out, as the favourite of the goddess Venus.

Qualis

The slow movement of that planet, which is called *Saturn*, would naturally suggest, that he was under the patronage of some Deity, distinguished by superior gravity and wisdom; and thence it was supposed to be the residence of the most ancient of the Gods, or time itself. Hence, as its symbol, they assumed the scythe, or the sickle, the peculiar attribute of that Deity. (See fig. 3. in the drawing). He is expressly called by *Ovid*, *Falcifer Deus*, (Fastor, lib. I. 233.) and *Juvenal* says that he assumed the sickle, when he was deprived of the imperial crown, by his son Jupiter.

> —————————————————— prinsquam
> Sumserit agrestem, posito Diademate, falcem
> Saturnus fugiens.   *Juv. Sat.* XIII. 38.

Hence he is commonly represented in medals and statues, holding an instrument of this kind in his hand.*

The red fiery appearance of the planet *Mars*, particularly, when he is in his most perfect

> Qualis ubi Oceani perfusus Lucifer undâ,
> Quem Venus ante alios astrorum diligit ignes,
> Extulit os sacrum Cælo, tenebrasque resolvit.
>   *Virg. Æn.* VIII. 589.

* See *Montfaucon*, Tom. I. Pl. 5. Fig. 1. and *Bryant*'s Mythology, vol. II. p. 259.

opposition to the sun, and at the same time in his perigeon,* might lead the early astronomers, to consider that planet as the residence of the God of war. Hence we need not be solicitous to seek for authorities, from ancient history or poetry, to explain the symbol of this planet, which is obviously borrowed from two of the chief instruments of war, the spear and the shield, (see fig. 4. in the plate.) It is worthy of remark, that we are told by *Varro*, that the Romans worshiped Mars under the simple representation of a spear, before they had any statues or images of their Gods. †

The rapid revolution and movements of the planet known by the name of *Mercury*, ‡ more particularly as he never moves, but a small

---

* It is not impossible that *Lucan*, in the following passage, alluded to this splendid appearance of Mars, when these circumstances occur in its revolution, where he describes it as reigning alone in the Heavens, giving dreadful omens of the calamities impending over the Roman state.

- - - - - - - - - - - - Tu, qui flagrante minacem
Scorpion incendis cauda, chelasque peruris,
Quid tantum, Gradive, paras? nam mitis in alto
Jupiter occasu premitur, Venerisque salubre
Sidus hebet, motuque celer Cyllenius hæret,
Et Cælum *Mars* solus habet - - - - - - - - -
Imminet armorum rabies, ferrique potestas
Confundet jus omne.   Luc. Pharf. Lib. I. 658.

† See *Montfaucon*, Tom. I. B. III. p. 125.

‡ Cyllenius *celer*. Lucan ut supra.

distance

distance from the sun, and returns quickly, as if engaged in the immediate execution of his commands, might lead the first astronomers to suppose, that this planet was sacred to the Deity, whom their mythology had made the servant, officer or messenger of the Gods; and, therefore, as its symbol, they chose the *Caducens* the staff of office, which that Deity was supposed to bear, (see fig. 5. in the plate.)

If this attempt, to explain the origin of these symbols, be admitted as plausible, the credit of their invention, and their first application must be ascribed to astronomy. But a greater difficulty now arises, to point out, by what principles the chemists were led to appropriate them to their art; an undertaking much more perplexed, and, which my attempts to illustrate, will require all the indulgence and favour of this learned Society. I give up entirely their pretensions to the invention of these characters, and, therefore, shall not pay any attention here to the attempts, which *Boerhaave* and others have made to explain them; but shall proceed upon a quite different plan.

The peculiar splendour of the sun and moon had without doubt been long noticed; and long before the introduction of chemical science, the language of poetry (and in the earliest ages almost all language was poetical, that is, figurative) had discriminated that of the former by epithets,

borrowed

borrowed from the analogous splendour and colour of gold; and that of the latter, by those borrowed, from the purer white lustre of the moon. A few instances, out of many, of their metaphorical mode of expression, are inserted in the margin.* The frequent use of these epithets might easily lead an enthusiastic mind to conceive, that a real analogy and correspondence subsisted, between these planets and the metals. This opinion to a strong and fertile imagination (improved too by the astrological notions, which might at the same time prevail, concerning the real or virtual emanations of the planets) might seem to receive confirmation, from innumerable circumstances, and ultimately suggest the employment of the same symbolical characters for the metals, which had before been appropriated to the planets. Hence

---

* Aurati Solis radii. *Virg.* Æn. XII. 164.
Solis aurata corona. *Statii* Thab. III. 414.
Sol auricomus. *Val. Flacc.* IV. 95.

Aureus axis erat, temo aureus, aurea summæ
Curvatura rotæ, says *Ovid* in his description of the chariot of the sun. *Metam.* Lib. II. 107.

Clara micante auro—of the palace of the sun. Id. line 2.
Sol aureus. *Virg.* G. I. 232.—G. IV. 50.
Niveos Luna levarit equos. *Ov.* Fast. IV. 374.
Nec candida cursum Luna negat. *Virg.* Æn. VII. 8.
Faveas; Dea candida, dixi.
    Ovid. Epist. Leander Heroni LXI.
Fulges radiis argentea puris. Id. LXXI.

gold came to be typified, by the circle of the sun, and silver by the crescent of the moon. The number of the metals, at that time known, agreeing exactly with the number of planets, would lead to an extension of this analogy to the whole; and every metal would easily be found, or supposed to have a relation to one or other of the seven planets, and receive as its mark the astronomical character of that planet. Some circumstances, which might give a foundation for these suppositions, shall now be enumerated. *Copper* was found, principally, or in the most considerable quantities, in the island of Cyprus, and the manufacture of brass was not only invented there, but carried to a degree of perfection unknown in other countries; insomuch that we are informed by Pliny,* that either the metal derived it's name from the island, or the island from the metal. As this island was supposed to be under the immediate dominion of Venus,† an obvious connection was dis-

---

* Nat. Hist. Lib. XXXIV. 2.

† Κυπρος δ'εισ αυγας Παμφυλιϰ ενδοθι κολπϰ
Κλυζει'; επηραιον αϛυ Διωναιης Ἀφροδιτης.
Cyprus autem ortum versus Pamphylium intra sinum
Albuitur, amabilis Urbs Dioneæ Veneris.
Well's Dionysius, 1240.

Ipsa Paphum sublimis abit, sedesque revisit
Læta suas: ubi Templum illi, centumque sabæo
Thure calent aræ, sertisque recentibus halant.
Virg. Æn. I. 419.

covered

covered, which justified the application of the symbol of the planet to the metal.

The use of *Iron*, in framing the instruments of war, presents so striking a relation, between this metal and the God Mars, that we need not wonder, that the symbol of that planet was applied to distinguish iron.

The mobility and unfixable nature of the metallic fluid *Quicksilver*, was naturally, by minds thus disposed to form analogies, compared with the rapid movements of the planet Mercury, and accordingly, the symbol of the planet was appropriated to the metal.

On the other hand, the slow motion of Saturn, the coldness of his situation, so far removed from the Sun,* and his dull aspect, which obtained him the epithets of *frigida, gelida, rigens*,† presented a sufficient resemblance to the obvious, as well as the medicinal qualities of *Lead*, to countenance the supposition of a relation between the metal and the planet, and to authorize the application of the symbol of Saturn to lead.

---

* Hence *Lucan*,

- - - - - - - - - - - - - - Summo si frigida Cælo
Stella nocens nigros *Saturni* accenderit Ignes.
Pharsal. B. I. 651.

† Plinii Nat. Hist. L. II. C. 6.

The analogy being extended thus far, without any great violence, the remaining symbol of Jupiter was applied to *Tin*, for which, the bright splendour of the planet and of the metal, might seem to give a plausible reason.*

This metal was not found in any of the countries of the ancient world, which were commonly known, and easy of access. It was imported by the Phœnicians from some of those regions, with which they traded in their voyages beyond the Pillars of Hercules; particularly, it was said to be brought from some islands, which were called *Cassiterides*. Whether the metal received the appellation of *Cassiteron*, (or *Cassiteros*, as Homer calls it) from these islands, or they were so called from the metal, is uncertain; nor is it less uncertain, what these islands were, and where they were situated. Some place them, on the western coasts of Spain, Portugal, or Africa: others suppose them to have been, the Scilly islands near the Land's end, in Cornwall.† It is not,

---

* It may be remarked, that *Homer* gives to Tin the same epithet φαεινος, which he frequently uses, to express the bright splendour of the moon, and planets. *Iliad* ψ 361.

† In *Wells*'s edition of *Dionysius*' Geography, it is positively asserted, that the *Cassiterides* were situated near the Land's end in Cornwall, and that they had their name from the Greek word Κασσιτερον, tin, which they produced in great plenty. *(Dionysii Geograph. par Wells.)*
Borlase

not, therefore, impossible, that the Phœnician Navigators, who were always remarkably secret concerning the country from whence they obtained their tin,* might insinuate, that this metal was discovered to them by the Deity, who presided over the sea, (not the Neptune of the Greeks and Romans, but the more ancient Oceanus, who was, in Egypt, Phœnicia, and even Greece, in its earliest periods, confounded with the Supreme Being.)†

May I therefore be allowed to conjecture, that there was a prevailing tradition, that Tin was discovered to the Phœnicians by Jupiter himself?

Borlase admits the truth of this position in general, but insinuates, that, probably, the name was derived from a Phœnician word of similar sound and import.

Borlase, Antiquities of Cornwall, Ch. VII.

* See some remarkable instances of this disposition in *Borlase*'s Antiquities, Ch. VII.

† Some of the ancient Greek writers expressly call Oceanus by the titles of the Supreme Being. We have in Homer the following expressions:

'Ωκεανε, οσπερ γενεσις παντεσσι τετυκται

Oceani, qui quidem Parens omnibus est.

        Hom. Iliad. XIV. 246.

'Ωκεανοντε Θεων γενεσιν. Id. V. 200.

Oceanumque Deorum Parentem.

And Plutarch, in his Isis and Osiris, says directly "'Ωκεανον Οσιριδα, that Osiris and Oceanus were the same." See further in Bryant's Account of Noah. V. II. 269.

If it were possible to prove, that any traces of such an opinion as this subsisted at the time when the Alchemical doctrines began to be prevalent, we should not be at a loss to determine, why Tin was honoured with the symbol of Jupiter. But on this point, I have no other support than mere conjecture, which I submit, with the rest of the Dissertation, to the candour of the Society, hoping they will not mark with the severity of critical accuracy or censure, my endeavours to deserve the honour of becoming one of their members. Before I conclude, allow me to mention, that in the above dissertation, though I might frequently have drawn my illustrations from the Greek authors, I have principally confined myself to the Roman, and those the most common and familiar, as supposing these were most likely to be known, if any were known, to the Alchemical authors, who first transferred to the metals the ancient astronomical characters of the planets.

I am, dear Sir,

With great Respect,

Your sincere Friend

and obedient Servant,

M. WALL.

REMARKS *on the* KNOWLEDGE *of the* ANCIENTS. *By* WILLIAM FALCONER, M. D. F. R. S. *Communicated by Dr. Percival. Read October,* 16, 1782.

THE superiority of the Moderns over the Ancients, in most branches of Natural Philosophy, is generally received as an acknowledged truth, and is, probably, well founded. Nevertheless, I am inclined to think, that the ignorance of the ancients has been over-rated, and, that several things were known to them, at least as facts, and matters of observation, which are not apprehended to be so, by the generality of people. Much learning and industry has been bestowed on this subject, by the Rev. Mr. Dutens, in his very ingenious Inquiry into the Origin of the Discoveries attributed to the Moderns, to which I beg leave to add a few remarks, that have occurred to me in the course of reading. And

I. I believe it is esteemed to be an original discovery of Dr. Black, That water which had been boiled was more easily frozen, than water that had not undergone that operation.

But, That water which had been heated, was by that means rendered easier to be cooled, was well known to the ancients.

Aristotle observes, "That water freezes the sooner for having been before heated; and, that this fact was even known to some barbarous people upon the Euxine Sea, who made use of Ice as a kind of cement for their huts; and that the water frozen for this purpose, was first heated, in order* that it might concrete the sooner." Pliny † also mentions it as a discovery of Nero, to boil the water that was intended to be frozen, as that hastened its concretion.

Athenæus‡ also remarks, "that in the Isle Cemolus they placed water in their Refrigeratories which had been heated by the rays of the sun, and, that they reproved their servants, if the water they provided for freezing was not previously heated."

There is to this purpose, a curious passage in Hippocrates, in the sixth book and fourth section of the Epidemics; which, though I am unable to clear up, I think has some reference to this subject. The words are as follows.

Ὕδωρ ἀφεψηθὲν, τὸ μὲν ὡς δέχηται τὸν ἀέρα, τὸ δὲ μὴ ἔμπλεον εἶναι, καὶ ἐπίθημα ἔχειν.

---

* Aristot. Meteorol. L. I. Cap. 12.
† Plinii Hist. Nat. L. XXXI. Cap. 3.
‡ Athenæi. Lib. III. p. 123, 124. Edit. Casaubon.

This direction is relative to the preparation of the water, to be drank by the patient, which is ordered to be, such as has been boiled; and part of the preparation was performed, with the water exposed to the air, and part, with the vessel closed up.*

The first, referred to the boiling or heating the water, and the latter, to the cooling of it; as I suppose, it was boiled, to throw out or expel the air, and then closed up, that it might not recover it again when cooling, which would have retarded its refrigeration, according to the modern theory. Galen, though he does not explain the meaning quite in the† same manner as I have done, imagines, that Hippocrates alludes to the boiling of water, that was afterwards to be drank cold, as, in the sentence just preceding the former, cold things had been recommended. Galen accounts for the obscurity of this passage, by informing us, that these works of Hippocrates were not written for publication, but as private notes to assist the memory.

---

* When water is boiled, care should be taken that air should be allowed admission to the vessel, that the vessel be not quite full, and that it have a cover. Farr's Transl.

† Galen, however, seems to think, that the water was to be boiled in an open vessel, and, when let down into the Refrigeratory, to be closed up, so as to exclude all air. Galen Comm. in Lib. VI. §. 4. Epidem. Hippocr.

Galen himself was personally well acquainted with this effect of boiling, in disposing water to cool more rapidly, and to a greater degree. "When," says he, "we wish to render water as cool as possible, we first heat it, then surround with snow the vessel containing it, or, if snow be wanting, we place it in the well or stream of a spring, and thus its temperature is more easily changed."

This he ascribes to the rarefaction the water had before undergone, which is evidently not the true cause, as, upon cooling, it would be as much condensed as before. Perhaps, the true cause may be, what is generally assigned, the discharge of the air. But how does this operate in promoting the refrigeration? Is it, that after the water has been freed of its air, any part of its latent heat has flown off with it, and thus rendered it more easily accessible to cold? Or, is the refrigeration more easy, on account of the discharge of air; as the air, being united with the water, and requiring to be disengaged in freezing, might, by its attraction to the water, require more cold to disengage it, than would have frozen the water, had it not had that attraction to overcome?

It must, however, be remarked, that Galen not only speaks of water that has been previously heated, being more easy to be *frozen*, but also says, such water is more easily cooled, even to any inferior degree: a fact worthy to be ascertained by experiment.

II. I believe the fact, Of the production of cold by the evaporation of fluids, is esteemed a modern discovery, as it justly may be: but it still appears (though the modern discoverers were not acquainted with it) that it was familiarly known to the ancients, and not only to the Greeks and Romans, but the Egyptians also.

Athenæus mentions, " that Protagorides, in describing the navigation of Antiochus upon the Nile, or Euphrates, relates the method used in that country, of cooling liquor, which was, by first heating it by exposure to the sun, and then straining it, and setting it in earthen jars, in the highest, and most open and exposed part of the building, whilst two boys were employed all the night, in keeping the outsides of the jars moist. After this, they preserved the coolness of its temperature, by covering the jars with straw. This, says he, cooled the water to so great a degree, that they felt no want of ice."*

Galen says, the method of cooling water, used at Alexandria, was as follows: "About sun-set, they poured water which had been first heated, into jars, which they hung up in the highest parts of the buildings, with the windows open, opposite to that point from whence the wind blew. Before sun-rise, they

* Athen. p. 124.

placed the jars upon the ground, and moistened the outside, and covered them with cool and succulent leaves, as of lettuce, &c. in order that the water might retain the cool temperature it had thus acquired."†

The modern method of making Ice in the East Indies, resembles the above in many respects. Pits are dug in large open plains, places most exposed to circulation of air, and of consequence, to evaporation: these are strewed with reeds, in order to admit the circulation of air on all sides, and on these are placed shallow pans of earth filled with water, and the texture of these pans is so porous, as to admit the water to percolate through them, in such a manner, as to keep the outside always moist, and of consequence, producing cold by evaporation. The water used for this purpose has also been previously boiled. It is needless to remark, how much this process resembles those before quoted, and how probable it is, from the immutability of ancient manners, that it was a custom derived from very remote antiquity.

III. Some other discoveries, such as, "The solution of water in air, and that this solution is assisted by heat and agitation," appear not to have been unknown to the ancients, though their notions hereupon were far from clear.

† Galen Comm. in Lib. VI. Epidem. Hippoc. Comm. IV.

"The moisture, says Aristotle, that is about the earth, being converted into vapours by the rays of the sun, ascends. When it has arisen, the heat, by whose assistance it had ascended, leaves the vapour (or, as Dr. Black would say, becomes sensible) and then, the vapour again assumes a consistence, and, from being in the form of air, becomes water." Meteorol. L. I. C. 9.

"The reason, says Aristotle, why dew and hoar frost do not concrete in elevated situations, is, that in them the air is much agitated, which dissolves * the consistence of the water. Ibidem. Cap. 10.

Dr. Black's doctrine of Latent Heat, seems not to have been altogether unknown to the ancients.

"Snow, says Aristotle, cannot be formed, without the cold prevails, much heat still remaining in it. For in a cloud, or vapour, there is much heat which remains of that fire, that has absorbed the moisture from the earth." Aristotle here mentions, that heat or fire was still contained in the cloud or vapour, and so far is agreeable to Dr. Black's system; but the latter discovered, that when the condensation took place, the heat, before latent, then became sensible.

---

* Ὃς διαλυει την τοιαυτην συστασιν.

N. B. Συστασις means the consistence, or solid form of any thing, in its primary signification, and is often applied to water. Vide Lex. Budæi. Vox Συστασις.

IV. The ancients perfectly knew the reason, why the air near the earth was more heated, than in higher situations. Aristotle explains this, from the reflection of the solar* rays from the surface of the ground; which cause is also assigned by Seneca.† This is, I believe, generally understood to be a discovery of Sir Isaac Newton.

V. Aristotle‡ assigns a cause for the sudden concretion of Hail Stones, to which he very properly attributes their largeness of size, which I have never before met with, and yet is, perhaps, the true one. He observes, "that hail generally falls most plentifully in hot weather:" and it is to this previous heat, which must have affected the vapour, and the water contained in it, that he ascribes the sudden congelation of the hail, in the same manner, as water, previously heated, is found to freeze more easily and suddenly.

VI. The fact ‖ likewise, of the separation of air

from

---

* —— εἰς τὸν ἄνω τόπον μᾶλλον ὄντα ψυχρὸν διὰ τὸ λήγειν ἐκεῖ τὰς ἀπὸ τῆς γῆς τῶν ἀκτίνων ἀνακλάσεις.

Meteor, Lib. I. C. 12.

† —— quod radii Solis a terra resiliunt et in se recurrunt. Horum duplicatio proxima quæque a terris calefacit. Quæ ideo plus habent teporis, quia solem bis sentiunt.

Seneca Nat. Quæst. L. IV. Sect. 8.

‡ Meteorolog. De Grandine.

‖ τὸ μὲν αὐτῦ λαμπρὸν καὶ κοῦφον καὶ γλυκὺ ἐκκρίνεται καὶ ἀφανίζεται, τὸ δὲ θολωδέςατον καὶ ςαθμωδέςατον λείπεται.

Hipp. de Aere Aquis et locis. §. XX.

from water, by freezing the latter, appears to have been not unknown to the ancients. Probably, this is what was meant by Hippocrates, when he says, "that the clear, light, and sweet parts of the water, are dissipated by freezing;" an opinion which Aristotle seems to have adopted, probably from this source.

Aulus Gellius* explains this passage of Aristotle, as if the air was pressed, as it were, from water, by its concretion; and Macrobius † expresses the same, in terms more plain and distinct, and seems to say, that it was necessary for water to part with its air, in order to its congelation.

VII. It is often imagined, that the fact, Of water rising to its level in pipes, was a modern dis-

Δαι τι απο χιονος και κρυςαλλων υδατα φαυλα εςιν; οτι παντος υδατος πηγνυμενϗ το λεπ]οτατον διαπνειται και κϗφοτατον εξαιμιζει.

Arist. Meteor.

* Quòniam cum aqua frigore aeris duratur, et coit, necesse est fieri evaporationem, et quandam quasi auram tenuissimam exprimi ex ea et emanare: id autem, inquit, in ea levissimum est quod evaporatur.

Aul. Gell. Noct. Attic. IX. 5.

† Omnis aqua, inquit, habet in se Aeris tenuissimi portionem, qua salutaris est: habet que terream faecem, qua est corpulenta post terram. Cum ergo Aeris frigore et gelu coacta calescit, necesse est per evaporationem velut exprimi ex illa Auram tenuissimam, qua discedente conveniat in coagulum.

Macrob. Saturn. L. VII. C. 12.

covery; but it appears to be by no means so: and that the Aquæducts built at such vast expence for the conveyance of water, were not constructed for want of knowing, that pipes would answer a similar purpose, but from the persuasion, that the water, in pipes of lead especially, was less wholesome, than water conveyed in an open channel. This appears very clear, from the following passage in Palladius.* " Si quis mons interjectus occurrerit, aut per latera ejus aquam ducemus obliquam, aut ad aquæ caput speluncas librabimus, per quarum structuram perveniat. Sed si se vallis interserat, erectas pilas, vel arcus usque ad aquæ justa vestigia construemus, aut plumbeis fistulis clausam dejici patiemur, et explicata valle consurgere. Ultima ratio est, plumbeis fistulis ducere, quæ aquas noxias reddunt." Vitruvius † expresses the same, though in terms rather more obscure; and Pliny‡ gives particular directions on the subject.

---

* Pallad. Mensi. August.

† Vitruv. L. VIII. C. 7.

‡ L. XXXI. C. 6.

An Enquiry *concerning the* Influence *of the* Scenery *of a* Country *on the* Manners *of its* Inhabitants. *By* William Falconer, M. D. F. R. S. *Read October* 23, 1782.

IT is an ancient maxim in Philosophy, attributed to Aristotle, and generally acquiesced in, That all mental ideas were primarily suggested, by sensible objects, through the medium of the senses. Whether this opinion be universally true, is not here meant to be discussed: but, that external objects influence our actions and conduct, and even direct our speculative sentiments, is too evident to bear dispute.

Animated beings, and, far above the rest, the human species, are the most powerful in producing these effects. We are naturally led to adopt the passions, and, to a certain degree, to imitate the character of those, to whose company and conversation we are daily habituated; and this disposition is so potent, that even error and prejudice are often introduced, and almost voluntarily entertained, by those, whose character and understanding, in other instances, should seem to afford the most complete security against such examples of human frailty.

A less potent, but a somewhat similar influence, is exerted by inanimate objects. Scenes of horror, even though composed of lifeless materials, impart gloomy and terrible ideas to the mind; and those of pleasure tend, on the conrrary, to exhilarate and refresh it. Hence we may infer, that the aspect or face of a country might contribute, in some measure, towards the formation of the manners, and character of the people.

The immediate and direct effect of the sight of objects, of either of the kinds above-mentioned, would be, I apprehend, but weak; but we should consider, that they must, from their nature, be almost constantly operating; and by their repeated action may make amends for the slightness of the impressions, distinctly considered.

As it is the natural property of beautiful objects to communicate pleasurable ideas to the mind, and to elevate the spirits, we may from thence infer, that the view of a fertile, pleasant, and cultivated country, would inspire sentiments of delight and satisfaction into those accustomed to survey it. A cultivated garden was the scene of delight, selected by that celebrated patron of sensual pleasure Epicurus; and the exhilarating effects produced upon the mind by the * survey of

---

* - - - - - - - - - - - - - - and now is come
  Into the blissful field, thro' groves of Myrrh,
  And flowering odours, Cassia, Nard, and Balm,
  A wilderness of sweets, for Nature here
                                 Wantons

of a beautiful scenery of country, are noticed by several of the poets, and particularly by Milton.

Is it not hence probable, that such a view would tend to inspire permanent chearfulness of temper, into those daily accustomed to behold it, both, as it presents great variety of subjects of attention and admiration, and as it fills the mind with representations of pleasing objects?

> Wantons as in her prime, and plays at will
> Her virgin fancies, pouring forth more sweet,
> Wild above rule, or art, enormous bliss.
> 				*Paradise Lost*, Book V.
> ------------ about me round I saw,
> Hill, dale, and shady woods, and sunny plains,
> And liquid lapse of murmuring streams: by these,
> Creatures that liv'd, and mov'd, and walk'd, and flew:
> Birds on the branches warbling: all things smil'd
> With fragrance, and with joy my heart o'erflow'd.
> 				*Paradise Lost*, Book VIII.
> Straight mine eye hath caught new pleasures,
> While the landscape round it measures,
> Russet lawns, and fallows gray,
> Where the nibbling flocks do stray:
> Mountains, on whose barren breast
> The labouring clouds do often rest:
> Meadows, trim with daisies pied:
> Shallow brooks, and rivers wide:
> Towers, and battlements it sees,
> Bosom'd high in tufted trees.
> 				*Milton*'s Allegro.
> Why sit we sad, when Phosphor shines so clear,
> And lavish nature paints the purple year?
> 				*Pope*'s First Pastoral.

T						Cicero

Cicero, in his Letters to Atticus,* speaks of the pleasures of a garden, as the best remedy for grief and concern of mind; and, in one of his philosophical dialogues,† he recommends attention to the natural beauties of a fine and cultivated country, as the proper study of the calm and serene period of old age.

* Deinde etiam ad καταβιωσιν mæstitiamque medendam nihil mihi reperiri potest aerius.
  Cic. Epist. ad Attic. L. XIII.

† Quid de pratorum viriditate, aut arborum ordinibus, aut vinearum olivetorumque specie, dicam? Brevi precidam. Agro bene culto nil potest esse, nec usu uberius, nec specie ornatius, ad quem fruendum non modo non retardat, verum etiam invitat atque allectat Senectus.
  Cicero. de Senect. §. LIII.

Vobis mehercule Martis viris cavenda et fugienda imprimis amoenitas est Asiæ, tantum hæ peregrinæ voluptates ad extinguendum vigorem animorum possunt.
  Livii, L. XXVII.

Loca amoena voluptaria facile in otio feroces militum animos molliverant.
  Sallust. Bell. Catilin.

Itaque ut frugum semina mutato solo degenerant, sic illa genuina feritas eorum Asiatica amoenitate mollita est.
  Flor. L. II. C. 11.

Effeminat animos amænitas nimia, nec dubie aliquid ad corrumpendum vigorem potest regio. Fortior miles ex confragoso venit.
  Senecæ. Epist. L. I. Ep. 51.

N. B. The word amoenus is applicable to what is pleasant or agreeable to the eye, in place or situation, and, of course, refers to the scenery or face of the country.

It is, however, probable, that the pleasures inspired by such a scenery as is above alluded to, which is rather of a luxurious tendency, may coincide with the effects of the climate, in which such prospects are mostly produced, in contributing to weaken and effeminate the mind and disposition. However whimsical this notion may appear, it has been adopted by writers, in the highest esteem for understanding and discernment. Perhaps, for the same reason, a beautiful and ornamented country has been thought to be favourable to the softer passions. "Love," says Agatho in the banquet of Plato, "resides not in a body or soul, or any other place, where flowers never spring; or, if they do spring, where they are fallen, and the spot quite deflowered. But, wherever a spot is to be found flowry and fragrant, he there seats himself, and settles his abode." The beauty of the country, must, no doubt, contribute to the improvement of the taste of the inhabitants, both in arts and science.

Taste, which is in other words, the faculty of discerning and relishing beauty, is acquired by the comparison of beautiful objects with one another, and, upon that account, is likely to be found in greater perfection, where those objects abound the most, and where, of course, such comparisons would be the most obvious and easy. Hence springs, in a good measure, I apprehend, the elegant and varied fancy of the eastern people, exemplified in some of their works of art, particularly the patterns of their manufactures. The diversified beauty of the vegetables, that cover the ground in those countries, could scarcely fail to suggest ideas, far superior to what could be imagined by those, who never had any opportunity of seeing such delicate productions.

The most admired passages in the eastern writings, especially the poetical, owe much of their power and effect, to the painting of the natural beauties of the country and climate. A late writer,[*] of no inconsiderable taste, as well as talent for observation, has remarked of the Spaniards, that the similies used by them, are universally taken from the beautiful objects of nature continually before their eyes. "The fragrance of the rose, the odour of the orange, the perfume of the myrtle, the murmuring of the cave inviting to slumber, the height of the mountains, the steepness of the rocks, the splendour of the rising sun, the coolness of the evening breeze, and the brilliancy of the stars by night, afford them endless allegories." Even Homer himself, that great master of our passions, is not a little indebted to his familiar acquaintance with the scenery of a beautiful country, for the ravishing

[*] Carter's Travels from Gibraltar to Malaga.

effects of many of his descriptions and comparisons.*

Milton appears to have been so sensible of this effect of Homer's picturesque representations, that he has ventured, perhaps improperly, to

* Glad earth perceives, and from her bosom pours
Unbidden herbs, and voluntary flowers:
Thick new-born violets a soft carpet spread,
And clustring lotos swell'd the rising bed;
And sudden hyacinths the turf bestrow;
And flamy crocus made the mountain glow:
Celestial dews descending o'er the ground,
Perfume the mount, and breathe ambrosia round.
Pope's Homer Iliad. B. XIV. L. 395.

Next this, the eye the art of Vulcan leads
Deep thro' fair forests and a length of meads,
And stalls, and folds, and scatter'd cots between,
And fleecy flocks, that whiten all the scene.
Homer's Iliad. Descr. of Achilles's Shield.

Elysium shall be thine, the blissful plains
Of utmost earth, where Radamanthus reigns:
Joys ever young unmix'd, with pain or fear,
Fill the wide circle of the eternal year:
Stern winter smiles on that auspicious clime;
The fields are florid with unfading prime;
From the bleak pole no winds inclement blow,
Mould round the hail, or shake the fleecy snow;
But from the breezy deep, the blest inhale
The fragrant murmurs of the western gale.
Homer's Odyss. B. IV.

adorn a scene laid in Britain, with productions peculiar to Asiatic climes.*

A beautiful scenery of a country contributes, I apprehend, to influence the sentiments of the people in some points respecting Religion. Thus, it is more than probable, that many of the ideas in the Roman and Greek mythologies, concerning a future state of happiness, were derived from this source. Homer's description of the Elysian fields,† and of the dwelling of the Gods,‡ is evidently borrowed from what he

---

* May thy lofty head be crown'd
  With many a tower and terras round,
  And here and there thy banks upon
  With groves of myrrh and cinnamon.
  Milton's Comus.

† See last page, Note *

‡ Without the grot, a various sylvan scene
  Appear'd around, and groves of living green,
  Poplars and alders ever quivering play'd,
  And nodding cypress form'd a fragrant shade,
  On whose high branches waving with the storm,
  The birds of broadest wing their mansion form;
  The chough, the sea-mew, the loquacious crow,
  And scream aloft, and skim the deeps below:
  Depending vines the shelving cavern screen,
  With purple clusters blushing thro' the green;
  Four limpid fountains from the clefts distil,
  And every fountain pours a different rill,
  In mazy windings wandering down the hill,
  Where blooming meads with vivid greens were crown'd,
  And glowing violets threw odours round;
  A scene, where, if a God shou'd cast his sight,
  A God might gaze and wander with delight.

had seen in a fine country: and Virgil,* and Tibullus,† seem to have taken their descriptions of the situation of the happy in a future life, from those natural beauties, with which they were familiar.

The same circumstances appear to have influenced the general opinions, concerning a place of future punishment. As the residence of the blest was supposed to be in a country exquisitely adorned with natural beauties, so that of the

---

* Devenere locos lætos, et amoena vireta,
Fortunatorum nemorum, sedesque beatas:
Largior hic campos Æther, et lumine vestit
Purpureo, Solemque suum sua sidera norunt.
Virg. Æneid. Lib. VI.

† Sed me, quod facilis tenero sum semper amori,
Ipsa Venus campos ducet in Elysios.
Hic choræ cantusque vigent, passimque vagantes
Dulce sonant tenui gutture carmen aves.
Fert casiam non culta seges, totosque per agros
Floret odoratis terra benigna rosis.
Tibull. Eleg. Lib. I. El. 4.

Propertius speaks of Elysian roses.
Mulcet ubi Elysias aura beata rosas.
Prop. Lib. IV. El. 7. L. 60.

Milton uses nearly the same expression:
On a bed
Of heapt Elysian flowers.
Milton Allegro. L. 146, 147.

Rolls o'er Elysian flowers her amber stream.
Par. Lost. III. 359.

miserable was placed in a region,* dark and uncultivated, foul and horrible, in which circumstances, the misery of those condemned to inhabit it was thought, in a good measure, to consist. Such are the effects we suppose producible by the beautiful face of a country.

Let us now see what would be the effects of one of a different appearance.

Hippocrates observes,† that the inhabitants of rough, mountainous, and uncultivated coun-

---

* Low in the dark Tartarean gulf shall groan.
Iliad. VIII. L. 16.

No sun e'er gilds the gloomy horrors there,
No chearful gales refresh the lazy air.
Iliad. VIII. 601 et.

At scelerata sedes jacet in nocte profundâ
Abdita, quam circum flumina nigra sonant.
Tibull. I. El. 4.

— — — — — — — — — tum Tartarus ipse
Bis patet in præceps tantum, tenditque sub umbras,
Quantus ad æthereum cœli suspectus Olympum.
Virg. Æn. Lib. VI.

— — diverso itinere malos a bonis loca tetra, inculta, fæda atque formidolosa habere.
Sallust. Bell. Catilinar.

Esse inferos Stoicus Zenon docuit et sedes prorsum ab impiis esse discretas et illos quidem quietas et delectabiles incolere regiones, hos vero luere pœnas in tenebrosis locis, atque in cæni voraginibus horrendis.
Lactantii. Lib. VIII. C. 7.

† De Aerib. aquis et locis. Cap. LV.

tries, are rude and ferocious in their disposition and manners. The people of Cynetha in Arcadia, who lived in a situation particularly * gloomy and disagreeable, were so remarkable for their unsociable qualities, that they were expelled from the Grecian cities. The Cimmerians, who inhabited a country dark and melancholy, subsisted upon robbery and plunder: and the country of the Cyclops, according to Homer's description, was somewhat of a similar appearance. The same disposition, of the people inhabiting the same region, is mentioned by Fazellus, a writer concerning Sicily, about two hundred years ago, and confirmed, by the later testimony of Mr. Brydone. The Indians also, discovered a few years since by Mr. Byron, in the Southern Hemisphere, were brutal and savage to an enormous excess.

May we not here suppose, with an elegant writer, that a stormy sea, together with a frozen, barren and inhospitable shore, might work upon the imagination of these Indians, so as, by banishing all pleasing and benign ideas, to fill them with habitual gloom, and with a propensity † to cruelty? And might not the tremendous scenes of Etna have had a like effect upon the

* Athenæi. Lib. XIV. Polybii. Lib. IV. C. 3.

† Harris's Philolog. Enquiries. p. 518.

Cyclops, who lived among smoke, thunderings, eruptions of fire, and earthquakes?*

If, then, these limited regions so influenced their natives, may not a similar effect be presumed from the vast regions of the north; may not its cold, barren, and uncomfortable climate, have made its numerous tribes equally rude and savage? Ovid, the Roman poet, who, unfortunately for himself, had but too many opportunities for observations of this kind, seems to have been of this opinion, from his so frequently connecting his account of the country with the manners of the inhabitants. Is it not probable, that the dreary aspect of the country, might be one cause of the devastations committed by these people, in their invasions of the Roman

---

* Frigida me cohibent Euxini littora Ponti:
Dictus ab antiquis Axenus ille fuit.
Nam neque jactantur moderatis æquora ventis,
Nec placidos portus hospita navis adit.
Sunt circa gentes, quæ prædam sanguine quærant,
Nec minus infidâ terra timetur aqua.
Illi, quos audis, hominum gaudere cruore,
Pæne sub ejusdem sideris axe jacent.
Ovid. Trist. L. IV. El. 4.

Sive locum specto, locus est inamabilis, et quo
Esse nihil toto tristius orbe potest.
Sive homines; vix sunt homines, hoc nomine digni:
Quamque lupi sævæ plus feritatis habent.
Ovid. Trist. L. V. Eleg. 7.

empire?* A desolate and uncultivated scene, which probably originally inspired the ferocious disposition of these people, was more congenial to their ideas and inclinations, than elegant buildings, and cultivated grounds, which, whilst they betrayed the unwarlike spirit of their possessors, evidenced their superiority in understanding and industry.

Miners, for the same reasons, are generally observed to be a hardy, ferocious, and cruel set of men. The scenes of horror, misery, and gloom, with which they are conversant, obliterate the finer sensations, and steel the heart against the sentiments of tenderness and compassion. The

---

* Ovid mentions in his time, that the Getæ destroyed all the buildings, and laid the country waste, wherever they went.

    Hostis equo pollens, longéque volante sagittâ
    Vicinam late depopulatur humum.
    Quæ nequeunt secum ferre aut abducere, perdunt,
    Et cremat insontes hostica flamma casas.
                      Ovid Trist. L. III. Eleg. 10.

Quicquid invenire poterat momento temporis parvi, vastabant, (Saraceni) milvorum rapacium similes.
                      Amm Marcell. L. XIX. C. 4.

The Franks destroyed forty cities upon the Rhine.
                      Zosim. L. III. C. 1.

Alaric destroyed all the cities in Macedonia, Thrace and Greece, except Athens, and Thebes. Attila preferred his house of wood on the Tibiscus, to all the splendid palaces he might have enjoyed. Zosim. L. V. C. 5.

emotions of the mind, in these instances, correspond with the wildness and ferocity of the surrounding chaos of objects, and require, in order to humanize them, a certain degree of adjustment, and even embellishment, of external appearances. We might reasonably conclude from hence, that a people so situated, would have their intellectual faculties considerably contracted, or depressed. The paucity of objects, and those of a disgusting, or terrible nature, would afford few motives for inquiry, and, of course, a narrow field for mental exertion.

The ancient Germans,* to whom letters were unknown, and who seem to have possessed very little thirst after knowledge, dwelt in a region, dark with forests, and foul with marshes; and the desolate and uncultivated face of the country contributes, I doubt not, to encourage the ignorance of the American Indians. We might, with still greater probability imagine, that such a people would be particularly defective in all matters that regard taste and sentiment. This, however, is not altogether the case. Their ideas are indeed melancholy, and their views of nature dark and gloomy; but, nevertheless, often par-

---

* Terra etsi aliquanto specie differt, est in universum, aut sylvis horrida aut paludibus fæda.
Taciti Germania.

Multis montibus aspera, et magna ex parte silvis et paludibus invia. Pompon. Mela.

take

take of a dreary magnificence, and sullen grandeur, that produce a deep and lasting impression upon the mind. These sentiments are congenial with the appearance of the country. The stupendous scenery of rocks, clouds, precipices, torrents, and deserts, continually exhibited to their senses, cannot fail to suggest a train of thoughts and expressions corresponding therewith; and the accidents, to which a life of hunting, in a country that gives occasions to so many dangers, is exposed, contribute still farther to increase the gloom, and throw a darker shade upon the imagination. Hence, sorrow and terror are the passions they are most naturally led to excite. Their music, as well as their poetry, is plaintive, and, I believe, mostly applied to the recital of melancholy tales, or unfortunate events. Even their superstitions are of a melancholy cast.

The noted faculty of prying into futurity, by means of a previous sight of events that were to take place, so noted in the Alpine scenes, both of Scotland and Swisserland, is held to be of a sad and uncomfortable nature, unlike the Seers of old, who were thought to be particularly favoured by such communications. This faculty has been regarded by those, who believed they possessed it, as a misfortune, on account of the many dreadful images it obtruded upon the fancy. This kind of prescience seems to have been principally, though not altogether, concerned

cerned in scenes of horror. Deaths, shipwrecks, storms, and famine, were much more frequently predicted, than the chearful and exhilerating circumstances of of life; which forms no inconsiderable presumption, that the ideas that occupied their minds, were principally of a gloomy and melancholy aspect.

The notions of people, concerning a future state, appear to be much influenced by the scenery of such a country. Some nations have been so sensible of the disadvantages and inconveniences attending it, that they have formed their system of future happiness, apart from any connection with the appearance of the country. Thus the Scythians, and the northern nations of Europe, held their Elysium to consist, in the joys of wine, and of company collected in a spacious building. The American Indians, for similar reasons, have selected such circumstances only, as served most to temper the gloomy and severe appearance of nature. Thus, they expect to be translated to a country, where the sky is always clear and unclouded, and a perpetual spring prevails. On the contrary, when they mean to describe a place of future torment, they figure it as possessing all the dreary appendages belonging to their own country, but in a greater degree. Thus the *Ifurin*, or hell of the northern nations, was supposed to be a place dark, gloomy, cold, and destitute of every convenience of life; the

former

former of which circumstances, as well as the latter, were imagined to constitute the misery inflicted by it.

A Tribute *to the* Memory *of* Charles de Polier, *Esq.* By Thomas Percival, M. D. *Read November* 13, 1782.*

THE contemplation of moral and intellectual excellence affords the most pleasing and instructive exercise, to a well constituted mind. By exalting our ideas of the human character,

October 30th, 1782.

* At a meeting of the *Literary and Philosophical Society* of *Manchester*, the following resolution passed unanimously.

"The Members of the *Literary and Philosophical Society* lamenting, with heartfelt concern, the death of their late much honoured brother, *Charles de Polier*, Esq; unanimously resolve, that *Dr. Percival* be requested to draw up a grateful and respectful Tribute to his Memory; to be inserted in the journals of the Society, with a view to record his distinguished merit, and to prolong the influence of his bright example."

November 13th, 1782.

At a meeting of the *Literary and Philosophical Society*, it was resolved unanimously, "That the Thanks of the Society be returned to *Dr. Percival*, for his Tribute to the Memory of *Charles de Polier*, Esq; and that he be desired to print the same."

it expands and heightens, the principle of benevolence; and at the same time is favourable to piety, by raising our views to the supreme Author of all that is fair and good in man. The wise and the virtuous have ever dwelt, with delight, on the meritorious talents and dispositions of their fellow-creatures: And an amiable philosopher drew, from this source, such sweet consolations, under the toils and distresses of life, that he warmly recommends the practice to our imitation. *" When you would recreate your-* *" self,"* says M. Antoninus, *" reflect on the lauda-* *" ble qualities of your acquaintance: On the magna-* *" nimity of one, the modesty of another, or the libera-* *" lity of a third."** Generous meditation! which every one, present, may indulge; and, by indulging, assimilate, to his own nature, the various perfections of others; transfusing, as it were, into his breast, the virtues which he contemplates.

But can we engage ourselves in such an exercise, without the most lively recollection of our late honoured and beloved colleague? His image presents itself before us; and we instantly recognise, the agreeableness of his form, the animation of his countenance, the vigour of his understanding, and the goodness of his heart. How graceful was his address; how sprightly, entertaining, and intelligent his conversation!

* M. Antonin. Lib. VI.

What rich stores of knowledge did he display; what facility in the use, what judgment in the application of them! Few have been the subjects of discussion in this Society, which his observations have not enlightened: and what he could not himself elucidate, he has enabled others to do, by the pertinency of his queries, and the sagacity of his conjectures. So quick was his penetration; so enlarged his comprehension; so exact the arrangement of his intellectual treasures! Learning, with some, is the parent of mental obscurity; and the multiplicity of ideas, which have been acquired by severe study, serves only to produce perplexity and confusion. But Mr. de Polier's thoughts were always ready at command. And he engaged, with perspicuity, on every topic of discourse; because he saw, at one view, all its relations and analogies to those branches of knowledge, with which he was already acquainted. With such felicity of genius, he was continually making large accessions to his stock of science, without laborious researches, or seclusion from the social enjoyments of life.

Of his abilities as a writer, he furnished us with a striking proof, in the Dissertation he delivered, last winter; which is equally distinguished by the justness of its sentiments, and the purity of its diction; and fully displays his perfect attainment, both of the idiom and embellishments of the English language.

But Mr. de Polier had merits, more estimable than those, which he derived from the vivacity of his fancy, the elegance of his taste, or the powers of his undestanding. And his friends will cordially unite with me in testifying, that, if honoured for his *intellectual*, he was beloved for his *moral* endowments. His heart was open to every generous sympathy; and the sensibility of his nature so enlivened all his perceptions, that the ordinary duties of social intercourse were performed, by him, with a warmth, almost equal to that of friendship. Nor was this the artificial deportment of unmeaning courtesy; but the generous effusion of a heart, which felt for all mankind. In such *philanthropy*, politeness has its true foundation: and of this joint grace of nature and education, " which aids and strengthens Virtue, where it meets her, and imitates her actions, where she is not," our lamented brother was a bright example. So engaging were his manners, and at the same time so sincere his disposition, that we may apply to him, with *honour*, what Cicero meant as a *reproach*; that he was qualified, *cum tristibus sevére, cum remissis jucunde, cum senibus graviter, cum juventute comiter vivere.* These powers of pleasing flowed from no servile compliances, nor
ever

ever led him into criminal indulgences. As a companion, he was convivial without intemperance, and gay without levity or licentiousness. His conversation was sprightly and unreserved; but, in the most unguarded hours of mirth, exempt from all indecency and profaneness. And the sallies of his wit and pleasantry were so seasoned with good humour, that they gave delight, unmixed with pain, even to those who were the objects of them. If the coarser pleasures of the bottle be banished from our tables; or if rational conversation, and delicacy of behaviour, with the sweet society of the softer sex, be now substituted in their room, this happy revolution has been rendered more complete by the influence of Mr. de Polier.

But though URBANITY, according to the most liberal interpretation of that term, was the *characteristic* of our excellent colleague, he possessed other endowments, of more intrinsic value. And I could enlarge, with pleasure, on his nice sense of rectitude, his inviolable integrity, and sacred regard to truth. These moral virtues were, in him, founded on no fictitious principle of *honour*, but resulted from the constitution of his mind; and were strengthened by habit, regulated by reason, and sanctioned by religion. For, notwithstanding the veil which he chose to cast over his *piety*, it was manifest to his intimate friends; and may be recollected by others, who have marked the seriousness, with which he discoursed, on every subject relative to the being and attributes of GOD. Defective indeed must be the character of that man, who can discern and acknowledge, without venerating, the divine perfections; and partake of the bounties of nature, yet feel no emotions of gratitude towards its benevolent Author. "*A little philosophy,*" says lord Verulam, "*may incline the mind to atheism; but depth in philosophy will bring it about again to religion.*"*

I have thus attempted to draw a rude sketch of the features, of our late honoured friend. A fuller delineation might furnish a more pleasing picture to strangers; but, to the Members of this Society, a few outlines will suffice to revive the image of the beloved original. This image, I trust, will be long and forcibly impressed on our minds; and that every one, now present, may adopt the language of Tacitus, on a similar occasion. "*Quicquid ex Agricola amavimus, quicquid mirati sumus, manet, mansurumque est in animis*

---

* The noble author subjoins a just reason, for this observation. "For while the mind of man," says he, "looketh upon *second causes* scattered, it may sometimes rest in them, and go no farther: but when it beholdeth the chain of them linked together, it must needs fly to Providence and Deity."

BACON's Essay on Atheism.

"*hominum.*"

"*hominum.*" "Whatever in Agricola was the object of our love and of our admiration, remains, and will remain, in the hearts of all who knew him."

Having taken a short view of the character of Mr. de Polier, curiosity and attachment concur in prompting us, to extend the retrospect; and we become solicitous to know something of his connections and education; and to trace the leading events of a life, in the conclusion of which we have been so deeply interested. But our friend was no egotist; and the zeal with which he entered into the concerns of others, precluded the detail of his own. I must content myself, therefore, with presenting to the Society, the following brief memoirs.

Charles de Polier Bottens was the son of the Reverend ——— de Polier Bottens, Dean of the Cathedral Church of Lausanne, President of the Synod of the Pais de Vaud, Member of the Society of Arts and Sciences at Manheim, and Citizen of Geneva. He was born at Lausanne, in the year 1753; and received the first part of his education, in the public schools of that city. As soon as he had acquired a sufficient knowledge of the classics, he was sent to an academy near Cassel, in Germany; from whence, after a residence of two years, he was removed to the university of Gottingen. In this celebrated seat of learning, he passed three years;

and being then inclined to a military life, he obtained a lieutenant's commission in the Swiss regiment of D'Erlact, in the French service. But he soon resigned his commission, and returned to Lausanne; where he had a command given him, in one of the Provincial regiments of dragoons. In this situation, his connection commenced with the Earl of Tyrone; who offered him the tuition of his eldest son, Lord le Poer, on terms equally honourable and advantageous. But before the engagement was completed, proposals were made to him by the duke of Saxe Gotha, to become governor to the hereditary prince, with an annuity, for life, of twelve hundred rixdollars; an apartment at court; and the post of chamberlain, or rank of colonel. These proposals, however, he declined in favour of lord Tyrone. And he executed the important trust, assigned to him, with such judgment, tenderness, and fidelity, as induced that respectable nobleman to commit three of his children to his sole direction. These amiable youths he brought to England, in the summer of 1779; and settled them at the school of a clergyman in Manchester, who is eminently distinguished by his virtues as a man, and abilities as a teacher.

At this period, our first acquaintance with Mr. de Polier was formed. By the laws of hospitality, he was entitled to our attention, as a
stranger.

stranger: but his personal accomplishments, and the charms of his conversation, soon superseded the ordinary claims of custom, and converted formal civility into esteem and friendship. He became our companion in pleasure; our assistant in study; our counsellor in difficulty; and our solace in distress. Amusement acquired a dignity and zest, by his participation; and he softened the austerity of philosophy, whenever he joined in the pursuit. The institution, which now celebrates his memory, owes to him much of its popularity and success; and, so long as it subsists, his name will be revered, as one of its founders, and most shining ornaments.

About the middle of last winter he was attacked by a complaint, which at first gave no disturbance to the vital functions. But being aggravated by the fatigues of a long journey to Holyhead, and of a voyage from thence to Dublin, at a time when he laboured under the *Influenza*, his malady rapidly increased after his arrival in Ireland; and put a final period to his valuable life on the 18th of October 1782.* The vigour of his faculties, and the warmth of his affections, continued even to the hour of his dissolution. And the amiableness of his behaviour, in the closing scene of trial and suffering

* At CURRAGHMORE, near WATERFORD, the seat of the Earl of Tyrone.

through which he passed, gave such completion to his character, that we may apply to him, what the Poet has said of Mr. Addison;

- - - - He taught us how to live; and, oh! too high
The price of knowledge, taught us how to die.*

On this affecting event, I cannot express your feelings and my own, in terms so forcible as those of the animated historian, whom I have before quoted. *Si quis piorum manibus locus; si, ut sapientibus placet, non cum corpore exstinguuntur magnæ animæ; placide quiescas, nosque ab infirmo desiderio, ad contemplationem virtutum tuarum voces, quas neque lugeri, neque plangi fas est! Admiratione te potius temporalibus laudibus, et si natura suppeditet, militum decoramus!*† "If there be any habita-
"tion for the shades of the virtuous; if, as
"philosophers suppose, exalted souls do not
"perish with the body; may you repose in peace,
"and recall us from vain regret, to the contem-
"plation of your virtues, which allow no place
"for mourning or complaint! Let us adorn
"your memory, rather, by a fixed admiration,
"and, if our natures will permit, by an imitation
"of your excellent qualities, than by temporary
"eulogies!"‡

* Tickell's Poem on the Death of Addison.
† Tacit. Vit. Agricolæ.
‡ See Dr. Aikin's Translation of the Life of Agricola.

THOUGHTS *on the* STYLE *and* TASTE *of* GARDENING *among the* ANCIENTS. *By* WILLIAM FALCONER, M. D. F. R. S. &c. *Communicated by Dr. Percival. Read December* 11, 1782.

THE moſt early account we have of a Garden, is contained in the Sacred Writings, in the deſcription of the habitation of our firſt parents. The form, diſpoſition, and arrangement are not particularly deſcribed. It is only ſaid, to have contained every tree, "that is pleaſant to the eye, and good for food;"* and that it was watered by a river, which, no doubt, added to the beauty of the proſpect, (which, in the expreſſion before cited, ſeems to have been particularly conſulted,) as well as to the fertility of the ſoil. Wood and water, therefore, both for ſhade† and ornament, the principal points aimed at in modern gardens, may be preſumed to have been here in the higheſt perfection. Farther than this, we are not informed.

The next hints concerning Gardens, that I can diſ-

---

* Geneſis, Chap. ii. ver. 9.

† And Adam and his wife hid themſelves from the preſence of the Lord, among the trees of the Garden.
Geneſis, Chap. iii. ver. 8.

cover in the Sacred Writings, are to be found in the Song of Solomon, part of the scene of which is, undoubtedly, laid in a garden.* Flowers and fruits are particularly spoken of, as the ornaments, and the produce of it; and besides these, aromatic vegetables† formed a considerable part of the gratifications it afforded. Fountains, and streams of water appear, also, to have had a share in the composition, and, probably, for ornament, as well as use. Statues, or paintings are not mentioned in these descrip-

---

* I am the rose of Sharon, and the lily of the vallies.
> Chap. ii. ver. 1.

A garden inclosed, is my sister, my spouse; a spring shut up, a fountain sealed. Thy plants are an orchard of pomegranates, with pleasant fruits, camphire, with spikenard, spikenard and saffron, calamus and cinnamon, with all trees of frankincense, myrrh, and aloes, with all the chief spices. A fountain of gardens, a well of living waters, and streams from Lebanon. Awake, O north wind, and retire thou south, blow upon my garden, that the spices thereof may flow out. Let my beloved come into his garden, and eat his pleasant fruits.
> Chap. iv. ver. 12. et.

† Aromatic plants are very often mentioned as a high gratification, and perfumes, to this day, are much admired in the east. " His cheeks, are a bed of spices, with sweet flowers, his lips like lilies, dropping sweet smelling myrrh." Ch. v. ver. 13. " I will get me to the mountain of myrrh, and to the hill of frankincense."
> Ch. iv. ver. 6.

tions,

tions, and, probably, had no place among their embellishments.

It is proper to remark, that all the beauties of these gardens were confined within themselves. No beauty of prospect, or variety of ground is mentioned, and for obvious reasons. The privacy of a place, destined, in a great measure, for the confinement of women, prevented the former, and the limited bounds of the extent of the garden, would not admit of the latter.

It appears probable, that, at that time, they were used to have houses in their gardens, wherein, particularly in hot weather, they were accustomed to sleep at nights, which, probably, was a great part of the gratification resulting from them. A dwelling is mentioned in the Song of Solomon, that seems to have stood in the garden, and was probably of this kind;* and it is likely, that "the pleasant houses," mentioned by Ezekiel,† were of a similar nature.

I am inclined to think, that some ever-green trees, particularly some of the terebinthinate

---

* Chap. v. ver. 1, &c.

† Chap. xxvi. ver. 12.

Dr. Russel says, that it is customary for the principal persons at Aleppo to live at their gardens during the month of April, and part of May. They live under tents, and perhaps tents might be used in the instance cited.

Russel's Aleppo, p. 135

kind, were favourite ornaments of the Jewish gardens.

The cedar is often mentioned, as a tree highly ornamental; and both that and the fir are spoken of in the book of the prophet Ezekiel,* as being frequent in magnificent gardens. Dr. Russel † likewise mentions, that, at present, at Aleppo a cypress tree is generally planted in the little gardens, in the inner courts of the houses, as well as in their more extensive ones.

The next description of a garden, in order of time, appears to be that of Alcinous by Homer. This has been, generally, esteemed to be a fruit garden for use merely, without any view to ornament. But, I do not take this to be altogether its character, though it seems to be so in a good measure. Something of parterre,‡ planted with flowers,

---

* The cedars in the garden of God could not hide him, the fir trees were not like his boughs. Ezekiel, xxxi.

† Russel's Aleppo, p. 5.

‡ Ενθα δε κοσμηται πρασιαι παρα νειατον ορχον
Παντοια πεφυασιν επηετανον γανοωσαι.

Homeri Iliad. L. VII.

Athenæus, and the Scholiast on Homer, understand pot herbs only to be meant in this place: but the words κοσμηται and γανοωσαι seems too ornamental to be so understood, and to be rather applicable to flowers. At any rate, they were planted in parterre-like division, as the word πρασιαι signifies.

" Ad

flowers, appears to have composed a part of it; and, probably, Homer would not have bestowed so particular, and laboured a description upon the trees, if they had not contributed to the beauty of its appearance, as well as to the furnishing of the table with fruits.

The hanging gardens of Babylon come next, I believe, in order of time. These seem, in many respects, to have been laid out with good taste. Their elevation, not only produced a variety and extent of view, but was, also, useful in moderating the heat, which, I suppose, might be the principal reason, why such a construction was fixed upon; though, another is assigned, referring only to the similarity of appearance. Such a situation would, likewise, suit a greater variety of trees, and plants, than a plain surface, and would contain a larger, as well as a more diversified extent.

The suiting of the situation, to the nature of the trees, seems, from the account given by

---

" Ad olerum consitionem quadratæ dispositiones quæ πρασιαι dicuntur in laterculi formam" Columella.

ως τα πλινθια—Scholiast. on Homer.

Was this division of the garden of Alcinous, similar to the garden of herbs, mentioned in the Book of Kings, into which Ahab wished to convert Naboth's vineyard?

Josephus,

Josephus, to have been one view,* in the erecting the building in such a manner. And the success seems to have been answerable, as the trees are said to have flourished extremely well,† and to have grown as tall as in their native situations. On the whole then, however different these may appear from modern gardens, I must confess, I think they were formed with judgment and taste, and well adapted to the situation and circumstances.

It appears, from the nature of the structure, that the trees, here, should be planted regularly, in rows and ranks; but this was also in the Persian taste. The garden of the younger Cyrus at Sardis, which was all planted with his own

---

* - - - εν δε τοις βασιλειοις τουτοις αναλημματα λιθινα υψηλα ανωκοδομησας και την οψιν αποδους ομοιοτατην τοις ορεσι καταφυτευσας δενδρεσι παντοπαδοις εξειργασατο και κατασκευασας τον καλομενον κρεμαστον παραδεισον

Joseph. contra Apionem, L. I. § 19. Extr.

† Το δε εδαφος εξωμαλισμενον πληρες ην παντοδαπων δενδρων των δυναμενων κατα τε το μεγεθος και την αλλην χαριν τοις θεομενοις ψυχαγωγησαι. Diod. L. II.

Stipites earum octo cubitorum spatium crassitudine æquent: in quinquaginta pedum altitudinem emineant, et frugiferæ æque sunt, ac si terra sua alerentur.

Quint. Curt. L. V.

hands, was laid out in straight lines,* and, at right angles, which was, no doubt, esteemed the established custom, of placing the trees in gardens.

It does not, as far as I can find, appear clearly, that flowers made a part of the ornaments of these gardens; but, we may conjecture, they did, from the odours mentioned to be exhaled from the plants growing there,† which were understood to constitute no small part of the pleasure they afforded.

It seems probable, from several circumstances, that the eastern gardens were adjoining to the house or palace, to which they belonged. Thus, King Ahasuerus goes immediately, from the banquet of wine, to walk in the garden of the palace. ‡ The garden of Cyrus, at Sardis, mentioned by Xenophon, ‖ was probably contiguous to the palace, as was that of Attalus,

---

* επει δε εθαυμαζεν αυτον ο Λυσανδρος ὡς καλα μεν τα δενδρα ειη, δι' ισου δε τα πεφυτευμενα, ορθοι δε οι ϛιχοι των δενδρων, ευγωνια δε παντα καλως ειη. Xenoph. Œconom.

† Οσμαι δε πολλαι και ηδ̓ιαι συνπαρομαρτοιεν αυτοις περιπατουσι. Ibidem Xenoph.

Και ταυτα μετ' ηδιϛων οσμων και θεαματων παρεχει. Ibidem Xenoph.

‡ Esther, Chap. vii. ver. 7. ‖ Œconom.

mentioned

mentioned by Justin.* The hanging gardens of Semiramis, at Babylon, were not so much adjacent to the palace, as a part of the palace itself, as several of the royal apartments were beneath them.†

Parks, also, which may be looked upon, somewhat, in the light of gardens, were common in the east. The younger Cyrus, we are told by Xenophon,‡ had a park at Celænæ in Phrygia, stocked with wild beasts, for the purposes of hunting. Plutarch ‖ speaks of another, belonging to Tissaphernes; and inclosures of a similar kind, are mentioned by other writers.§

---

* Justin. L. XXXVI. C. 4.

† Αι δε ευριγγες τα φωτα δεχομεναι ταις δι αλληλων υπεροχαις πολλας και παντοδαπας ειχον διαιτας βασιλικας.
         Diodor. Lib. II.

‡ Ενταυθα Κυρω βασιλεια ην και παραδεισος μεγας αγριων θηριων πληρης, ἅ εκεινος εθηρευεν απο ιππου οποτε γυμνασαι εαυτον βουλοιτο τε και τους ιππους. Anabas. L. I.

‖ Vita Alcibiadis.

§ Παραγινεται δε και εις περιβολον, ον βασιλεως θηραν εκαλουν. ην δε τι τειχιον χωριον απειληφος ενδον πολυ, δενδρεσι πεφευτευμενον παντοδαποις. εν τουτω θηριων παντοιων εναποκλειομενα γενη, τροφης τε ουκ ηπορευοντο, δια το και ταυτην επεισαγεσθαι, και παρειχον τω βασιλει του θηραν, ηνικα αν βουληθειη, ραστονην.
         Zozimi. L. III. C. 23.

Venationes Regis esse in Babylone, et omnis generis bestias murorum ejus tantum ambitu coerceri.
        Sanct. Hieronym. in C. XIII. Esaiæ.

What, the taste for gardening was, among the Greeks, I do not understand. The Academus, we know, was a woody shady place;* and the trees appear to have been of the olive species.† It was situated, beyond the limits‡ of the walls, and adjacent to the tombs of the heroes. I do not, however, find any particular account in ancient history, of the manner, in which this grove was disposed or laid out. It appears, however, to have been an elegant ornamented place.§ At the entrance, was an altar dedicated to Love, which was said to be the first erected to that Deity. Within the Academus, were the altars of Prometheus, of the Muses, of Mercury, Minerva, and Hercules; and, at a small distance, was the tomb of Plato. So that, in all probability, it was highly adapted by art, as well as nature, to philosophic reflection and contemplation.

We are told by Plutarch, that before the time of Cimon, the Academus was a rude and un-

---

* Atque inter Sylvas Academi quærere verum.
    Horat. Epist. L. II. Ep. II. l. 46.

† Αλλ' εις Ακαδημιαν κατιων, υπο ταις μοριαις αποθρεξεις.
    Aristoph. Νεφελαι. Act. III. Sc. 3.

‡ - - - γυμνασιον προαστειον αλσωδης.
    Diog. Laert. Vit. Platon.
Non longe a Muris Academia est. Pausan. Attica.

§ Pausaniæ Ibidem.

cultivated spot: but that it was planted by that General, and had water conveyed to it;* whether this water was brought merely for use to water the trees, or for ornament, does not appear. It was divided into gymnasia, or places of exercise, and philosophic walks, shaded with trees. These are said to have flourished very well, until destroyed by Sylla,† (when he besieged Athens) as well as those in the Lyceum.‡

Near the Academy, were the gardens of the philosophers,§ of Plato,‖ and of Epicurus,¶ which, however, were probably but small.

The scene of Plato's Dialogue concerning Beauty, is elegantly described, as being on the

---

* Την Ακαδημιαν εξ ανυδρου και αυχμηρας καταρρυτον αποδειξας αλσος ησκημενον υπ' αυτου δρομοις καθαροις και συσκιοις περιπατοις. Plutarch Vit. Cimon.

† Επεχειρησε τοις ιεροις αλσεσι, και τηντε ακαδημιαν εκειρε δενδροφορωτατην πρασειων ουσαν, και το λυκειον. Vit. Syllæ.

‡ The trees in the Lyceum were probably Plane trees. Varro quotes Theophrastus, for the relation of the large size and extent of the roots of one in that place.
De re rustica, Cap. XXXVII.

§ Ομοιως δε και η ακαδημια και οι κηποι των φιλοσοφων.
Strabon. L. IX.

‖ - - - - cujus (Platonis) enim hortuli propinqui non memoriam solum mihi afferunt, sed ipsum videntur in conspectu meo ponere. Cicero de finib. L. V.

¶ In Epicuri hortis, quos modo præteribamus. Ibidem.

banks of the river Iliffus, and under the fhade of the Platane; but no artificial arrangement of objects is mentioned, nor any thing which will lead us to imagine the profpect to be any other than merely natural. The beauty of this defcription was fo much admired, by fucceeding writers of philofophic dialogues,* that it was frequently imitated, and, at laft, to fuch a degree, that it appeared ridiculous and difguftful, as we may fuppofe from the caution given by Plutarch † againft fuch attempts, in the proems to difcourfes.

The Romans feem to have early imbibed fomewhat of a tafte for gardens.

Tarquin the Proud, is faid to have communicated his intentions to his fon, concerning his conduct to the people of Gabii, ‡ by ftriking off the heads of the flowers in his garden.

---

* Cicero was a great admirer of this paffage in Plato.

Quæ (Platanus) videtur non tam ipfa aquula quam Platonis oratione creviffe. De oratore, Lib. I. § 15.

† Αφελε τȣ λογου το νυν εχον εμποιων τε λειμωνας και σκιας και αμα και λακκων διαδρομας και οσα αλλα τοιουτων τοπων επιλαβομενοι γλιχονται τνν Πλατωνος Ιλισσον και τον αγνον εκεινον και την ηρεμα προσαντη ποαν πεφυκιαν προθυμοτερον η καλλιον επιγραφεσθαι. Plutarch Amator. ad Initium.

‡ Livii Lib. I. Cap. 54. Luc. Flor. C. 8. Dionyf. Itallic.

It appears from all thefe accounts, that the garden was adjacent or contiguous to the palace.

I see but little mention made of a garden, otherwise than as a matter of utility, to produce articles of food, for many years after; though I think it probable, they might be as matters of pleasure also. The writers, however, on husbandry, Cato, Varro, Columella, and Palladius, make not the least mention of a garden, as an object of pleasure, but solely, with respect to its productions of herbs and fruits; and I do not imagine it was among the earliest articles of Roman luxury. The Lucullan gardens seem to be the first I can find mentioned, of remarkable magnificence; though, probably, from the height of extravagance to which these were arrived, they were not the first. Plutarch speaks of them, as incredibly expensive, and equal to the magnificence of kings.* They contained artificial elevations, of ground to a surprizing height, of buildings projected into the sea, and vast pieces of water made upon land. In short, his extravagance and expence was so great, that he acquired from thence the appellation of, the Roman Xerxes.

---

* Plutarch. Life of Lucullus.

Sallust is thought to have alluded to the Villa of Lucullus when, in describing the Roman luxury, he says, "Nam quid ea memorem, quæ, nisi his qui videre, nemini credibilia sunt; a privatis compluribus subversos montes, maria constrata esse." Bell. Catilin.

It is not improbable, from the above account, and from the consideration of Lucullus having spent much time in Asia, in a situation, wherein he had an opportunity of observing the most splendid constructions of this kind, that these gardens might be laid out in the Asiatic style.

The vast masses of building, said to have been erected, might have born some resemblance, in the arrangement and style, to the Babylonian gardens; and the epithet of the Roman Xerxes might be applicable to the taste, as well as the size and expence, of his works.

The Tusculan Villa of Cicero, though often mentioned, is not, as far as I can discover, any where described in his works, so as to give an adequate idea of the style, in which his gardens or grounds were disposed.

There is but little in Virgil, that I can find, relative to this subject. Pines,* it seems probable, were a favourite ornament in gardens, and flowers,† roses especially, were much esteemed.

---

* Fraxinus in sylvis pulcherrima, pinus in hortis,
Populus in fluviis, abies in montibus altis:
Sæpius at si me, Lycida formose, revisas,
Fraxinus in sylvis cedet tibi, pinus in hortis.
    Virgil, Eclog. VII. l. 65. &c.

† Forsitan et, pingues hortos quæ cura colendi
Ornaret, canerem, biferíque rosaria Pæsti:
Quóque modo potis gauderent intyba rivis,

esteemed. Some plants also, of the culinary kind, as the endive, the parsley, and the cucumber, were sometimes either planted as ornaments, or else intermixed with plants of that kind, contrary to modern practice.

I apprehend that flowers and shrubs were planted full as much among the Romans, for the sake of their odour, as the beauty of their appearance.* Perfumes were always highly valued in warm climates. Virgil places Anchises† in Elysium, in a grove of bays, and is careful to remark, that they were of the sweet scented kind.‡ The Pæstan roses were chiefly valued for their excellent perfume; and the same quality appears to be the cause, why they were placed by Tibullus ‖ as ornaments to the Elysian fields.

Et virides apio ripæ, tortúsque per herbam
Cresceret in Ventrem cucumis; nec sera comantem
Narcissum, aut flexi tacuissem vimen acanthi,
Pallentésque hederas, & amantes litora myrtos.
Georgic, L. IV. L. 118.

* See Athenæus passim, & Anacreon.
Jactat odoratos Vota per Armenios. Tibulli, L. I. Eleg. 5.

† Inter odoratum lauri nemus. Virg. Æneid. VI.

‡ Calthaque Pæstanas vincet odore rosas.
Ovid. Ep. de Pont. L. II. El. 4.

‖ Floret odoratis terra benigna rosis.
Tibulli L. I. Eleg. 3.

Athenæus speaks of the rose, entirely with a view to its odour. L. XV. p. 681, 682, edit. Casaubon.

I must

I must not pass over one piece of Roman luxury, relative to gardens, which is equally prevalent at present, viz. the endeavour to produce flowers at seasons of the year, not suited to their time of blowing.

Roses were then, as at present, the principal flowers, upon which these experiments were tried, as appears from Martial and others.*

The next accounts of ancient gardens I can meet with, are those of Pliny, which, we may conjecture, were not only laid out according to his own taste, but that, also, of the age in which he lived.

---

* Ut nova dona tibi, Cæsar, Nilotica tellus
  Miserat, hibernas ambitiosa rosas.
  Navita derisit Pharios Memphiticus hortos,
  Urbis ut intravit limina prima tuæ.
  Tantus veris honos, et odoræ gratia Floræ,
  Tantaque Pæstani gloria ruris erat.
  Si quacumque vagus gressum oculosque ferebat,
  Textilibus sertis omne rubebat iter.
  At tu, Romanæ jussus jam cedere brumæ,
  Mitte tuas messes, accipe, Nile, Rosas.

       Martial. Epigr. L. VI. Ep. 80.

Dat festinatas Cæsar tibi bruma coronas:
Quondam veris erant, nunc tua facta rosa est.

     Epigr. L. XIV. Epig. 127.

Æstivæ nives, hibernæ rosæ. Lamprid. Vit. Elagab.

His account of his Laurentine Villa,* relates but little to the external arrangement of gardens and ground, but is confined chiefly to the house.

It appears, however, that the Gestatio,† or place for horse exercise, was bordered with box, and where that was defective, with rosemary intertwined with vines. It appears, also, that the Gestatio surrounded the garden.‡ The Xystus ‖ likewise, or place for foot exercise, was planted with violets, which seem to have been placed there, on account of their odour. His description of his Tuscan Villa ** is more particular. This seems to have possessed great natural beauties, to which its possessor attended with great judgment. Its situation appears to have been healthy, and remarkably cool; insomuch, that the olive and the myrtle would not thrive, nor perhaps, even grow there. This

---

* The Laurentine Villa, we are told by Pliny himself, was calculated more for use than ornamenet. " Villa usibus capax, non sumptuosa tutela."

Plin. Epist. L. II. Ep. 17.

† Gestatio buxo aut rore marino ube deficit, buxus ambitur. Adjacet gestatione interiore circuitu vinea tenera et umbrosa. Ibidem Plinii.

‡ Hortum et gestationem videt quâ hortus includitur.
Ibidem Plinii.

‖ Ante Cryptoporticum Xystus violis adoratus. Ibidem.

** See Pliny's Letter to Apollinaris.

Lib. V. Epistol. 6.

circumstance, owing, probably, to its proximity to the Appennine mountains, fitted it for a summer residence. It was placed in the midst of a vast natural amphitheatre, surrounded with hills crowned with lofty and venerable woods: Small rising grounds of great fertility here and there occurred, which were planted on their sides with vines, and surrounded with shrubs and under-wood. The lower grounds were full of flowers and plants, always green and flourishing, and, probably, on account of the difference of temperature of the situation, varying from those of the surrounding country. What added to the beauty of this scene was, that it was plentifully watered by many rivulets from the adjacent hills, which the coolness of the situation prevented being dried up by the summers heats. No marshy places were, however, to be found, but the whole of the superabundant moisture was carried off into the Tyber, which ran through the middle of the prospect, and completed the beauty of the scene, not only as a piece of water, but also, as a navigable river. The Villa of Pliny was situated upon one of those rising grounds before mentioned, and enjoyed a distant and varied prospect; though the ascent to the place on which it stood was so gradual, as scarcely to be sensible to those who went up to it.

After this account of the natural beauties of this elegant situation, which its noble possessor seems to have been thoroughly sensible of, and to have entered into with the highest taste and delight, we are surprized and sorry, to see the artificial part of the prospect, form so disgraceful a contrast. The Xystus, or court before the portico, for walking and exercise, was parted into numerous divisions of diverse shape, all edged with box. The slope lawn, or descent from thence, was bordered on the sides with figures of beasts, cut in box trees. The interior space seems to have been planted (probably here and there only) with acanthus. These were surrounded by a walk, shaded by ever-greens, shorn into different shapes: and the whole again incircled by a riding path, which was secured on the outside by a wall, or rather mound of earth, covered with box trees, rising one row above another, in form of steps. Opposite to the middle of the portico, there was a small court, surrounded by a summer-house, and shaded by four plane trees, in the midst of which, a fountain arose into a marble bason, and running over the edges, sprinkled the trees and the grass underneath. In the front of the buildings, lay a plantation of trees, in form of an Hippodrome, open in the middle, in order that its whole extent might be perceived at one view, and incircled with plane trees, covered with ivy, in such a manner,

manner, as that they appeared, in their lower parts, to be compofed of that fhrub, while their tops flourifhed, in their native verdure and foliage.

The ivy, fpreading from one tree to another, connected them together into an uniform appearance. Between each of the plane trees, box were planted, and behind thefe, bay trees, which blended their fhade with that of the planes. This plantation formed a ftreight boundary on each fide of the Hippodrome, and, at the end, bent into a femicircular form, bordered with cyprefs trees, which ferved to vary the profpect, and to caft a deeper and more gloomy fhade; whilft the internal circular walks, feveral of which there were, planted with rofes, formed a contraft to the fhade of the others. Thefe winding paths terminated in a ftreight walk, which again divided into feveral others, feparated from one another by box hedges. In one place, there was a little meadow; in another, the box was cut into a thoufand different forms; fometimes, into letters, expreffing the name of the mafter; fometimes, that of the artificer; whilft here and there, little obelifks arofe, intermixed alternately with fruit trees; and in the midft of this regularity of arrangement, fo fuited to the tafte of the inhabitants of a great city, there arofe an unexpected fcene, refembling the natural beauties of the

the country, in the center of which lay a spot, surrounded with dwarf plane trees.

Beyond these, was placed a plantation of acanthus, and, as you proceeded, the trees were cut out into various figures and shapes. At the termination, was an alcove seat, of white marble, supported by four small Caryſtian marble pillars. Underneath the seat, the water gushed out, through several small pipes, as if pressed out by the weight of those who reposed themselves upon it. This water was again collected into a stone ciſtern beneath, and received, from thence, into a polished marble baſon, so artfully contrived, as to be always full without overflowing; though the means, by which this was brought about, were not obvious to the view. We are also told, that this baſon served, sometimes, as a table at supper, the larger dishes being placed on the edge, whilſt the smaller swam about, in form of little ships, and wild fowl. Correſponding to this was a fountain, inceſſantly filling and emptying; the water being thrown up to a great heighth, and falling back into the baſon, from whence it ran off. Fronting the alcove, stood a marble Summer-houſe, with folding doors, projecting and opening into a green incloſure, so that, from the upper and lower windows you might diſtinguiſh a variety of different verdures. Seats of marble, with fountains by their ſides, were diſperſed through the
gardens;

gardens; and throughout the whole Hippodrome, streams of water were conveyed in pipes, to different spots, to water and refresh the trees and verdure.

It is obvious, that the above descriptions bear, a striking resemblance to the taste in gardens that prevailed in this country, and indeed throughout Europe, towards the beginning of the present century. The walks bordered with box and rosemary; the terrace planted with violets, at the Laurentine Villa; and the court divided into parterre divisions, edged with box; the figures of animals cut out in box trees, placed opposite each other, upon the slope; with the surrounding walk, inclosed with tonsile evergreens cut into shapes, point out the same resemblance, in the gardens at the Tuscan Villa. The circular amphitheatre of box, cut into figures, and the walk, covered with graduated shrubs, are all exactly in the same style. The fountains overflowing; the marble basons; the little jets d'eau about the seats, and under the alcove; the sudden disappearance of the water; the spouts in the grass; the regular disposition of the trees in the Hippodrome, in lines straight, and regularly curved; together with the arrangement of the different kinds behind each other, make one think, Pliny was rather describing a Villa of king William, or Louis XIV. than one of a Roman nobleman, and senator, seventeen hundred years ago.

Some circumstances, in the above description, appear in many respects, absurd and exceptionable. But let us not be too hasty in our censures; but consider, whether the nature of the climate and country may not vindicate them, in several respects, from the imputations which might have been justly ascribed to them, under different circumstances. The walks, bordered with box, a tree of close growth, and said to flourish extremely in that situation, formed a convenient shelter from the torrid rays of an Italian sun. The shearing of the trees, contributed also to thicken their shade, and to render them more commodious for this purpose; though, I confess, it was not necessary, for this end, that they should be clipped into awkward imitations of animals, &c. which, it is surprizing, a man of the taste of Pliny could approve. The fence to the garden was, in Pliny's Villa, concealed by trees, an improvement on the modern taste referred to; a long range of bare brick walling having been often esteemed an object of beauty or magnificence.

Fountains, likewise, and jets d'eau, however useless, and therefore absurd and unnatural, in Great Britain and Holland, may still be in perfectly good taste in Italy. The dispersion of moisture cools the air, by the evaporation it produces;

duces; and the very murmur of the falling of water, gives the idea of coolness, by association of sensations. They seem here to have been disposed with judgment, some of them being situated near the alcove, and resting places, as a refreshment to those fatigued with heat, and exercise; and others, dispersed through the grass, not to cause a foolish surprize, and to endanger the health of those passing that way, by wetting their cloaths, but to water the trees, cool the ground, and refresh the verdure; circumstances indispensable to the beauty of the scenery and prospect, in a hot climate.

The same apology may, I think, be made for the regularity of the walks, in the Hippodrome, and the minute parts and divisions, in which it was disposed.

It is probable, the extent of ground itself was not large. Distant walks would be fatiguing in an Italian summer, and would be too much trouble and expence to keep as closely shaded, as would render them sufficiently agreeable. They were, therefore, in a manner, compelled to make as much as possible, out of the space of ground; which they accomplished, by dividing it into as many walks and paths as possible.

The parterre, likewise, parted into beds of various shapes, was necessary for flowers, which were highly valued in warm climates for their perfume, but do not thrive, unless kept distinct and

and free from the proximity of other trees, or plants.

It is remarkable here, that the taste of the author, for the beauties of nature, breaks out among his description of the most artificial ornaments. Immediately after describing the fence of the garden, covered with graduated box trees, he adds, that the adjoining meadow, was as beautiful by nature, as the garden had been rendered by art; and, in another place, mentions the contrast of the beauties of rural nature, with those of art,* as one of the chief ornaments of his garden. The same apology that has been made for the style, in which Pliny's gardens were laid out, is applicable to the eastern gardens in general, and holds, still more strongly, as the heat becomes more constant and intense. We may farther observe, that this mode suits the disposition of the eastern people, in many other respects. The regularity

---

* Juvenal appears to have possessed a good taste in gardening, and laying out grounds, from what he says of the artificial grottoes at Aricinum, and the attempt to ornament the water, by substituting marble, in place of its natural boundary of herbage.

In Vallem Egeriæ descendimus, et speluncas
Dissimiles veris: quanto præstantius esset
Numen aquæ, viridi si margine clauderet undas
Herba, nec ingenuum violarent marmora tophum?
      Juvenal. Satyr. III. L. 17.

and formality of their manner of living, and manners, corresponds with their taste for regular figures, and uniformity of appearance, in the laying out of ground. It may not, perhaps, be too great a refinement to remark, that such a taste is conformable also to a despotic government, which is jealous of all innovations, and, of course, affords no opportunity for exertions of genius, in any capacity. It is worthy of observation, that the regular taste, above referred to, prevailed in this country, at a time when our system of manners, dress, and behaviour was extremely ceremonious, formal, and reserved, and approaching to those of the eastern countries. As this stiffness wore off, the taste of the people improved. Shakespeare was no longer censured for inattention to dramatic strictness; the turgid, but regular bombast of Blackmore, fell into disrepute and ridicule, and a more easy and natural style was adopted, both in sentiment and writing.

The general method of laying out grounds, in this country, seems at present to be very rational. Natural beauties, or resemblances thereof, are chiefly attempted; which are the more proper, as being more conformable to the climate and situation of the country, and disposition of the people, who are best pleased with great and sublime objects, which are to be found only in nature. The close walk, however

ever delightful in Italy, or Perfia, is here judiciously exchanged for the open grove, and the moisture of grass for gravel. The tonsure of trees is also laid aside; not only as impairing their beauty, but also, as thickening their shade, more than would be necessary or agreeable, where a free intercourse of air is so requisite, to dispel damps and exhalations. Fountains, on the same account, are laid aside, and we are content with the natural current of streams, which exhale less moisture, and produce less cold, than water spouted into the air by the fantastic, but less beautiful distribution of it by a jet d'eau. The gardens, or pleasure grounds, in our country, are likewise very properly of much larger extent, than those in hot climates. Pleasure, in the latter, is always combined with somewhat of indolence and inaction; in the former, it is connected with exercise and activity. A large scope of ground, therefore, that afforded opportunity for the latter, would be more conformable to the genius of the people, as well as to the climate in which the luxurious indulgence, so delightful when the heat is intense, could very seldom be safely practised. On the whole, I am inclined to believe, that, notwithstanding our want of the ornaments proper for hot climates, in our gardens and pleasure grounds, Great Britain is capable of affording more real and genuine beauty in views of

this

this kind, than is, perhaps, any where elfe to be met with. The fine and regular verdure, which always cloaths both the earth and the trees; the variety of the herbage, and the fize to which oaks and other foreft trees, congenial to the country, will arrive, impart a beauty and magnificence to our profpects, and afford opportunities for the judicious interpofition of art, far fuperior to what is to be met with, where thefe advantages do not occur.

We are ftruck with claffic defcriptions, and affected by the circumftances which, by their connection, they recall to the memory; but fetting thefe afide, I make no doubt, a grove of Englifh oaks would be a more beautiful, as well as a more magnificent object, than "the olive grove of Academe," or that of plane trees in the Athenian Lyceum.

After all, it is poffible to err in too clofely following Nature, as it is in neglecting her. There are beauties of the artificial kind, as well as natural, which are proper to be introduced into fcenes of this kind. Statues, buildings, and other ornaments, in good tafte, and well executed, may unite with great propriety with natural objects, and heighten their effect. I do not speak of thefe ornaments, as to any particular beauties they may individually poffefs, but merely as coinciding with the general effect, and nature of the profpect. They are, however, to be be employed cautiously, since, if injudiciously, or even too frequently introduced, they give an air of frivolousness and affectation to the whole, which renders it an object of contempt and ridicule, rather than of admiration.

More, I think, might be said against excluding parterres of flowers, which were so constant attendants upon the old gardens, and so rarely seen at present. We all know, that several kinds of flowers are exquisitely beautiful, and that their beauty and perfection depends on certain circumstances, relative to their culture. Great care is necessary, and a separation from other plants, both of which suggest the parterre as the most proper and convenient way of producing them. I confess, parterre divisions possess no remarkable beauties in themselves, but I think, at the same time, that they have nothing so shocking, to the most delicate taste, that should hinder their being employed, when they are the harbingers of such beautiful productions of nature. A square, or an oblong border, has nothing obviously absurd or disgusting in its appearance; and as to its being artifical, it may be said in defence of it, that it is not an imitation of any thing in nature, nor meant to be so, but solely calculated for utility, as an instrument necessary to the production of beauty; and, considered in this view, we might, with equal reason, object against a house, as an

unnatural,

unnatural, and therefore, an improper object, as against the divisions of a flower parterre.

I grant, indeed, that they have been whimsically, and often absurdly arranged, and fashioned; but such I do not here defend. I only maintain the cause of parterres, on account of the beauties, which they are necessary to produce; not of any they themselves possess.

On the REGENERATION *of* ANIMAL SUBSTANCES. *By* CHARLES WHITE, *Esq.* F. R. S. *&c. Read December* 18, 1782.

THE great Author of the creation has endowed the animal world with a wonderful power of repairing and recruiting its various compound machines, and not only filling up and making good lost substances, but in some instances, of even totally regenerating parts; but we must not from hence accuse him of partiality, in not doing it in every instance; for the further we carry our researches into the secrets of Nature, the more we shall be convinced of the great and unbounded wisdom of God, and of the extraordinary resources he has placed in her possession;

> ------ "The first Almighty cause
> Acts not by partial, but by general laws.
>   Pope's Essay on Man.

The Deity has drawn the line, has fixed the limits, and has said to Nature, hither shalt thou go, and no further.

If this order does not appear to us to be uniformly preserved, we must not conclude that it is not really so, but that it is owing to our slender capacities, that we are unable to trace his hand through all his ways,

> "See and confess, one comfort still must rise,
> " 'Tis this, tho' man's a fool, yet God is wise."
>   Loc. citat.

The antients knew that a fresh broken bone would unite by a callus, that wounds of the flesh would fill up by what is called incarnation, and would be healed over with skin, by what is called cicatrization. But all vain-glorious boasting man must not from hence pretend, that he can make a single fibre grow: this is the act of Nature only. The ablest surgeon living, can do no more than assist her, remove the present obstacles, and prevent others being thrown in her way.

> "Yes Nature's road must ever be preferr'd;
> Reason is here no guide, but still a guard."
>   Loc. citat.

The moderns have carried this matter further.

I did myself the honour to lay before the Royal Society, a remarkable case of a broken bone,

bone, which was inferted in the Philofophical Tranfactions, vol. LI. part the fecond, for the year 1760, in which Nature was difappointed of her ufual method of throwing out a callus, and after more than fix months had elapfed, without an union; when all obftacles were removed, by cutting off the ends of the bone, the offeous matter fhot out as freely as if it had been from a recent fracture, and the broken bone was perfectly united. Since the publication of this cafe, a great number of fimilar ones have occurred, both to myfelf and others, which inconteftably prove, that though Nature is difappointed in her work, even for a long time together, yet, when all obftructions are removed, fhe is ever ready to exert herfelf.

In the year 1768, I cut off the upper head of the os humeri of Edmund Pollitt, aged fourteen, whofe cafe is related in the LIX. volume of the Philofophical Tranfactions. This was much corroded with matter, part of it confumed, and followed by an exfoliation of a large piece of the whole fubftance of the bone; yet the head, neck, and part of the body of it were actually regenerated, and the entire ufe of the joint preferved.

Mr. William Johnfton, furgeon at Dumfries, has given us a cafe in the Edinburgh Medical Effays,* where the whole tibia, the principal

* Vol. V. p. 452.

bone of the leg, being cast off by exfoliation, was regenerated, and was, in a little time, as useful as the old one.

Mr. Le Cat mentions a case in the Philosophical Transactions,* of a child of three years old, from whom he extracted the entire tibia, exostosed and carious in its whole extent, between the two articulations; which had remained sound: this great deficiency of bony substance was entirely supplied again by nature, and the patient regained a new tibia, much firmer than that which he had lost.

In the same place, he relates the case of an adult person where he took out three inches and ten lines of the bone of the upper arm, which was followed by a regeneration of bony matter. In this case the form of the bone, as well as its natural length, was preserved.†

Both in compound luxations and in caries,‡ the heads of the principal bones, and considerable portions of their bodies have been sawn off, and regenerated, such as the tibia, fibula, humerus, radius, ulna, thumb, and finger; the bones were little or no shorter, and new joints were formed, with such a degree of motion, that the patients found little or no inconvenience, and were able to follow their business as well as ever.

* Vol. LVI. p. 270.
† Gooch's Cases, vol. I. p. 323.
‡ Phil. Transf. vol. LIX. p. 39.

Dr. Hunter, in his reflections on cutting the symphysis of the pubis,* says, "as to any property which living ligaments possess of stretching, under violence, permitting dislocations without laceration, I have long taught, that though a very general opinion, it seems not to have been founded in observation. Ligaments will not allow of dislocations in dead bodies without laceration; and elasticity to any degree either in ligaments or tendons, would ill agree with their use in living bodies, which is to keep the parts strongly together; and accordingly, since this opinion has roused attention and examination, every case of a recent dislocation that I have known examined, has been found complicated with a laceration of the ligaments."

Mr. John Hunter, in his Chirurgical Lectures goes further, and says, "that a luxated bone not reduced, by pressing against another bone, digs a cavity for itself, which gets cartilaginous edges and cartilage on all its surface; nay, a synovial gland secreting synovia, and a new joint is set up. In the fracture of a bone, though the parts be thrown at some distance, a callus is formed, which unites them. It is agreeable to the same uniformity of operation, that when a bone is broken, which was originally formed in a nidus of cartilage, the renovated bone also forms in cartilage; while a bone, originally formed in membrane, when it is partially destroyed, is re-

* Letter to Dr. Vaughan, p. 86.

produced in membrane." All furgeons muft have obferved this, that in old diflocations which have not been reduced, there is always fome degree of motion more or lefs in the diflocated joint, except it has been complicated with a fracture.

In a converfation I lately had with Dr. Monro, he confirmed Dr. Hunter's opinion, with the relation of the two following diffections. He immerfed a dead child in warm water, till it was perfectly foft and flexible; he then diflocated the fhoulder. Upon diffecting the parts, he found the capfular ligament lacerated.

A man in Edinburgh was killed by a fall from a horfe, and his fhoulder was at the fame time diflocated. Upon diffection in this cafe alfo, he found the capfular ligament lacerated.

Dr. Monro told me, he did not in the leaft doubt what Mr. John Hunter had advanced on this fubject; and informed me, that he had a cafe, laft winter, of a patient who had an exfoliation of half the lower jaw, particularly of the whole condyle on the left fide; the loft part was regenerated, he had the entire ufe of the jaw, and the joint was as perfect as on the other fide, except being a little fuller, and attended with a trifling degree of hardnefs. I had the fatisfaction of feeing the exfoliated bone amongft his valuable collection, and found the head of the bone perfect, except a little carious on one fide.

In the same collection I saw an astragalus, (one of the bones of the foot) which had come away entire, and the patient, as Mr. Fyfe informed me, had the perfect use of his foot and ancle. I likewise saw in the same place, a thigh bone, which had been broken, the ends had not coaptated, but had overshot each other three inches, and were perfectly united. Cases of this sort I have often seen, and have now a thigh bone by me, united in the same manner; but in that bone in the possession of Dr. Monro, there is this circumstance, which I had never before observed, that the sides of the bone had not approximated each other, but in one point. The callus had shot out in such a manner as to form cancelli, and the void space had all the appearance of having contained a medullary substance. Dr. Monro told me he had a whole chest of regenerated bones in his possession. He likewise described to me the following experiment, he had made.

He laid open the abdomen of a pig for several inches, in such a manner, that the intestines protruded; which convinced him, that all the integuments were completely divided. He then reduced the intestines, and sewed up the wound. After it was perfectly united, he killed the pig. He then made incisions above and below, and on one side of the cicatrix; after which he injected the aorta; and, though there was not a possibility of the injection entering but on one side of the cicatrix, yet the arteries, on both sides, were perfectly injected, a convincing proof, that they must have regenerated, for it cannot be supposed that the mouths of so many small vessels could possibly have coaptated, so as to have continued the circulation through the cicatrix. I had the satisfaction of seeing both the preparation and an engraving from it, which, it is hoped, the doctor will favour the public with, together with the several other valuable experiments.*

Teeth have regenerated in every period of life. Mr. Thornton, a very ingenious medical student at Edinburgh, informed me, that he had a sound tooth drawn by mistake some years ago, which as soon as he found out he immediately replaced. It grew again, and was as good in every respect as any other. But in process of time, this tooth began to decay, and give him pain, which became exquisite whenever the tooth was touched, even in the slightest manner. He therefore had it drawn, and one of the fangs was found to be carious. From this it is very evident, that nerves will grow again, after being disunited.

* Since this paper was read before the Society, Dr. Monro has published his useful and ingenious observations on the nervous system, with the engravings of these preparations. Vid. Tab. XLVI. and Tab. XLVII.

Mr. Cruikshanks, in his Letter to Mr. Clare, p. 87, says, "Not only the brain, but the nerves also, appear to have other properties than we have hitherto apprehended. Some years ago, I demonstrated, by experiments on living animals, that nerves divided unite again; and that when portions had been cut out, they were regenerated: in both instances the animals perfectly recovered. These experiments I hope soon to be able to lay before the public; meantime I am happy to find, they have been recently confirmed by so great authority, as the Abbè Fontanà, to whom I communicated my discovery, and shewed my preparations of united and regenerated nerves."*

Mr. Gooch has given us a remarkable case of the cuticle and nails,† being frequently cast off and regenerated, particularly in the feet and hands, sometimes twice in a year. Those of the hands where cast off whole, and we are furnished with an engraving of a pair of these cuticular gloves.

---

* Dr. Monro, in the work before mentioned, has given a plate (Vid. Tab. XIV.) to shew the regeneration of the sciatic nerves, which had been divided in living frogs, and dissected twelve months after. The regenerated parts are of a darker colour than the original nerves, which proves, that there was not a mere coaptation of the divided ends.

† Philosophical Transactions, vol. LIX. p. 281.

There is another similar case related by Mr. Latham,* but with this difference, that this patient did not cast her nails.

By performing the operation for the cure of the aneurism, several inches of the trunks of the principal arteries, both of the arm and the thigh, have been destroyed; yet in a few days, the circulation through the whole limb, has been carried on, as perfectly, as before the operation. The method, which nature has taken for accomplishing this business, may be seen by an engraving † from a preparation which I made, and which Dr. Hunter has done me the honour to give a place amongst his valuable collection.

There is a very extraordinary history of a glans penis regenerated after amputation, related by Mr. Jamison, surgeon at Kelso, and inserted in the Edinburgh Medical Essays.‡ The young man was married, in that country, about two years after the cure, has had two children, and complains not of want or defect even in sensation.

Crabs and lobsters cast their shells, both from their bodies, legs, and claws, and even cast their stomachs, generally every year, which are immediately regenerated. The shell is renewed by a fluid, which they eject; and it invests their whole body, growing hard and dry, in a short

---

* Philos. Transactions vol. LX. p. 451.
† See my Cases in Surgery, p. 140.
‡ Vol. VI. p. 434.

time, and becoming as strong a shell, as that which they had before. But, what is more extraordinary, they frequently lose a leg or a claw in their combats, which are very frequent and furious: the lost part will be regenerated in about three weeks, and be almost of its natural size. Brown, in his history of Jamaica, informs us, that the claw of the violet crab, in seizing its food, catches such an hold, that the animal loses its limb sooner than its grasp; the claw continuing its retentive power for above a minute, whilst the crab is moving off.

In the polypus, not only young ones will grow out like warts from different parts of the body, drop off, live, and grow; but you may cut them into a thousand pieces, and turn them inside out, and they will still live, and do well; this is accounted for by its whole body being composed of stomach and parts of generation. The latter not being peculiar organs, but merely particles of the stomach, which are its body, each part of which has the power of producing the like. Its food is converted into chyle, in the stomach; absorbents opening into the part, take up the chyle, and these, at some distance from their mouths, become arteries.

If the *Actinia Urtica Marina, Animal flower*, or *Sea-Anemone* be cut through the middle, either transversely or longitudinally, both parts will survive the operation. Nay further, if you tear them

them from the rock or shell, to which they generally adhere, and a shred is left behind, it will become a fresh and perfect animal.

The earth-worm and sea-worm will live after being cut in two; but, what is most surprizing, the small red headed earth-worm, being cut in two, both extremities survive the operation; the head produces a tail, with the anus, the intestines, the anular muscles, and the prickly beards: the tail on the other hand, is seen to shoot forth the noble organs, and, in less than three months, sends forth a head, heart, together with all the apparatus and instruments of generation. These parts, as may be easily supposed, were produced much slower than the former; a new head taking nearly three months for its completion; a new tail shooting forth in less than as many weeks. The lizard, and also the viper cast their skin, and some say their tail, and even their eyes; and the sea-slug is said to cast its head; all which are regenerated.

The buck casts its horns every spring, which are reproduced in a few months. But if he be castrated when young, he will have no horns at all, or small buds only, and those soft to the touch, like velvet, and void of firmness. Dr. Russel informs us, that he had two old bucks castrated at the end of February, and their horns dropped off, the twenty-first of March following; so that the fall of their horns was anticipated five

five weeks at leaſt. Theſe horns were renewed, next year, and were longer than the buck's of the ſame age; but the palms, or collateral branches, were leſs and ſhorter, and neither the velvet of the horns, nor the horns themſelves, were ever caſt afterwards.

I ſhall now beg leave to lay before the Society, two caſes, that have not been publiſhed, in order to prove ſtill further the doctrine I have been endeavouring to eſtabliſh.

Roger Nuttal, of Bury, twenty years of age, was admitted an in-patient of the Mancheſter infirmary, under my care, on the 23d of January, 1775, for a tumor on his back. Upon ſtripping off his ſhirt, to ſhew me the tumor, I was ſtruck with a very ſingular appearance of a ſtump of the right humerus. I aſked him, if he was born with it in that form, or whether his arm had been taken off. He informed me, that Mr. Kay Allen had taken his arm off cloſe to the ſhoulder, when he was but four years old, and that the ſtump was grown again to that length, which ſeemed to be about eight inches longer than he deſcribed it to have been, immediately after the amputation. I enquired both of his mother, and Mr. Allen, as to the truth of his relation, which they both confirmed; and the latter, with this addition, that the arm was taken off, as near the ſhoulder, as the application of the tournequet would permit. The bone had every degree of firmness, and solidity, and the stump was warm to the extreme point, and he informed me, was perfectly sensible when touched. Along with this, you will receive a drawing of the young man, and the appearance which the stump made, executed by your ingenious Secretary Mr. Bew, at the time the patient was at the Infirmary.

Some years ago, I delivered a lady of rank of a fine boy, who had two thumbs upon one hand, or rather, a thumb double from the first joint, the outer one rather less than the other, each part having a perfect nail. When he was about three years old, I was desired to take off the lesser one, which I did; but to my great astonishment it grew again, and along with it, the nail. The family afterwards went to reside in London, where his father shewed it to that excellent operator, William Bromfield, Esq. surgeon to the Queen's household, who said, he supposed that Mr. White, being afraid of damaging the joint, had not taken it wholly out, but he would dissect it out entirely, and then it would not return. He accordingly executed the plan, he had described, with great dexterity, and turned the ball fairly out of the socket; notwithstanding this, it grew again, a fresh nail was formed, and the thumb remains in this state.

The conclusions I would draw from these facts, are, that, in the human species, not only

flesh,

flesh, skin, and bones, may be regenerated, but membranes, ligaments, cartilages, glands, blood vessels, and even nerves; and this for the wisest purposes, that every part may be repaired in its own kind, and in some manner restored by the coagulable lymph, which is poured out, and becomes vascular, and forms organized parts.

By this wise provision of nature, the many accidents to which we are continually exposed, are often more compleatly repaired, than art could be able to accomplish.

In some animals, we see this regenerating and living principle, carried still to a much greater length, where not only whole limbs, but even the more noble organs are reproduced.

The study of nature is not only engaging and pleasant to a high degree, but it inspires us with such a respect and admiration of the Almighty Being, that it is impossible either for a Naturalist or an Anatomist to be an Atheist.

They have constantly before their eyes so many wonderful living machines, differently wrought, yet so compleatly fashioned, and all tending to one great point, the preservation of themselves and their species; in which, there are so many orders of vessels, one depending upon another, yet compleat in themselves; capable of repairing injuries they may sustain, and even of restoring lost substances; that men, who daily see such objects, must be convinced,

vinced, that these admirable fabrics cannot have proceeded from chance, but must have been the work of an Omnipotent Creator, who has formed them with the most perfect wisdom, and attention to their several interests and situations;

"And spite of pride, in erring reason's spite,
One truth is clear, Whatever is, is right."
Pope's Essay on Man.

P. S. Mr. Parke, of Liverpool, in a Pamphlet he has lately published, intitled, "an Account of a new Method of treating Diseases of the Joints of the Knee and Elbow," has given us a case, which fell under the care of Mr. Wainman, of Skipton in Craven; and, as it is perhaps the fullest confirmation, that can possibly happen, of the regeneration, of not only the head of a bone, but of the capsular ligament, and synovial glands, and even every appendage of a joint, it may, perhaps, be thought to be a proper supplement to this paper. I shall therefore give the case in Mr. Wainman's own words. He describes it, as "a violent luxation of the cubitus, occasioned by a fall from a horse in full speed, which forced the os humeri, through the common integuments, a considerable length into the ground, and the bone was quite denudated." He adds, "There was not a possibility of reducing it, and I thought it most eligible to take off the limb,
which

which the family objected to. I called in Dr. Taylor, who was of my opinion; but it would not be complied with. We then judged it best to saw off the os humeri, which I did, about an inch above the sinus that receives the olecranon. I then placed the arm, in such a position, as I thought would be most advantageous, prognosticating, that an anchylosis would ensue, in which I was mistaken; the person is now living, and can perform all the motions of the joint, which is as flexible, as if nothing had ever been amiss."

An ESSAY *on the* DIVERSIONS *of* HUNTING, SHOOTING, FISHING, *&c. considered as compatible with* HUMANITY. *Read January* 15, 1783.

WHILST the general constitution of society remains, such as that no man, however obscure, can be considered as unconnected with the rest of his species; whilst, in every situation, our conduct and sentiments, in some degree, invariably produce an influence on those of others; no inquiry, which respects the genuine motive of such actions, as are frequently committed,

mitted, whether their object be, the pleasure of the individual, or the benefit of society, ought to be regarded as unworthy of serious attention.

The prevailing, though much to be lamented propensity of individuals, to justify their own failings, by the detection of similar weakness in superior characters, renders such an investigation the more necessary; and if, in the prosecution thereof, it should appear, that unworthy motives have been erroneously ascribed to some actions, which may be traced to a different source; or that, from the peculiar constitution of human nature, some weaknesses are inseparable from kindred excellence; such discoveries would prove useful acquisitions to our fund of knowledge; they would tend to rectify the mistaken conceptions of the ignorant, or to improve the discriminating faculty in those, who are most easily seduced by the influence of example.

In reasoning concerning a species of animals, which we suppose, governed by a principle superior to that of instinct, it is desirable to trace a consistency between sentiments and actions, as on this alone, our claim to virtue and to reason seems founded. On a superficial survey, however, such a consistency appears but ill supported in the conduct of those, who, whilst they discharge all the moral duties, and in an especial manner, practise the virtues of hospitality, humanity, and benevolence, are

yet

yet capable of discovering considerable pleasure from those amusements, the professed object of which is, to deprive of life an innocent animal, unacquainted with those desires which spring from luxury, and asking no more of the bounties of our common Parent, than is necessary to its own support and existence.

To be prompted to such actions, not from any necessity to gratify the wants of nature, but solely from the desire of amusement, appears, at first view, repugnant to every principle of humanity, and seems more characteristic of the ferocity of a savage, than of the clemency of a civilized being. What then shall we conclude! Are there no characters exempt from inconsistency? Or is virtue an empty name, without precise meaning? The mind shrinks with aversion from either conclusion. Let us therefore take a more intimate view of the motives to such actions, and, perhaps, they may admit a solution, less repugnant to our feelings.

From the attributes justly ascribed to the benevolent Author of our existence, we may safely conclude, that every propensity, with which the human mind is endowed, is not only necessary, but even conducive to our happiness, whilst indulged in a proper degree. This is not more true, of the mild and gentle dispositions, those which seem to be nourished by the "milk of human kindness," than of our more active and lively propensities, those which excite to the most vigorous and toilsome exertions.

The love of fame gives a glow, an enthusiasm, to the feelings of the possessor, when circumscribed within proper limits, which leads him to combat fatigue and danger, to triumph over toil and difficulty, and smile amidst the anguish of pain and death. Yet the same passion, uncontroled by reason, hath prompted the most abject submission, the most licentious excess; it hath produced the most baneful disorders in society, and, instead of deifying human nature, hath made earth the abode of those spirits, which the poets have assigned to the confines of Tartarus.

We may remark the same, of every other disposition of the human mind, in the exercise of which, the excess, or the deficiency alone is injurious; but there is none, the limited use whereof, doth not contribute to the happiness of the individual, and the good of society.

Not to wander, however, too far from our subject, let us, for a moment, consider man in a state of nature, whilst he is yet unacquainted with the blessings which spring from civilization, or has conceived an idea of pleasure, superior to that which arises from the gratification of his appetites. His own personal safety, with that of those who are dependent on his protection, joined to the daily cravings of nature, first dictate the necessity of waging war with many of those animals,

animals, with whom he hath hitherto lived "joint tenant of the shade."

Perhaps these necessities, however, would not always be sufficient to overcome that love of ease, which is so natural to a state, wherein men seem only a small degree elevated above the rank of brutes. Perhaps, if other inducements were not superadded, he would not be studious to plan, bold to resolve, and active to engage in those dangers and enterprizes, without which, he must frequently be deprived of this species of food, and obliged to substitute others, more easily gained, but less adapted to the health and vigour of the animal œconomy. Without insisting too much on these presumptive reasons, it is certainly a kind provision in the constitution of man, that those exertions, which are dictated by necessity, should also be inspired by inclination; and that, whilst his employment is made subservient to the means of his existence, it should also become a principal instrument of his pleasures.

These remarks, however, principally apply to the rude and savage state of man, which, happily for society, is now almost unknown. There is no longer a necessity for an individual to be himself the executioner of the animal destined to his subsistence; yet, as hunting, shooting, angling, &c. are still pursued, with as much avidity as formerly, it is necessary, if we propose to justify these diversions, to attempt it on principles, which apply to a state, wherein men are humanized, by laws and government, and by the refining influence of arts, sciences, and religion.

It will be generally allowed, that the health and vigour of the intellectual, as well as of the corporeal system, require frequent exercise, and that their very existence almost depends upon it. It is also pretty evident, that to induce such a degree of exertion as will promote these ends, there must be something to stimulate and incite; the final cause being too remote an object. Hence, every amusement which exercises the powers and faculties of man, if not improperly expensive, nor necessarily attended with a neglect of more noble and important pursuits, is, in this point of view, not only not censurable, but meritorious.

Such, however, is the constitution of man, that health alone will not satisfy his aspirations after happiness; and it is clear, that exercise is not more necessary to the perfection of his faculties, than to the promotion of his pleasures. In the words of an elegant writer, equally distinguished for depth of thought, and benevolence of character.* "Labour is the chief ingredient of the felicity to which man

---
* See the Stoic. Hume's Essays.

aspires, and all his enjoyments soon become insipid and distasteful, when not acquired by fatigue and industry. See the hardy hunters rise from their downy couches, shake off the slumbers which still weigh down their heavy eye-lids, and ere Aurora has yet covered the earth with her flaming mantle, hasten to the forest. They have behind, in their own houses, and in the neighbouring plains, animals of every kind, whose flesh furnishes the most delicious fare, and which offer themselves to the fatal stroke. Laborious man disdains so easy a purchase. He seeks for a prey, which hides itself from his search, or flies from his pursuit, or defends itself from his violence. Having exerted in the chase, every passion of the mind, and every member of the body, he then finds the charms of repose, and with joy compares its pleasures to those of his engaging labours."

If exercise, then, be necessary to the health and well-being of man; if it be also necessary to those pleasures, for which nature hath inspired him with the thirst; and if hunting, shooting and fishing furnish stimulating motives, which, in their absence, it would not be easy to supply; these diversions may be esteemed both innocent and virtuous, whilst considered solely with respect to the agent; and it remains only to examine, how far, to the united motives of pleasure and advantage to man, other reasons may be added, in juftification of actions, which refpect the lives and happinefs of the brute creation.

Man, as lord of the creation, regards every other animal as intended for his neceffary ufe, and fubfervient to his reafonable purpofes. This prerogative feems to have been intended for him in the original conftitution of things; and it is fully evident, that the proper exercife of it, is not more favourable to his own, than to the general good. Of fome animals he prolongs the lives, and provides for the fupport, to make them conducive to his own convenience. Others, doomed to contribute to his fuftenance, are cut off ere they attain maturity.* Even if it were not expedient to facrifice thefe to the indifpenfible *wants* of man, *neceffity* would equally prompt him to their deftruction; fince, if they were left uninterruptedly to provide for their own fupport, and to propagate their fpecies, their increafe would foon be incompatible with his exiftence, and probably, with that of their own.

It would, perhaps, be too hafty an affertion, to affirm, that death to brutes is no evil. We are not competent to determine, whether their exiftence, like our own, may not extend to fome

* In the laft clafs may be enumerated moft of the victims to the diverfions we fpeak of.

future mode of being, or whether the present limited sphere is all in which they are interested! On so speculative a question, little could be advanced with precision; nor is it necessary for the investigation of the subject before us. If we may be allowed to reason only from what we know, it may safely be conjectured, that death to brutes is no positive evil; we have no reason to believe, they are indued with the gift of foresight, and therefore, even admitting that with them the pleasures of life exceed its pains and its cares, in terminating their existence, they only suffer a privation of pleasure.

Though the tie of natural affection is, perhaps, not less strong in brutes, than in the human species, yet it is often necessarily dissolved, and and of much shorter continuance. It is also to be remembered, that, on the present plan of pursuing these diversions, such a regard is had to the circumstances and situation of animals, that no helpless, feeble progeny is left to bewail the loss of an affectionate parent; or, from the want of its providence and protection, to perish from exposure to rapacious animals, or the more cruel attacks of want and famine. The fate of an individual may, therefore, be considered as unconnected with that of any of its species; and if it be allowed, that an untimely period of its existence is not to it any evil; the mode of its suffering death, will not only be no objection to the diversions we speak of, but will furnish reasons of considerable weight in their favour.

The tie of natural affection, it hath already been observed, is not weak amongst brute animals; but it may be remarked, that, though in many cases it is so strong in parents towards their progeny, the reflected attachment seems to subsist, only whilst the young offspring are incapable of providing for themselves. When they attain to maturity, the connection is, in most cases, dissolved, and the relationship forgotten. How pitiable then must be the situation of that animal, whom age, with its attendants, weakness and disease, hath reduced to a feeble and helpless state, incapable of providing for itself the necessary subsistence, a prey to continual apprehension from those animals whose attacks it is unable to fly from or repel; and at length languishing to the period of its existence, consumed by famine and wasted by disease? Compare with the fate of such an animal, that of the timid hare. She meets the opening morn in health and vigour, and with playful frolic wantons on yon upland hill, enlivened by the beams of the rising sun. No feeble pulse, or languid eye, indicate a disordered frame; no anticipation of her approaching fate inspires her with apprehension. All is gay and lively, like the prospect around her. On a sudden, however, the scene is changed,

the

the echoing of the horn refounds from the adjacent valley, and the cry of the deep-mouthed hounds thunders towards the hills. She becomes motionlefs with fear, when a fecond alarm roufes her from her trance; fhe flies, and with eager fteps feems to outftrip the winds. Men, horfes, and dogs inftantly join in the chace, and the foreft echoes to the wild uproar. The hare doubles—the fwiftnefs of her fpeed abates—fear, more than fatigue, retards her flight—fhe faints at the noife of the approaching hounds—redoubles to elude their purfuit—her feeble limbs are unable to perform their office—and now—breathlefs and exhaufted, fhe is overtaken, and torn in pieces by her mercilefs purfuers.

Such a doom feems fevere, and hard is the heart which doth not commiferate the fufferer. Its apparent feverity will, however, be much mitigated, if we confider the quick tranfition, from perfect health to the expiring conflict. Death, brought on by difeafe, or the decay of nature, would be much more to be dreaded; and compared therewith, the fate of the partridge from the gun of the fowler, or of the trout by the rod of the angler, is mild and enviable.

To recapitulate then what hath been advanced on this fubject—We have feen the human mind, in every age, endowed with a ftrong, natural inclination to thefe diverfions. In the favage ftate, we have feen, that the fituation of man

renders

renders such a propensity absolutely necessary; we have seen it become, at once conducive to his convenience, and his pleasures; we behold him emerge, from a state of uncivilization, into polished life. This propensity still accompanies him; it stimulates him to exercise the efficient cause of health; it inspires him with a love of industry and activity, the certain source of true pleasure; he becomes habituated to fatigue and exertion, despises danger and difficulty, nor dreads exposure to those elements, from whose severity he acquires strength of body, with vigor and firmness of mind. We have seen, with respect to brute animals, that, being destined for the use of man, in depriving them of existence, he disturbs not the order and intention of nature; that, in sacrificing them to his pleasures, he neither destroys nor diminishes their portion of enjoyment; and that, in exercising the prerogative with which he is invested, if he were not thus prompted by inclination, he would be compelled by necessity.

It may be urged, if not as an argument in favour of these diversions, yet as a circumstance which should incline us to caution in condemning them, that they are pursued by many individuals, who are distinguished for those virtues of the heart; which seem totally inconsistent with thoughtless or with intentional cruelty; and which

which are at once the ornament and the blessings of society.

The Patriot, or the Citizen, who, anxious for the good of his country, and of mankind, bends all his thoughts and all his faculties to the promotion of the public weal; who sacrifices the comforts of ease and of repose, foregoes the sweets of domestic bliss, nor is with-held by the charms of social converse, when his exertions can tend to relieve the unfortunate from the burden of affliction, and to enliven the face of sorrow with smiles of joy; will yet, when leisure, from these more noble occupations permits, join in the pleasures of the chase—arrest the pheasant in his aërial flight—or ensnare the inhabitants of the dimpled lake. And surely the heart, that makes "all human weal and woe its own," cannot rejoice in acts of inhumanity—Surely the generous passions of philanthropy and benevolence, can never inspire or accompany a cruel deed!

It would exceed the limits of this Essay, to take a comprehensive view of the human mind, which yet is not unnecessary in the investigation of this subject. It might then, perhaps, appear, that amidst all the variety and eccentricity, which the contemplation of a given character presents, the primary dispositions, the original motives, and springs of action, are extremely few. If this were proved, the seeming inconsistency between many of the actions of an individual must disappear; as it would be unfair to reason from any partial view of his character.

Perhaps the dispositions, which incline us to these diversions, are the same which, under other circumstances, incite to the most heroic actions. The courage gained in the field, may be exerted to restrain the insolence or ambition of a tyrant; exposure to fatigue, and the inclemency of seasons, qualify us for those exertions, which our stations, as members of society may demand; and he who, fearless of danger, is emulous of distinction in the chase, may equally pant for glory, when the invasion of his country prompts him to repel her foes.

We may further observe, that if Nature, with a liberal, but not lavish hand, hath bestowed on all her offspring, those powers and propensities only, which their own necessities, or the general order and œconomy of the system require, we shall be unable to discover her intention in the gifts of scent to the hound, swiftness to the grey-hound, and sagacity to the pointer; these being amongst the number of innate, instinctive faculties, which can only be exercised in some of the diversions we speak of, and for which purposes, we may therefore reasonably presume they were given.

Upon

Upon the whole, may we not then conclude, that man, by co-operating with such animals, employs both his and their faculties on the purposes for which they were partially designed: thus tending to complete the bounteous scheme of Providence; the happiness and well-being of all its creatures?

Observations *on* Longevity. *By* Anthony Fothergill, M. D. F. R. S. *Communicated in a Letter to Dr. Percival. Read January* 15, 1783.

DEAR SIR,

I HAVE often thought, it would be an useful undertaking to collect into one point of view, the memorable instances of long-lived persons, whose ages are recorded by monumental inscriptions, biographical writings, or even by the public prints. The only judicious attempt I have yet seen of this kind, was by the ingenious Mr. *Whitehurst*, a few years ago, in his Inquiry into the Origin and Formation of the Earth. To the examples of longevity mentioned by him, as collected by a person of veracity from the above sources, I have now added sundry remarkable instances of a similar kind, as they have occurred to me in the course of reading; and have annexed the authorities, (so far as was practicable) that you may be enabled to judge of the degree of credibility, that may seem due to the respective facts, and of the allowance which it may appear necessary to make, for that natural propensity, which mankind have ever betrayed for the marvellous. Now, admitting that many of the ages may have been somewhat exaggerated, yet still there can be no possible doubt, that even these have extended far beyond the ordinary period of life, and may therefore be entitled to a place in the following tables, which I submit to your consideration, as a small specimen of what might be more worthy your attention, if conducted hereafter on a larger scale, and pursued with chronological accuracy.

TABLE I.

OF LONGEVITY.

Names of the Persons.	Ages	Places of Abode.	Living or Dead.
Thomas Parre	152	Shropshire	Died Nov. 16, 1635 Phil. Transf. No. 44.
Henry Jenkins	169	Yorkshire	Died Dec. 8, 1670 Phil. Transf. No. 221.
Robert Montgomery	126	Ditto	Died in - 1670
James Sands	140	Staffordshire	} Do. Fuller's Worthies,
His Wife	120	Ditto	} p. 47.
Countess of Desmond	140	Ireland	Rawleigh's Hist. p. 166.
------- Ecleston	143	Ditto	Died - - 1691 (a)
J. Sagar	112	Lancashire	- - - 1668 (b)
-- Laurence	140	Scotland	Living - - - (c)
Simon Sack	141	Trionia	Died May 30, 1764
Col. Thomas Winslow	146	Ireland	—— Aug. 26, 1766
Francis Consist	150	Yorkshire	—— Jan. - 1768
Christ. J. Drakenberg	146	Norway	—— June 24, 1770 (d)
Margaret Forster	136	Cumberland	} Both living 1771
------ her Daughter	104	Ditto	
Francis Bons	121	France	Died Feb. 6, 1769
John Brookey	134	Devonshire	Living - - 1777 (e)
James Bowels	152	Killingworth	Died Aug. 15, 1656 (f)
John Tice	125	Worcestershire	—— March 1774 (g)
John Mount	136	Scotland	—— Feb. 27, 1776 (h)
A. Goldsmith	140	France	—— June 1776 (i)
Mary Yates	128	Shropshire	- - - 1776 (k)
John Bales	126	Northampton	—— April 5, 1706 (l)
William Ellis	130	Liverpool	—— Aug. 16, 1780 (m)
Louissa Truxo, a Negress in S. America	175	Tucuman, S. America	Living Oct. 5, 1780 (n)
Margaret Patten	138	Lockneugh near Paisley	Lynche's Guide to Health
Janet Taylor	108	Fintray, Scotland	Died Oct. 10, 1780
Richard Loyd	133	Montgomery	Lynche's Guide to Health
Susannah Hilliar	100	Piddington, Northamptonshire	Died Feb. 19, 1781 (o)
James Hayley	112	Middlewich, Cheshire	—— March 17, 1781 (p)
Ann Cockbolt	105	Stoke-Bruerne, Northamptonshire	—— April 5, 1775 (q)

William Walker, aged 112, not mentioned above, who was a Soldier at the Battle of Edge-Hill.

(a) *Fuller's* Worthies, p. 140.
(b) Phil. Transf. abridged by Lowthorp, vol. III. p. 306.
(c) *Derham's* Physico Theology, p. 173.
(d) Annual Register.
(e) Daily Advertiser, Nov. 18, 1777.
(f) Warwickshire.
(g) Daily Advertiser, March 1774.
(h) Morning Post, Feb. 29, 1776.
(i) Daily Advertiser, June 24, 1776.
(k) Ibidem, Aug. 22, 1776.
(l) See Inscription in the Portico of All-Saints Church.
(m) London Even. Post, Aug. 22, 1780.
(n) London Chronicle, Oct. 5. 1780.
(o) Northamp. Mercury, Feb. 19, 1781.
(p) Gen. Evening Post, March 24, 1781.
(q) Well known to Persons of Credit at Northampton.

If we look back to an early period of the christian æra, we shall find that *Italy* has been, at least about that time, peculiarly propitious to longevity. Lord *Bacon* observes, that the year of our Lord 76, in the reign of *Vespasian*, was memorable; for in that year was a taxing, which afforded the most authentic method of knowing the ages of men. From it, there were found in that part of *Italy*, lying between the *Appennine* mountains, and the river *Po*, one hundred and twenty four persons who either equalled, or exceeded one hundred years of age, namely:

TABLE II.

	54 Persons	of	100	Years each.
	57 - -	of	110	
	2 - -	of	125	
	4 - -	of	130	
	4 - -	of	136	
	3 - -	of	140	
In *Parma*	3 - -	of	120	Years each.
	2 - -	of	130	
In *Brussels*	1 - -	of	125	
In *Placentia*	1 - -	of	131	
In *Faventia*	1 - -	of	132	
	6 - -	of	110	
	4 - -	of	120	
In *Rimino*	1 - -	of	150	Years, viz. Marcus Aponius.

Mr.

Mr. *Carew*, in his survey of *Cornwall*, assures us, that it is no unusual thing, with the inhabitants of that county, to reach ninety years of age and upwards, and even to retain their strength of body, and perfect use of their senses. Besides *Brown*, the Cornish beggar, who lived to one hundred and twenty, and one *Polezew* to one hundred and thirty years of age, he remembered the decease of four persons in his own parish, the sum of whose years, taken collectively, amounted to three hundred and forty. Now, although longevity evidently prevails more in certain districts than in others, yet it is, by no means, confined to any particular nation or climate; nor are there wanting instances of it, in almost every quarter of the globe, as appears from the preceding, as well as the subsequent table.

TABLE III.

OF LONGEVITY.

Names of the Persons.	Age.	Places of Abode.	Where recorded.
Hippocrates, Physician	104	Island of Cos	Lynche on Health, Chap. 3.
Democritus, Philosopher	109	Abdera	Bacon's History, 1095.
Galen, Physician	140	Pergamus	Voss. Inst. or Lib. 3.
Albuna Marc	150	Ethiopia	Hakewell's ap. Lib. 1.
Dumitur Raduly	140	Haromszeck Transilvania	Died Jan. 18, 1782. Gen. Gazetteer, April 18th.
Titus Fullonius	150	Bononia	Fulgosus, Lib. 8.
Abraham Paiba	142	Charles-town, South Carolina	General Gazetteer.
L. Tertulla	137	Arminium	Fulgosus, Lib. 8.
Lewis Coronaro	100	Venice	Bacon's Hist. of Life, &c. p. 134.
Robert Blakeney, Esq.	114	Armagh, Ireland	General Gazetteer.
Margaret Scott	125	Dalkeith, Scotland	See Inscrip. on her Tomb in Dalkeith Ch. Yard.
W. Gulstone	140	Ireland	Fuller's Worthies.
J. Bright	105	Ludlow	Lynche on Health.
William Postell	120	France	Bacon's Hist. p. 134.
Jane Reeves	103	Essex	St. J. Chron. June 14, 1781.
W. Paulet, Marquis of Winchester	106	Hampshire	Baker's Chron. p. 502.
John Wilson	116	Suffolk	Gen. Gaz. Oct. 29, 1782.
Patrick Wian	115	Lesbury, Northumberland	Plempius Fundammed. Sect. 4, Chap. 8.
M. Laurence	140	Orcades	Buchanan's Hist. of Scot.
Evan Williams	145	Carmarthen Workhouse, still alive	Gen. Gazetteer, Oct. 12, 1782.

The Antidiluvians are purposely omitted, as bearing too little reference to the present race of mortals, to afford any satisfactory conclusions; and the improbable stories of some persons, who have almost rivalled them in modern times, border too much upon the marvellous, to find a place in these tables. The present examples are abundantly sufficient to prove, that longevity does not depend so much, as has been supposed,

on any particular climate, situation, or occupation in life. For we see, that it often prevails in places, where all these are extremely dissimilar; and it would, moreover, be very difficult, in the histories of the several persons above-mentioned, to find any circumstance common to them all, except, perhaps, that of being born of healthy parents, and of being inured to daily labour, temperance, and simplicity of diet. Among the inferior ranks of mankind, therefore, rather than amongst the sons of ease and luxury, shall we find the most numerous instances of longevity; even frequently, when other external circumstances seem extremely unfavourable: as in the case of the poor sexton at *Peterborough*, who, notwithstanding his unpromising occupation among dead bodies, lived long enough to bury two crowned heads, and to survive two complete generations.*
The livelihood of *Henry Jenkins*, and old *Parr*, is said to have consisted chiefly of the coarsest fare, as they depended on precarious alms. To which may be added, the remarkable instance of *Agnes Milburne*, who, after bringing forth a numerous offspring, and being obliged, through extreme indigence, to pass the latter part of her life in St. Luke's work-house, yet reached her

---

* *Fuller*'s Worthies, p. 293, from a Memorial in the Cathedral at *Peterborough*.

hundreth and sixth year, in that sordid, unfriendly situation.* The plain diet, and invigorating employments of a country life, are acknowledged, on all hands, to be highly conducive to health and longevity, while the luxury and refinements of large cities are allowed to be equally destructive to the human species: and this consideration alone, perhaps, more than counterbalances all the boasted privileges, of superior elegance and civilization, resulting from a city life.

From country villages, and not from crouded cities, have the preceding instances of longevity been chiefly supplied. Accordingly it appears, from the London Bills of Mortality, during a period of thirty years, viz. from the year 1728 to 1758, the sum of the deaths amounted to 750,322, and that, in all this prodigious number, only two hundred and forty two persons survived the hundreth year of their age! This overgrown metropolis is computed, by my learned friend Dr. *Price*, to contain a ninth part of the inhabitants of England, and to consume annually, seven thousand persons, who remove into it from the country every year, without increasing it. He moreover observes, that the number of inhabitants, in England and Wales, has diminished, about one fourth part, since the revolution, and so rapidly of late, that,

* *Lynche*'s Guide to Health, C. III.

in eleven years, near 200,000 of our common people have been loſt!* If the calculation be juſt, however alarming it may appear in a national view, there is this conſolation, when conſidered in a philoſophical light, that without partial evil, there can be no general good; and that, what a nation loſes in the ſcale of population at one period, it gains at another; and thus, probably, the average number of inhabitants, on the ſurface of the globe, continues, at all times, nearly the ſame. By this medium, the world is neither overſtocked with inhabitants, nor kept too thin, but life and death keep a tolerably equal pace. The inhabitants of this iſland, comparatively ſpeaking, are but as the duſt of the balance; yet, inſtead of being diminiſhed, we are aſſured by other writers, that, within theſe thirty years, they are greatly increaſed. †

The deſire of ſelf-preſervation, and of protracting the ſhort ſpan of life, is ſo intimately interwoven with our conſtitution, that it is juſtly eſteemed one of the firſt principles of our nature, and, in ſpite even of pain and miſery, ſeldom quits us to the laſt moments of our exiſtence. It ſeems, therefore, to be no leſs our duty, than our intereſt, to examine minutely

---

* Obſervations on Population, &c. p. 305.

† The Rev. Mr. *Howlet*, Mr. *Wales*, and others.

into the various means, that have been considered as conducive to health and long life; and, if possible, to distinguish such circumstances as are essential to that great end, from those which are merely accidental. But here, it is much to be regretted, that an accurate history of the lives of all the remarkable persons, in the above table, so far as relates to the diet, regimen, and the use of the *non-naturals*, has not been faithfully handed down to us; without which, it is impossible to draw the necessary inferences. Is it not then a matter of astonishment, that historians and philosophers have hitherto paid so little attention to longevity? If the present imperfect list should excite others, of more leisure and better abilities, to undertake a full investigation of so interesting a subject, the enquiry might prove not only curious, but highly useful to mankind. In order to furnish materials for a future history of longevity, the bills of mortality, throughout the kingdom, ought first to be revised, and put on a better footing; agreeably to the scheme which you pointed out some time ago, and of which Manchester and Chester, have already given a specimen, highly worthy of imitation. The plan, however, might be further improved, with very little trouble, by adding a particular account of the diet and regimen of every person, who dies at eighty years of age, or upwards; and mentioning,

ing, whether his parents were healthy, long-lived people, &c. &c. An accurate register, thus established throughout the *British* dominions, would be productive of many important advantages to society, not only in a medical, and philosophical, but also in a political and moral view. It is therefore to be hoped, that the legislature will not long delay taking an object, of such great utility, into their serious consideration.

All the circumstances, that are most essentially necessary to life, may be comprized under the six following heads.

1. Air and climate.
2. Meat and drink.
3. Motion and rest.
4. The secretions and excretions.
5. Sleep and watching.
6. Affections of the mind.

These, though all perfectly natural to the constitution, have by writers, been styled the *non-naturals*, by a strange perversion of language; and have been all copiously handled under that improper term. However, it may not be amiss, to offer a few short observations on each, as they are so immediately connected with the present subject.

1. Air, &c. It has long been known, that fresh air is more immediately necessary to life than food; for a man may live two or three days without the latter, but not many minutes without the former. The vivifying principle
contained

contained in the atmosphere, so essential to the support of flame, as well as animal life, concerning which, authors have proposed so many conjectures, appears now to be nothing else but that pure dephlogisticated fluid lately discovered by that ingenious philosopher, Dr. *Priestley*. The common atmosphere may well be supposed to be more or less healthy in proportion, as it abounds with this animating principle. As this exhales, in copious streams, from the green leaves of all kinds of vegetables, even from those of the most poisonous kind, may we not, in some measure, account why instances of longevity are so much more frequent in the country, than in great cities; where the air, instead of partaking so largely of this salutary impregnation, is daily contaminated with noxious animal effluvia, and phlogiston?

With respect to climate, various observations conspire to prove, that those regions, which lie within the temperate zones, are best calculated to promote long life. Hence, perhaps, may be explained, why *Italy* has produced so many long livers, and why Islands in general are more salutary than Continents; of which *Bermudas*, and some others, afford examples. And it is a pleasing circumstance, that our own Island, appears from the above table, (notwithstanding the sudden vicissitudes to which it is liable,) to contain far more instances of longevity than could well be imagined. The ingenious Mr. *Whitehurst*, assures us, from certain facts, that Englishmen are, in general, longer lived than North Americans; and, that a British constitution will last longer, even in that climate, than a native one.* But it must be allowed in general, that the human constitution is adapted to the peculiar state, and temperature, of each respective climate, so that no part of the habitable globe can be pronounced too hot, or too cold, for its inhabitants. Yet, in order to promote a friendly intercourse between the most remote regions, the Author of Nature has wisely enabled the inhabitants to endure great and surprizing changes of temperature with impunity.†

2. Foods and drink. Though foods and drink, of the most simple kinds, are allowed to be the best calculated for supporting the body in health, yet it can hardly be doubted, but variety may be safely indulged occasionally, provided men would restrain their appetites within the bounds of temperance. For bountiful nature cannot be supposed to have poured forth such a rich profusion of provisions, merely

---

* Enquiry into the Original State, and Formation of the Earth.

† See remarkable instances of this, in the Account of Experiments in a heated room, by Dr. *George Fordyce*, and others.

Phil. Transf. vol. LXIX.

to tantalize the human species, without attributing to her the part of a cruel step-dame, instead of that of the kind and indulgent parent. Besides, we find, that by the wonderful powers of the digestive organs, a variety of animal and vegetable substances, of very discordant principles, are happily assimilated into one bland homogeneous chyle; therefore, it seems natural to distrust those cynical writers, who would rigidly confine mankind to one simple dish, and their drink to the mere water of the brook. Nature, it is true, has pointed out that mild, insipid fluid, as the universal diluent; and, therefore, most admirably adapted for our daily beverage. But experience has equally proved, that vinous, and spirituous liquors, on certain occasions, are no less salutary and beneficial, whether it be to support strength against sickness, or bodily fatigue, or to exhilarate the mind under the pressure of heavy misfortunes. But alas! what Nature meant for innocent and useful cordials, to be used only occasionally, and according to the direction of reason; custom and caprice, have, by degrees, rendered habitual to the human frame, and liable to the most enormous and destructive abuses? Hence, it may be justly doubted, whether gluttony and intemperance, have not depopulated the world, more than even sword, pestilence, and famine. True, therefore, is the old maxim, "Modus

utendi

ûtendi ex veneno facit Medicamentum, ex Medicamento, venenum."

3. and 4. Motion and rest, sleep and watching. It is allowed, on all hands, that alternate motion and rest, and sleep and watching, are necessary conditions to health and longevity; and that they ought to be adapted to age, temperament, constitution, temperature of the climate, &c. but the errors which mankind daily commit, in these respects, become a fruitful source of diseases. While some are bloated and relaxed with ease and indolence, others are emaciated, and become rigid, through hard labour, watching, and fatigue.

5. Secretions and excretions. Where the animal functions are duly performed, the secretions go on regularly; and the different evacuations so exactly correspond to the quantity of aliment taken in, in a given time, that the body is found to return daily to nearly the same weight. If any particular evacuation happen to be preternaturally diminished, some other evacuation is proportionally augmented, and the equilibrium is commonly preserved; but continued irregularities, in these important functions, cannot but terminate in disease.

6. Affections of the mind. The due regulation of the passions, perhaps, contributes more to health and longevity, than that of any

other of the *non-naturals*. The animating paffions, such as joy, hope, love, &c. when kept within proper bounds, gently excite the nervous influence, promote an equable circulation, and are highly conducive to health; while the depreffing affections, such as fear, grief, and despair, produce the contrary effect, and lay the foundation of the most formidable diseases.

From the light which history affords us, as well as from some instances in the above table, there is great reason to believe, that longevity is, in a great measure, hereditary; and that healthy, long-lived parents would commonly transmit the same to their children, were it not for the frequent errors in the *non-naturals*, which so evidently tend to the abbreviation of human life.

Whence is it, but from these causes, and the unnatural modes of living, that, of all the children which are born in the capital cities of *Europe*, nearly one half die in early infancy? To what else can we attribute this extraordinary mortality? Such an amazing proportion of premature deaths is a circumstance unheard of, among savage nations, or among the young of other animals! In the earliest ages, we are informed, that human life was protracted to a very extraordinary length; yet how few persons, in these later times, arrive at that period, which nature

nature seems to have designed! Man is, by nature, a field-animal, and seems destined to rise with the sun, and to spend a large portion of his time in the open air, to inure his body to robust exercises, and the inclemency of the seasons, and to make a plain homely repast, only when hunger dictates. But art has studiously defeated the kind intentions of nature; and by enslaving him to all the blandishments of sense, has left him, alas! an easy victim to folly and caprice! To enumerate the various abuses, which take place from the earliest infancy, and which are continued through the succeeding stages of modish life, would carry me far beyond my present intention. Suffice it to observe, that they prevail more particularly among people, who are the most highly polished and refined. To compare their artificial mode of life, with that of nature, or even with the long livers in the list, would, probably, afford a very striking contrast; and, at the same time, supply an additional reason, why, in very large cities, instances of longevity are so very rare. Of late years, the increasing luxury and dissipation of the age, no longer confined to the metropolis, have spread their contagion far and wide into the country, so as to afford the sage divine, and speculative moralist, a more melancholy prospect of the apparent degeneracy of the human race, than, perhaps, was ever before exhibited!*

That so complicated a machine, as the human body, so delicate in its texture, and so exquisitely formed in all its parts, should continue, for so many years, to perform its various functions, even under the most prudent conduct, is not a little surprizing: but that it should ever hold out to any advanced period, under all the rude shocks it so often meets with from riot and intemperance, which lay it open to all the various " ills that flesh is heir to," is still more truly miraculous! But here, perhaps, it may be alledged, that it never can be supposed, all the long livers pursued one uniform, regular course of life, since it is well known, that some of the most noted ones were sometimes guilty of great deviations from strict temperance and regularity. Let not this, however, encourage the giddy libertines, of the present age, to hope to render their continued scenes of intemperance

---

* I say *apparently*, because mankind, in reality, have been equally prone to vice and folly in all ages; only these have assumed different appearances, according to the taste and manners of the times: not that the human heart has been successively growing more and more depraved, as the Poet satyrically exclaims,

  Ætas parentum, pejor avis, tulit
  Nos nequiores; mox daturos
  Progeniem vitiosiorem! *Hor.* Lib III. Ode 6.

and debauchery, compatible with health and longevity. The duties and occupations of life, will not, indeed, permit the generality of mankind to live by rule, and subject themselves to a precise regimen. Fortunately, this is not necessary: for, the divine Architect, has, with infinite wisdom, rendered the human frame so ductile, as to admit of a very considerable *latitude of health*; yet this has its bounds, which none can long transgress with impunity. For, if old *Parr*, notwithstanding some excesses, and irregularities, arrived at so astonishing an age, yet we have reason to suppose, that these were far from being habitual; and may also conclude, that had it not been for these abuses, his life might have been still considerably protracted.

On the whole, though some few exceptions may occur, to what has been already advanced, yet, it will be found, in general, that all extremes are unfriendly to health and longevity. Excessive heat enervates the body; extreme cold renders it torpid: sloth and inactivity clog the necessary movements of the machine; incessant labour soon wears it out. On the other hand, a temperate climate, moderate exercise, pure country air, and strict temperance, together with a prudent regulation of the passions, will prove the most efficacious means of protracting life to its utmost limits. Now, if any of these require more peculiar attention than the rest, it is, undoubtedly, the last: for the social passions, like gentle gales, fan the brittle vessel calmly along the ocean of life, while, on the other hand, rough, turbulent ones dash it upon rocks and quicksands. Hence, perhaps, it may be explained, why the cultivation of philosophy, music, and the fine arts, all which manifestly tend to humanize the soul, and to calm the rougher passions, are so highly conducive to longevity. And, finally, why there is no sure method of securing that habitual calmness and serenity of mind, which constitute true happiness, and which are, at the same time, so essential to health and long life, without virtue.

" *Æquanimitas sola, atque unica felicitas.*"

I hope you will excuse the prolixity of this letter, and believe me to be, with the highest esteem,

    Dear Sir,

        Your sincere Friend

            and faithful humble Servant,

                A. FOTHERGILL.

LONDON, *Nov.* 23, 1782.

On the INFLUENCE *of the* IMAGINATION, *and the* PASSIONS, *upon the* UNDERSTANDING. *By the Rev.* THOMAS BARNES, D. D. *Read Feb.* 12, 1783.

A SENTIMENT was advanced in conversation several evenings ago, in this place, which, to some Gentlemen, appeared strange, or rather, *false*. The respect I owe to this Society, and above all, to Truth, obliges me to endeavour to defend a point, which appears to me, to be, not only just, but very important.

In the conversation before alluded to, it had been asserted, "That an energy, imparted to "*one* power of the human mind, will often com- "municate a degree of energy to the *rest*, and "thus assist and quicken *their* operation."

In proof of this, it was maintained, "That "in many cases, the vigour of IMAGINATION will "give correspondent vigour to the JUDGMENT," and " That a degree of warmth and SENSIBILITY, "will be greatly favourable to the *clearness*, as "well as to the *celerity*, of the perceptions of the "UNDERSTANDING."

This sentiment will, probably, alarm those who have implicitly received what is so generally asserted, "That pure and simple truth has nothing "to do with imagination, feelings, or paffions; and, that he will bid the faireft for fuccefsful inquiry into any fubject, who can diveft his mind moft entirely of all *affections*, and bring it into a ftate of abfolute *indifference*, and *apathy*."

It is not uncommon, to hear the Imagination condemned as a criminal of the moft dangerous nature, whofe province is, at the beft, only to amufe, who is a fworn enemy to truth, and whom Reafon wifhes to banifh as far as poffible from her throne. How often have we known, what was *very dull*, for want of fome feafonings of imagination, fuppofed to be, for that reafon, *very deep?* Whilft, on the other hand, what was enlivened by the animation of an active fancy, was cenfured, as flimfy, and irrational? As if a brilliant imagination could not poffibly become the companion, and affiftant of the pureft underftanding!—That it *may,* is the point which this paper attempts to prove.

In fupporting this hypothefis, I beg leave to hazard a defcription of the human mind, which fome may not very readily admit. In judging of the mental powers, it does not appear to me philofophically juft, to defcribe the foul, as confifting of feveral diftinct and difcordant faculties, of which, fome are commiffioned perpetually to oppofe and contradict the others. The proper idea of human nature feems seems to be, " That it is ONE UNCOMPOUNDED " ESSENCE, continually in motion, and receiving " different denominations, according to the " different *modes* and circumstances of its move- " ment." Instead of considering the understanding, memory, passions, and will, as *distinct* and *opposite powers*, or, as unconnected tenants under the same roof, would it not be more just, to consider them all as *modes* of the MIND ITSELF, and as each of them bearing the common nature and character of the whole united spirit? We should then consider, the *mind itself* as understanding, the *mind itself* as judging, remembering, feeling, willing. And this idea would be exactly consonant to many facts, and phenomena of human nature, which will be hereafter mentioned.

However the common representation of human nature, as consisting of *several contending* powers, may have been *figuratively* adopted, in order to solve some appearances, such as, the experience of *conflicting passions*, or of *opposite tendencies* in the soul, yet, it is not founded in philosophical truth, and, if not properly guarded, by being always considered merely *as a figure*, it may lead to falsehood, and absurdity.

The full elucidation of all these positions, would swell this paper to a length, far beyond the limits wisely appointed for our communications, which, being intended only as subsidiary

diary to conversation, should rather contain *hints*, than a regular composition of finished and artificial sentences. I may add, this subject would have received its *best* illustration and support from MORALS, and RELIGION. But, as these would lead me too much into a professional line, I shall endeavour to draw the arguments from those lower subjects, of TASTE, CRITICISM, and POLITE LITERATURE, by which, it appears to me, to be unanswerably supported.

The points we undertake to defend, are these; " That the imagination and passions *may*, within " proper limits, be of the utmost service in " giving strength and clearness to the under- " standing. And, that this arises,—from the " nature, and office of the imagination,—and " from the principle before-mentioned, that the " energy of *one* power may be communicated to " the *rest*, with the greatest advantage."

It is owing to the narrowness of our faculties, that we do not comprehend the *substance* of the human mind. Of its *operations*, however, we can speak with certainty. I represent it to myself, as *one uniform and simple essence*, liable to be *moved* or *affected* by the various objects around it, or, by the flow of ideas continually passing before it—and, according to the state and temperament of the *whole indivisible mass*, judging, feeling, willing, acting. Hence, it will follow, that it will judge, and feel, and act, not
according

according to the impulse of *some distinct and unconnected* faculty, but according to the state and disposition of the *whole mind*.

And, is it not true in *fact*, that men *do thus* judge, and feel, and act; not, according to the movement of a single power; but, according to the *general character* and complexion of the heart? The poet has beautifully illustrated and enforced this sentiment.

> ------ " The difference is as great between
> " The OPTICS seeing, as the OBJECTS seen.
> " All manners take a tincture from our own;
> " Or come difcoloured, *through our paſſions* shewn.
> " Or Fancy's beam enlarges, multiplies,
> " Contracts, inverts, and gives ten thousand dyes."
>   Pope.

Do not all Politicians judge upon every article of news, according to their prepossessions? Is it not of equal importance, in EDUCATION, to give a proper bias to the *heart*, as to furnish proper ideas for the *head*, in order to produce *rectitude of mind*? Hence, the sanctity of *error*. Hence, the different manner in which you judge of the same actions, in a *friend*, and in an *enemy*. Hence, all the advantages of *manner*, of *oratory*, of *address*. And hence, all that fascination of the *graces*, upon which, if a noble author has said true, so much depends. In all these cases, the understanding acts, not as a single insulated principle, but as taking its tinge and impression,

from

from the feelings, the imagination, and the heart.

This fact will probably not be contested. But it will be said, " That these passions are the " sources of all our errors, and that, if we could " entirely lay aside imagination and affection, " we should judge upon every subject, more " impartially, and therefore, more truly."

Allowing, that truth is ever one and the same, yet if, as the foregoing facts evince, the same truth will appear very differently to different minds, and to the *same* mind at *different* times; if the disposition and frame of the mind be a kind of *medium*, through which the same object shall appear amazingly diversified, most amiable to one, most disgusting to another: Then, it should seem to follow, that what is most desirable to a right judgment, is, not, that the mind be divested of *all* its affections, that the imagination be laid asleep, and that the understanding *alone* be employed in the contemplation. To me, all this appears to be, neither necessary, nor possible. But, that the *whole united mind*, considered as comprehending all its various powers, shall be in a *proper state* for the investigation and reception of truth, and, that the imagination and passions shall be of such a temperament, as to assist the judgment in its determination. This is not a state of absolute inaction; but of action suited to their proper nature and office, in

subordination

subordination to the higher powers of reasoning and judgment.

If the understanding were that pure and simple principle, which many represent it to be, entirely distinct from all the passions, and able to judge *best* of every truth, when most separate from their influence, we should not, surely, observe so much diversity of judgment, such amazing variety of opinions, upon almost every subject of human life. Wherever it is *possible* for human affections, interests, or feelings to insinuate themselves, we find a *tinge* of their nature, in the judgment. If we suppose the *mind itself* to judge, according to *its nature and character*, we shall immediately perceive, that its sentence *must* be coloured and diversified—that the judgment will fashion itself to the state of the heart—and that, in almost every instance, a false *taste* or *feeling*, will lead to false opinion, whether in poetry, painting, music, criticism, oratory, or art in general. Is there not an almost universal conformity between the feelings and the judgment? Even *vice itself*, in the paroxysms of temptation, for a moment, seduces the understanding, and blinds the reason. At *that* moment, the sinner promises himself impunity, and enjoyment. Nor is it, till the temptation is *past*, that the mind sees *again* the deformity and danger of vicious conduct.

But,

But, it will be asked, "Are not the *passions*, then, the *causes* of our wrong judgments?" Most certainly they *are*. But, upon the same principle, that *wrong* passions lead to wrong judgments, *right* passions would lead to true. If the mind were properly *affected*, it would *judge* properly.

But, let us inquire more particularly, into the nature and office of the *Imagination*—for these are, I persuade myself, very commonly, and very greatly, mistaken.

Imagination is that *power*, or more properly, that *act* of the mind, which assembles, compounds, divides its ideas, *not* in the order in which they first came into the mind, for *that* is the province of *memory*, but, in *any* order, and upon *any* principles it chooses. It ranges abroad, through the immense magazine and repository of ideas, treasured up there, and joins together, or separates, at pleasure, ideas, qualities, and forms. It may be called, the *servant* or *labourer* of the mind, continually employed, to bring before it, from its amazing storehouse, *materials*, with which to build up its conclusions. It is the ever busy, patient, indefatigable *drudge*, toiling for the common benefit and assistance of all the other powers; and does not *deserve* the indignities and reproaches, it is continually receiving. How often is it forced to be *present*, and even to give *assistance*, in the condemnation and execution of *itself?* How many, with declamation most extravagant, with ideas most deranged, with apprehensions most fanciful, have abused the poor imagination, whilst all their censure and alarm have had no better, than an *imaginary* foundation?*

A mind *too imaginative* does, indeed, often join its ideas together in wild and ridiculous associations. One who is called, *a wit*, joins only those which appear *odd* and fantastic. But he, whose *judging* are exactly poised by his *imaginative* powers, who is, according to our scheme, *at once*, lively to conceive, and sober to judge, collects together only *those* ideas, which are proper to set the subject before him in such a light, as to enable him to form an exact determination. The power of *imagining*, is, therefore, in its place, as necessary, as the power of *judging*. Suppose a mind which could only *remember*—It would fall, at once, into the track marked out by *others*, and would never employ its *own* powers, by reasoning and determining for itself. Accordingly we find, that persons of the strongest memory have generally the weakest judgments.

If these principles are just, a mind, which could not *imagine*, could not *reason*. It would have no *materials* before it, on which to form its decision. Its view of any subject would be narrow and defective. Observe, on the other

* - - - "turbida terret imago." Virgil. Æn. IV. 353.

hand, a mind, keen and fervent in the profecution of a favourite fubject, viewing it attentively on every fide, catching every ray of light, which can illuminate, and every kindred fentiment, which can illuftrate it. Without animation and ardour, *thefe* would never have been difcovered; without imagination and affection, the underftanding would have lain torpid and inactive. Fancy, that noble and neceffary power, has placed the fubject in every poffible combination of form and circumftance, has called in to its aid ideas, images, and analogies, which, at firft, feemed moft foreign and inapplicable; and has thus beheld it in afpects, which the dull plodder would never have *imagined*. By this means, a knowledge is acquired, various, extenfive, and exact, beyond what *could*, otherways, have poffibly been obtained. The office of the underftanding, is, merely that of a *judge*, to pafs *fentence* upon the caufe before it. The imagination collects and arranges the *evidence*, and brings it before the deciding power, in fuch a form, as may lead to an accurate and judicious determination.

This influence of the imagination and paffions upon the judgment muft, however, differ greatly, according to the different *kinds* of *evidence*, of which different *fubjects* are capable. In *mere mathematics*, where the mind has to contemplate *pure demonftrative* truth, little more is neceffary, than

than such a degree of *memory*, as to keep in view the steps of the process, and so much *understanding*, as to be able to apply the plainest axioms, and to see the truth of *demonstration*. Surely, no *great* exertion or exaltation of mind is necessary to *this*. You would not call that a *superior spirit*, which was able to see, with infallible certainty, truths, of which, when properly understood, it is impossible to doubt.

Here, we grant, high degrees of imagination, sensibility, taste, are *not* necessary. A mind, which *could not* see the certainty of *such* conclusions, if able to trace, and to remember the steps by which it had proceeded, would *hardly* deserve to be called rational.

Those, certainly, are the *greatest* and *noblest* spirits, who can exert the *whole collected powers* of their minds, upon the contemplation of important subjects, and determine, with clearness and truth, where the evidence is *not* so irresistible, as that the conclusion cannot possibly be mistaken. The most *common*, the most *important*, the *greatest* subjects which can come before the human mind, are not capable of *demonstrative* evidence. Yet, they *have* evidence of a peculiar kind, which can only be discerned, in its full proportion, by a mind, properly prepared to receive it. Besides memory and understanding, you must call in *other powers.*

powers. The *heart* must be in right order. The mind must *feel* and *imagine* justly, in order to a perfect sentence.

Let us take, for an illustration, one of the most respectable and useful professions—that of a Physician. The science *he* professes, is not, surely, that of demonstration. He will himself acknowledge, that it is only, a science of probability. Suppose him devoid of imagination, and of feeling. How ill qualified would a merely mathematical mind be, to prescribe, in cases which demand, and almost *every* case in *some* degree demands, presence of mind, largeness of thought, a view to remote and possible consequences, together with that quickness, penetration, and sagacity, which must unite together, to constitute the *skilful physician!*—Take common life. What is *Prudence*, but another name, for an ability to *imagine* all the possible or probable consequences of such or such a conduct, of foreseeing such and such difficulties, and of balancing the good and evil, in such a manner, as, upon the whole, to avoid the greatest evil, and to obtain the greatest good? But how could this possibly be done, without a lively, active, and well directed imagination?

Nay, we may go farther and say, that even a Mathematician will make very little progress in *demonstrative* science, without the aid of this noble, but much mistaken and abused faculty.

Here,

Here, it is true, imagination has the narrowest range: but it would be false to say, it has no range at all. For what are the subjects of his boasted reasonings? They are *points, lines, superficies,* all of which he can only *imagine.* A *Point* has neither length, breadth, nor thickness. A *Line* has length, but neither breadth, nor thickness. A *Superficies* has length, breadth, but not thickness. Are then Lines, Points, or Superficies, objects of vision, or of sense? By no means. They are the mere creatures of fancy. His *Figures* likewise of circles, squares, &c. are not perfect. They contain innumerable excrescences, and deformities; and yet, his reasonings suppose figures exact and faultless.

And, how often must imagination present before him, distances, heights, orbits, &c. which he has not immediately under his eye, which he *cannot possibly* conceive, without the aid of fancy? The application of mathematics to Astronomy, Navigation, &c. demands the *same* assistance. Who would scruple to say, that Sir Isaac Newton, enjoyed a *brilliant imagination?* In sketching the outlines of his amazing system—in roving through the pathless wilds of space—in contemplating

"The dependencies,
"The bearings, and the ties"

of this stupendous universe, must he not have possessed a fancy of the *boldest wing,* yet accompanied, in all its flight, by the most wise and watchful reason? Let me just mention another exalted character, in proof of the same point—Mr. Locke. No where do you perceive stronger lines of a vigorous and active fancy, than in the writings of this immortal philosopher. His stile is *full* of imagery and allusion, the most beautiful and happy. He has all the signatures of a *glowing*, and, at the same time, of a *sober* and *cautious* mind. For *such* imagination only do I plead—under the *command*, and employed in the *service*, of that judgment, whose province it is, to direct, and to control.

Even in the act of REASONING, which is generally esteemed the most solemn and serious process of the mind, imagination is essentially necessary. For, if the mind be not able to chuse with advantage those intermediate ideas, on which its reasonings depend; if it is not able, by means of this excursive power, to range abroad, to view its subject on every side, to catch minuter, as well as larger similitudes and differences; if, in one word, it has not activity, comprehension, quickness, all which depend chiefly upon imagination, it will not possess, in any considerable strength, that ILLATIVE POWER, which we acknowledge to be so noble a faculty of human nature.

If the preceding observations are true, with respect to mathematics—the region of science which seems *most remote* from the fairy land of fancy,

fancy, there will be little difficulty in proving our point with respect to *those* provinces, which lie nearer to its confines. And, in its *own province*, in all that extensive and beautiful domain, in which *the pleasures of the imagination* grow, as in their *native* soil, it would be ridiculous to ask, whether imagination be not conducive to exactness of judgment. It would be just the same, as to inquire, whether a man must have *eyes*, to judge of *visible* objects; or *ears*, to judge of *sounds*. Through all the wide empire of criticism, of taste, of poetry, of painting, of music, of arts, fancy reigns with almost sovereign sway. A poet, or an artist, without *imagination*, might as well be without *ideas.* Mr. Hayley has very justly observed, " That three things " are necessary to constitute a sound critic— " Good *understanding*—lively *imagination*—refined " *sensibility.*"* *In general*, to judge well upon *any* subject, you must have a *kindred* spirit. If the *poet* must be " alive to fancy," a *reader* of poetry must inherit a *portion* of the *same* inspiration.

Let us suppose a critic, such as, perhaps, the world has sometimes seen assuming the name, to pass sentence upon Milton's Paradise Lost. Does he relish and enjoy this divine performance? Does he taste its exquisite beauties? Does his imagination glow with its descriptions? Does

---

* Hayley's Essay on Epic Poetry. Notes to the first Book.

he fensibly feel the sweetness, richness, and loftiness of its language? Is he alive to all the superior charms of its subject, its scenery, and its execution? Alas! No. Like the fly on St. Paul's Cathedral, he stumbles at a straw, or a hair. But, is this cold-blooded *thing*, whose scanty soul cannot expand itself to the dimensions of such a subject, who cannot take in, at one grand and ennobling view, its whole extent and adjustment, the connection of its parts, the characters, the machinery, the end—is *he* the proper critic of Milton?*

---

* " How did Garrick speak the soliloquy last night?" " Oh! Against all rule, my Lord, most ungrammatically. Between the nominative case, which, your Lordship knows, should govern the verb, he suspended his voice a dozen times; three seconds, and three fifths, my Lord, each time." " Admirable grammarian!" " But, in suspending his voice—was the sense suspended likewise? Did no expression of attitude or countenance fill up the chasm? Was the eye silent? Did you narrowly look?"— " I looked only at the stop-watch, my Lord."—" Excellent observer!"

" And what of this new book the whole world makes such a rout about?"—" Oh! it is quite out of all plumb, my Lord.—Quite an irregular thing! Not one of the angles at the four corners was a right angle.—I had my rule and compasses, my Lord, in my pocket."—" Excellent critic!"

" And for the epic poem your Lordship bid me look at—upon taking the length, breadth, height, and depth of it, and trying them at home upon an exact scale of Bossu's—'tis out, my Lord, in every one of its dimensions"—" Admirable connoisseur!" Sterne.

Imagination is neceffary to reprefent to the mind, all things *diftant, future, invifible,* and even *paft,* when they are not *exactly* recalled by *memory.* How wide! How important its province! In RELIGION, the happinefs of Heaven, the nature, character, and employment of fuperior beings, the folemn proceffes of Judgment—Eternity—and even the Deity himfelf, *can only* come before us, as drawn by the imagination.

In *Hiftory,* you continually *imagine* characters, events, times, places, circumftances, which you have never feen. Thefe are portrayed to your fancy, by the pen of the hiftorian; and your pleafure and improvement will very much depend upon the clearnefs and celerity, with which you *paint* to yourfelf the different fcenes, which are paffing before you. All the pleafures of *Tafte* depend abfolutely upon a vigorous and cultivated imagination. Even in the *actual contemplation* of the *fcenes of nature, imagination* is as neceffary, to refined pleafure, as the *eye.* Perhaps we might, without great impropriety, call it, the *eye of the mind.* If any perfon fhould think, this appellation would *better* belong to the *underftanding,* let him recollect, that the eye of the *body* can give no *exact* information, till *rectified* by the judgment. It is fo with the imagination. The ideas *it* prefents muft be brought before the higher tribunal of the understanding, and receive their sentence, according to its superior determination.

I shall, perhaps, be told of the *lover*, who sees in his mistress an *imaginary* idol, decked all o'er with charms, perfect and matchless, in every air, and in every attribute. I shall be told, of the amazing *change* in his judgment, when time and better knowledge have taken the glare from the object, stripped the idol of her divinity, and faded her charms, even to ugliness. But, against this exception we meant to guard, by maintaining only, a *due poise* and *degree* of the imaginative quality.

"The *lover*, the *lunatic*, and the *poet*, are
"Of imagination ALL COMPACT."   Shakespeare.

Minds, so *excessively imaginative*, cannot be judicious.

But, on the other hand, suppose a person to contemplate excellence, *female excellence*, without imagination—just as he would, a mathematical problem. Would he do *more exact* and impartial justice to the subject?

Would the fairer sex consent to abide the sentence of *such a judge*? Would they not *justly* complain, that though he wore the *form*, he had not the sentiment, the *soul* of a human being? Would they not appeal—and who would not *justify* the appeal—to the decision of a *mind*, capable of feeling, and of fancy, and therefore

rational,

rational, and *alone* competent to judge of that excellence, which is fitted to cheer and captivate the heart?

But it has been the hard fate of imagination to be, in general, spoken of, in its *excess*. We seldom hear it mentioned, by those who declaim against it, without hearing of the *flights* of fancy, the *extravagance*, the *agitation*, the *wildness*, the *sallies*, the *fervours*, the *excentricities*, of a *heated* imagination. The *fervour*, the *glow*, however, belong rather to *passion*, than to *imagination*. The imagination indeed may *excite* the passion; and thus they ascribe the attributes of the *effect* to the *cause*.

That imagination *may*, that it often *does* transgress its proper bounds, we most readily acknowledge. That it is necessary to hold it in with a *tight rein*, that it may not run away with the understanding, and lead to conclusions fanciful and groundless, we allow, in its fullest extent. We contend only for *that degree*, which will consist with the exactness of judgment.

The vivacity and strength of imagination, in children, is astonishing. Their knowledge of objects being very slight and superficial, a few faint resemblances are sufficient to realize and embody them. By degrees, as their knowledge becomes more extensive and exact, their power of *imagining* declines, the power of *judging* is improved, and when these two powers have

attained

attained their *proper balance,* the mind has attained its higheſt capacity.

That "*great wits are to madneſs near allied.*" That "great genius's are too imaginative," proves only, that the mind, when in a frame too *creative* and *fanciful,* is not ſufficiently judicious. But, ſurely, a *degree* of warmth may be *neceſſary* to a tool, for its *proper* action; and yet, that warmth may be increaſed, till it is improper for ſervice.

It will, perhaps, be ſaid, that lunatics and madmen are under the dominion of fancy, and that upon this account their judgments are erroneous. It is anſwered, that, in general, if you will but grant their *premiſes,* they will reaſon from them, with aſtoniſhing quickneſs and clearneſs of argumentation. Unhappily, their minds are, in ſome particular points, by wrong aſſociations, become deranged and extravagant. This is their *diſeaſe.* But the fervour imparted to their minds, ſeems rather to have ſharpened, than impaired, their reaſoning powers.

Let, then, *underſtanding* and *judgment* ever be conſidered as the *preſiding faculties* of the human ſpirit. To their control, let every other power ultimately ſubmit. Let the *imagination* and the *paſſions* be conſidered merely as their *ſervants,* obedient to their command. But, whilſt they are thus obedient, let them have the praiſe of *good* and *uſeful* ſervants; and above all, let them not be compelled to criminate and condemn *themselves*. Or, according to the just simile of the poet.

"Whilst *reason* holds the helm—
"Let *passion* be the gale." Pope.

And let *imagination* fly abroad to collect the various scattered breezes, which, thus united into *one* strong current, may carry the the vessel forward, across the ocean of life, under *such a* pilotage, with safety, and satisfaction.

An Essay *on the* Ascent *of* Vapour. By A. Eason, M. D. &c. *Read Nov.* 27, 1782.

— — — — — — — — — Unde serenas
Ventus agat nubes, quid cogitet humidus
Auster, Sol tibi signa dabit.
Virg. Geo. C. I. ver. 461.

THERE are few phenomena in nature, which have puzzled philosophers more, than the ascent of vapour: and the different theories laid down by Doctors *Halley* and *Desaguliers*, have been rejected, while another, not less liable to objections, has been almost universally received.

This theory, which I shall presently mention, was at first invented by a French Gentleman, Monsieur

Monsieur le Roi, and afterwards revived by Lord *Kaimes*, and Doctor *Hugh Hamilton*. It is this—That the air dissolves water, as water does saline substances: the solution being perfect, the air will become transparent.

Objections. 1. Were this theory true, evaporation could not be performed without air; but Mr. Watt, contrary to the theory supported by Lord Kaimes and Dr. Hamilton, has proved, that when water in vacuo was boiled with a degree of heat very little greater than that of the human body, the steam came over, and was condensed in the refrigeratory. But he relates, that the evaporation was not quicker than in the open air.

2. Were the doctrine of solution true, the air would be heavier, the more water it contained; and, as clouds contain a great portion of water, they ought to float on the surface of the earth, and not in the higher regions, as we daily observe.

3. We never could expect any rain, unless the air were supersaturated with water; and it would only yield to us, what it could not retain in solution.

4. It is universally allowed, that heat contributes, very much, towards converting water into vapour, which is again condensed by cold. In what manner, will the doctrine of solution account for the spontaneous evaporation of water, and its being suspended in air, in the coldest weather,

weather, even when the thermometer is below the freezing point? Though I cannot allow of such a solution as above mentioned, I can, however, readily admit of a strong attraction betwixt air and water: for no air is found without water, and no water without air.

Water, which is eight hundred times heavier than air, by a very small degree of heat, may be converted into vapour, which vapour is one thousand eight hundred times lighter than air, according to Mr. Watt. It consequently follows, that vapour will rise up in the atmosphere, to the height of its own specific gravity; but, long before it could reach to so high a region, it would be condensed by cold, and return to the earth in rain, were it not for the latent heat* it contains, and the electric matter in the air.

Whatever I mention concerning Electricity, is from facts, and not from any theory, written about it, which is above my comprehension. But as the terms now in use, viz. positive and negative, or plus and minus, are generally best understood, I shall express myself by them.

* That heat enters into vapour, and becomes an ingredient in it, is certain. For example: if we distil a pound of steam, the water in the refrigeratory will be heated by it, as much as by a pound of water heated one thousand and twelve degrees; so eight hundred degrees of heat appear, though the steam is not sensibly hotter than boiling water, which is two hundred and twelve. *Exp.*

The able Nollet has proved, that water electrified, will evaporate faster, than water which is not electrified. Does it not follow, that the more electric matter is in the air, the quicker the evaporation of water will be? And Mr. Cavallo has proved, that at all times the atmosphere is electrified, but much stronger in frosty, than in warm weather, and by no means less in the night than in the day: it is likewise stronger in elevated, than in low places. From these facts, we may be enabled to account, why evaporation is carried on during very cold weather. All the heat contained in water, above what is sufficient to keep it in a fluid state, will convert it into vapour; which, in a north or north east wind, when the electric matter greatly abounds, will be carried off with much rapidity; and, by the power of electricity, will be rendered still lighter, the higher it ascends; each particle repelling each other, and preventing the cold from condensing the vapour, in its ascent through the cold regions of the atmosphere. The higher it rises, the more space there is for expansion; and the more it is expanded, the clearer will the atmosphere appear, and, probably, the higher the mercury will rise in the barometer.

It likewise appears, that the electric matter is more sensible near the surface of the earth, in cold northern countries, than in warm southern places. Mr. Volta, with a very simple apparatus, on the upper gallery of St. Paul's, produced an electric spark, which, he told me, in Italy, could not be done, but on a very high mountain, or in a situation greatly elevated. This seems a wise provision in nature, that the electric matter should appear near the surface of the earth in cold climates, to raise up and suspend the vapour in the air, which otherways, would be condensed by the cold; whereas, in warm countries, the heat of the earth will be sufficient to raise vapours to a great height, which are afterwards carried still higher, by the electric matter in the upper regions. This, perhaps, is the cause, why the air is so clear and transparent in warm climates.

By making some observations on the falling of rain, we shall have other proofs, that the electric matter is the great cause, by which vapour is supported in the atmosphere. Here I must observe a fact, well known to all present, that bodies electrified, by the same electric power (no matter whether positive or negative) repel each other; and, when electrified by the different powers, that is, the one plus and the other minus, attract each other: on coming into contact, an equilibrium is restored, and neither of them will shew any signs of electricity.

From this it follows: If two clouds are electrified by the fame power, they will repel each other, and the vapour be fufpended in both; but, when one is pofitive and the other negative, they will attract each other, and reftore an equilibrium. The electric power, by which the vapour was fufpended, being now deftroyed by the mutual action of the clouds on each other, the particles of water will have an opportunity of running together into each other, and, as they augment in fize, will gain a greater degree of gravity, defcending in fmall rain, or a heavy fhower, according to circumftances.

A cloud, highly electrified, paffing over a high building or mountain, may be attracted by, and be deprived of its electricity, without or with a violent explofion of thunder. If the cloud is electrified plus, the fire will defcend from the cloud to the mountain; but, if it be electrified minus, the fire will afcend from the mountain to the cloud. In both cafes, the effect is the fame, and generally, heavy rain immediately, or foon after, follows: this is well known to the inhabitants of, and travellers among, mountains.

From this, we can eafily account, why thunder-fhowers are often partial, falling near, or among mountains, and the rain in fuch quantities, as to occafion rivers to be overflowed; whilft, at the diftance of a few miles, the ground continues parched

parched up with drought, and the roads covered with dust.*

It often happens, that one clap of thunder is not sufficient to produce rain from a cloud, nor even a second: in short, the claps must be repeated, till an equilibrium is restored, and then the rain must, of consequence, fall. Sometimes we may have violent thunder and lightning without rain, and the black appearance of the heavens may be changed to a clear transparent sky, especially in warm weather. To account for this, it must be remembered, as I lately said, that one or more claps of thunder are not always sufficient to produce rain from the clouds: so, if an equilibrium be not restored, little or no rain will fall, and in a short time, the electric matter, passing from the earth to the clouds, or the superabundant quantity in the air, will electrify those black clouds, by which means the particles of vapour will be expanded, raised higher, and the air become clear. Clouds may be melted away, even when we are looking at them, by another cause, that is, by the

* Sæpe etiam immensum cœlo venit agmen aquarum.
 Et fædam glomerant tempestatem imbribus atris
 Collectæ ex alto nubes.
 Ipse pater, mediâ nimbrorum in nocte, coruscâ
 Fulmina molitur dextrâ, quo maxima motu
 Terra tremit. - - - - -   *Virg.*

heat of the sun. We know, that transparent bodies are not heated by the sun, but opaque ones are; the clouds being opaque bodies, are warmed by the rays of the sun shining on them, and any additional quantity of heat will rarify the vapour, and occasion its expanding in the air, which will soon become transparent. When vapour is made to expand, more than it would otherwise do, a certain quantity of absolute heat is necessary to keep it in the form of vapour; therefore, when the receiver of an air-pump is exhausting, it appears muddy, and a number of drops are found within it; the moisture contained in the air, in the form of vapour, being made to occupy a greater space than what is natural to it, and receiving no addition of heat, a part of it is condensed.*

If, therefore, the air is suddenly rarified, a few drops of rain will descend, as may often be observed in the summer season.

I have repeatedly observed, especially during the summer, when the wind is at north east, that the weather is, in general, cold and dry, with a clear atmosphere. Should the wind sud-

---

* On this principle, we can readily account for the mist, which appears, on discharging an air-gun: the condensed air in the chamber of the barrel, on being set free, will expand suddenly, occupying a larger space, and no additional heat being acquired, the vapours must necessarily be condensed in the form of mist.

denly change to south west, in a few hours, black clouds begin to gather, vegetables look sickly, and droop their leaves; and, soon after, comes on a violent storm of thunder, with heavy rain.*

This change, I imagine, is not so much owing to the south west wind bringing rain, as to the atmosphere's being changed from an electric state, capable of suspending vapour, to a state of parting with its moisture. As soon as the storm is going off, vegetables revive from their languid state, and the air recovers its usual aspect. From this we may conclude, that no instrument can be made to ascertain the quantity of moisture in the air: all that is, or ought to be expected from a hygrometer, is to shew, whether the air be in a state to retain, or part with its moisture. In apparent dry weather it may point to rain; and when it rains, it may point to fair. For this reason, the stones of halls, and smooth substances, are often bedewed with wet, in dry warm weather, (that is, the air is in a state to part with its moisture) and, *vice versâ*, they will dry in the time of rain.

Lest this paper should exceed the common limits of time in reading, I shall pass over those observations, which might be made on fogs or mists; a few excepted, which I shall subjoin in a

---

* "Ingeminant Austri, et densissimus imber." *Virg.*

note.* I shall, therefore, conclude with a short summary of the whole.

1. That, heat is the great cause, by which water is converted into vapour, which is condensed by cold.

2. That, electricity renders vapour specifically lighter, and adds to its absolute heat, repelling its particles; which particles would be condensed by cold: and that, electricity is the great agent by which vapour ascends to the upper regions.

---

* Fogs are produced by two causes as different as their effects are opposite. A fog may be produced by a precipitation of rain, in very small particles, like a cloud floating on the surface of the earth. In this case the air is moist and damp, and never fails to wet a traveller's cloaths; the stones of the street, painted doors, and hard, cool, smooth bodies are generally covered with moisture, which often runs in large drops: this, I dare say, has been observed by every person. Secondly, a fog may be produced by the absorption of moisture, when the air is too dry, and differs from the other just described; for it will not impart any of its moisture even to dry bodies, no damp is to be met with on stones, polished marble, &c. This fact is well known to the inhabitants on the sea coast of Fifeshire, who, during their summer months, have frequent opportunities of observing a fog in the afternoon, driving up the Firth of Forth, with a drying east wind, which often blasts the trees and young vegetables, and therefore, in a small degree, resembles the Harmattan in drying up the ground, and robbing vegetables of their moisture.

3. That, when the electric power, by which vapour is suspended in the atmosphere, is destroyed, a heavy mist, small rain, or thundershowers, will be the consequence. Had the advocates for the doctrine of solution, made heat and electricity, the solvents, their theory would have been less exceptionable.*

On the COMPARATIVE MERIT *of the* ANCIENTS *and* MODERNS, *with respect to the* IMITATIVE ARTS. *By Mr.* THOMAS KIRSHAW. *Read February* 19, 1783.

> Vitaque tam longæ brevior non sufficit Arti.
> Fresnoy de arte Graphicâ.

THE life of man being too short, and the extent of human abilities too confined, to make considerable improvements or inventions in any art, we ought to view the performances of celebrated men, with all the candour, and generosity, they so well merit.

Even, after all the advantages we have received from the united studies of ages, we may, with great justice say, how small and imperfect is all our boasted wisdom, and, how much to be regretted is it, that we have not made a greater

* This paper is, through accident, placed out of the order in which it should have been inserted.

progress in the spacious field of science!—This short essay is intended to point out the excellencies of the ancients in the imitative arts: yet, at the same time, to allow the moderns their due share of fame, in having, not only made some improvements, but inventions, of which the ancients were entirely ignorant.

There is not a doubt, but the ancients possessed a polished taste, and a critical knowledge of the various and exquisite forms of beauty: they knew the arts, could only receive their perfection from ideal beauty, superior to what is ever found, in individual, and imperfect nature. There is no man equal, in strength and proportion to the Farnesian Hercules: nor, any woman comparable, for symmetry of form, to Medicean Venus.

These instances seem to prove, that the authors of the finest remains of antiquity formed to themselves ideas of *perfect* nature, and collected from *various* individuals, what *no one* could supply.

It is said, that Zeuxis, when he painted his Helena, selected five of the most beautiful virgins that could be found; and, whatever nature had formed most perfect in each, he united in a single figure.

Thus painters, and sculptors, render their ideas more perfect, and exalt their Art above

Nature

Nature herself. In this manner, by contemplating grand and exquisite forms of beauty, the operations of the hand are directed by the image in the mind: but how far to proceed, and when to stop, must be left to the judgment of the artist.

That the ancients bear the palm from the moderns in sculpture, will not be contested: their religion sanctified and encouraged that branch of science. Gods, Demigods, and Heroes, all conspired to bring it into the highest repute: and their images were often deposited in buildings of the most exquisite taste, to commemorate particular occurrences. The rage for highly ornamented edifices, perhaps never rose to a greater height, than amongst the Romans. These sons of fortune acquired so much wealth, and, by plundering distant climes, had so collected the riches of whole kingdoms into one city, that there was no way left to dissipate such immense sums, but by engaging in the most expensive works of art. Each ambitious conqueror, desirous to transmit his own actions, and those of his ancestors to posterity, called in to his aid the sculptor, and the architect, whose utmost skill was exerted, to blazon their atchievements in the solidity of stone and marble.

This shews, in some measure, why Sculpture outstripped her sister Art; for the specimens of ancient Painting are much inferior to modern productions. They are deficient in colouring, chiaro-obscuro, and keeping. Several of the *Classics** tell us, there were but four colours or pigments in use amongst the ancient artists, viz. black, white, yellow, and red. Now, it is impossible to produce, from those colours only, the variety of tints necessary to equal even a tolerable colourist of the moderns. Although this evinces nothing against the *abilities* of the ancients, we may fairly conclude, that the rich and luxuriant descriptions, handed down to us, are inflated with hyperbole, sufficient to make us doubt the veracity of some of their authors. Unfortunately for these warm advocates, the discoveries of Herculaneum have spitefully contradicted their assertions, and furnished us with means to draw our own conclusions. It is very possible they might admire, and be surprized at a sight of, what appeared to them the ultimatum of perfection.

The stories of Zeuxis, and Polygnotus raise a smile. The former is said to have painted fruits so naturally, that birds attempted to eat them; the latter to have delineated the character and features of the face so truly, that physiognomists, upon sight of the portrait, could foretel the precise time of the party's death. Sir Joshua Reynolds, who may be justly considered as the first artist in the world, thus delivers his opinion.

* Pliny, Cicero.

"In antique paintings, there are not the
"smallest traces to make us think, that what
"we call light, and shade, or a distribution of
"the work into masses, claimed any part of their
"attention: these may be ranked amongst the
"defects of the learned *Poussin*,* as well as of
"the antique paintings: and the moderns have
"a right to that praise which is their due, for
"having given so pleasing an addition to the
"splendour of the art. *Poussin*'s pure and cor-
"rect stile was a direct contrast to the florid
"and inaccurate stile of *Rubens*;* yet the luxu-
"riant brilliancy and harmony of the latter, so
"dazzles the eye, that we cannot help thinking
"all his deficiencies are fully supplied." *Poussin*
carried his veneration for the ancients so far,
as to give his works the air of antique paintings.
It is certain he copied some of them, particularly
the marriage, in the Aldrobrandini palace at
Rome; which, in the opinion of that great artist
before mentioned, is the best relique of those
remote ages, that has hitherto been found.
Those of the antique paintings which stand
foremost, are fine, and correct imitations of
improved nature; with the chastest outline;
formed upon such certain principles as no one

* *N. Poussin*, an eminent French painter. It should have been noticed, whether it was *Nicholas*, or *Gasper Poussin*.

* *Rubens*, a famous Flemish painter.

has yet dared to controvert. "But they have "a remarkable dryness of manner, which is, by "no means, recommended for imitation." The compositions of the ancients appear to be much better calculated for the chissel, than the pencil.

Chiaro-scuro, or the art of distributing the lights and shadows in a picture advantageously, as well for the repose, and satisfaction of the eye, as for the effect of the whole together, seems to be a modern invention. By the assistance of this part of science, objects receive more relief, truth, and soundness. The masses of light and shade are formed by a proper distribution of objects, which, by an artful management, are so disposed, that all the lights are on one side, and the shades on the other. Sometimes, reflected lights are necessary; at other times they are used, with a pictorical liberty, to produce the desired effect; it is the knowledge of this that animates the canvas, and gives the appearance of corporeal substance to a flat surface. *Rembrandt*,[*] so far from selecting the most beautiful and graceful parts of nature, frequently made a bad choice from among the subjects she affords. And, although he possessed a very moderate portion of true taste, yet the fire and spirit, with which his pictures are finished, cannot be seen without surprize; and the effect produced by his colour-

---

[*] *Rembrandt*, a great artist of the Flemish school.

ing, and expression, demand our admiration. His etchings are collected at a great expence for the cabinets of the curious. The same spirit, which flowed from his pencil, guided his needle. Had this eminent artist visited Rome, and refined his taste, it is supposed, with his profound knowledge of chiaro-scuro, and colouring, he would have been one of the first masters in the world.

That part of the art, termed *keeping*, the ancients seem to have been but little acquainted with, and without a due management of this, every picture would be filled with confusion. Instead of a proper subordination, each groupe or figure, would seem to contend for precedence. This want of order destroys all dignity, and prevents the artist from forming an agreeable whole.

Any attempts in antique landscape, with which we are acquainted, are executed wretchedly. In that part of the art, the superiority of the moderns is manifest.

We have the authority of *Fresnoy** to say, "that, Michael Angelo surpassed not only all the moderns, but the ancients in architecture, he quotes the St. Peters at Rome, the Palazzo Farnese, and the St. Johns at Florence, as proofs of his opinion."

* *Fresnoy*, a French artist well known for his Latin poem de Arte Graphicâ.

Etching, engraving, mezzotinto, and aquatinta are all of modern invention, and of great utility. They deliver down to us accurate copies from the works of eminent men at a small expence; and diffuse abroad the bright flame of science, so that even those, who are far distant from the centre of the arts, may rouse their souls to action, and enlighten that spark of genius, which might hitherto have lain dormant. From these meritorious, and ingenious improvements, we can judge, with great certainty, of the various merits of an artist, and every part, but the colouring, may be critically examined.

The stile of the Italian, Flemish, or French schools, may be pointed out by these copies, and frequently the very manner of pencilling, by particular artists, is faithfully represented. These arguments are not meant to depreciate the antiques, they will always engage our admiration, and most highly merit it.

The advantages, received by the moderns, from studying the ancients, are freely acknowledged. It is no uncommon thing to hear some people lament the decay of genius, and the decline of arts, in these times, when compared with the Augustan age. However that may be, the moderns have a right to claim their full portion of fame, in many arts in which the ancients could not instruct them.

From the candour of this learned Society, the writer of this Essay claims protection, and hopes, an attempt to investigate truth, will not be deemed audacity.

On the IMPROPRIETY *of allowing a* BOUNTY *to encourage the* EXPORTATION *of* CORN, *&c. By* JOSEPH WIMPEY.

IN the conversation on a paper read before this Society some time since, respecting the propriety of keeping œconomical registers; their use was questioned in respect to one of the principal objects, upon a supposition, that a necessity for it did not exist; because it had been obviated by measures adopted for that purpose. The object alluded to, is the exportation of corn. Notwithstanding all that was urged against it, the writer is fully persuaded, the measure recommended is well founded, the object of it of very great importance, and that men of very good abilities, have had their judgments misled by inveterate popular prejudices, or false reasoning. Imprest with an idea of the great importance of the subject, he begs leave to submit the following observations to the consideration of the Society.

To maintain an argument, not founded on juſt principles, is like putting to ſea without compaſs or chart. As the veſſel would be the ſport of the waves and winds; ſo would ſuch a reaſoner lie at the mercy of the boiſterous ſtorms of his paſſions, and the uncertain bias of his inclinations. To avoid both, let us premiſe certain propoſitions, where truth is not only conſonant to reaſon, but confirmed by experience, and acknowledged facts.

PROPOSITIONS.

1. The prime object of civil ſociety, is the happineſs of the members of whom it is compoſed. No government can be juſt, whoſe ſupport and defence do not extend to the equal, and indiſcriminate benefit of the whole.

2. Though the good and protection of each individual, is either virtually implied, or formally conditioned or articled for; yet it cannot juſtly extend further, than may be conſiſtent with public good: for, the rights of all men are the ſame, and it is ſhocking to common ſenſe to ſuppoſe, that one man, or one claſs of men, might, with juſtice, be made rich, great, and happy, by the miſery and ſufferings of a hundred men, or at the expence of the reſt of the community. No government ever intended men ſhould live *upon* one another, but be equally advantaged

advantaged by the mutual affiftance, given to the common fupport, of which every individual is entitled to an equal fhare.

3. Public good is the barometer, or, if I may ufe the expreffion, the political balance, by which the fpecific gravity, the intrinfic worth, or fterling value, of every meafure, refpecting the public, is to be determined and afcertained. Therefore, every meafure, which has a tendency to promote public good, is right and defirable: every meafure, which is inimical to the public intereft, is a wrong meafure, and fhould be reprobated. To fay otherwife, would be repugnant to common fenfe, therefore falfe and abfurd.

4. The projects of individuals, in which the good of the public is ultimately included, have been very defervedly countenanced by public encouragement: but fuch encouragement cannot confiftently be continued longer than the eftablifhment of fuch projects; for if they could not fupport themfelves, and reward the projectors, they would be abfurd projects, and fhould be abandoned, as by propofitions fecond and third; the individual is not to be enriched, at the unjuft expence and lofs of the public. Now, all the bounties, of whatever nature or kind, whether they refpect produce, manufactures, or commerce, are public encouragements; and their origin and exiftence depend, upon the reafonable

expectation

expectation of their being subservient to public good; if they are found not to answer that purpose, they should be execrated and abandoned as public evils, as appears by the foregoing propositions.

5. Cheap and dear are relative terms; and are measured or estimated, by their rise or fall above the medium value. The medium value of things may be estimated, at the price they stand the grower, the breeder, or the manufacturer in, with a reasonable profit on the same, for the maintainance of himself and family, be the commodity whatever it may. If it deviates from that standard, it will be dear, in proportion to its advance above it, or cheap, as it falls below it. But cheap and dear, being relative terms, they must depend on something else for their existence; and this is very well known to be scarcity and plenty. If the demand for any commodity is increased, beyond the quantity adequate to the supply, its price is necessarily advanced. But if the quantity exceeds the demand, the price as necessarily falls; and it is not in human power to prevent it. From hence follows

6. Proposition. Whatever measure, rule, or law, increases the quantity of any commodity, in proportion to the demand for it, necessarily makes it cheaper; and whatever increases the demand,

demand, in proportion to the quantity, as necessarily renders it dearer.

Now, there is hardly any public question respecting agriculture, manufactures, or commerce, but its expedience and use may be ascertained by some one, or more, of these propositions.

The question before us is of the greatest importance: there is not a *subject* in the *realm*, whose interest is not affected by it. Nothing can be more interesting, than that proper measures should be taken respecting an article, upon which the people depend for their daily subsistence. It is a measure, however, in which men of good sense have been deceived and deluded; by which *millions* have been foolishly thrown away, to the advantage of our neighbours; and which, to this hour, has its advocates, who contend, not only for its continuance, but also for its extension. But the effects of popular prejudice are indeed very surprizing.—Let us first take a cursory view of its history, and then try its merit by the foregoing propositions.

Patriotism, genuine patriotism, is a word of noble signification. But, a true patriot, one who, in all things, at all times, and upon all occasions, prefers the good of the community to his own private interest, would be as singular a phenomenon in the political world, as a Phœnix in the natural. It is an object one may contemplate with pleasure; but rarely be indulged with the sight of. Legislators, like Judges, should be incorrupt: their ears should be open to no voice, but that of truth. But where shall we find those, who have no interest in the laws they enact; or those, who can divest themselves of the influence of such interest?

Unhappily, the landed interest of the country is placed in opposition to that of commerce, and they contemplate each other with an evil eye. This has a pernicious tendency; since they are connected together, like links in a chain, and since their safety and interest depend upon their union. Neither could subsist long without reciprocal aid.—But to proceed to facts.

One of the calamities of the civil war was, a scarcity and dearness of provisions. When peace was restored, men betook themselves to their civil occupations, and agriculture was encouraged by men of ability. In 1687, wheat was at a lower price, than it had been at any time in the century; somewhere from three shillings, to three and four-pence a bushel. The circumstances of the farmers, of those days, were very different from the present. If the prices were low, they were, notwithstanding, obliged to go to market: nor could they keep large stocks, for a change of times, and an advance of price. Therefore, when corn sold low, their rents were ill paid, and the land-owner was affected by, and partook of, the distress of his tenant.

tenant. To remedy this, the bounty was devised, and a market was procured abroad: for it was clearly seen, as the demand increased, the price *must* do so too; and the event fully evinced the policy of the measure, for the year following, the price was nearly double. Could this relief have been given to the farmer and land-owner, without injury to the rest of the community, it would have been just: but, when it is considered, that there is no one, even in the lowest circumstances of life, who is not taxed to pay the bounty, perhaps it will appear rather cruel, to oblige poor wretches, who, with the greatest care and industry, cannot provide bread sufficient to support their families, to contribute towards the enriching of the farmer, and increasing of the rent of the land-owner.

But, what says the advocate for the bounty? Why, he tells you, that the time of granting it is the great æra, from which, improvements in agriculture are to be dated. That at the same time, it has benefitted the land-owner and the farmer, has added to the riches of the nation, and has lowered the price of corn, which is a common blessing to all. That it has been very beneficial to the land-owner and farmer, we not only admit, but have proved; but that it has added to the riches of the nation, is denied: and that it should be the means of lowering the price of corn, is contradictory, absurd, and impossible. But it is said, it *has* lowered the price, and the fact is indisputable.—Facts, indeed, are stubborn things, and not to be warped to accommodate any body. But, be it remembered, assertions are not facts: and any one, who is remarkable for *fearlessness* of assertion, can never be depended upon for facts.

What effect the bounty had upon the price of corn, can only be known, by comparing the prices for a considerable number of years, before that measure was adopted, with the same number of years after. This, and this only, is the true method of ascertaining the fact. But to compare plentiful years with years of scarcity, can only serve to expose the fraud and artifice of the writer, and to impose upon the credulity of the reader. The following is a true state of the fact, as any one may satisfy himself, who will be at the trouble of inspecting the Windsor Tables, which he may find in Bishop *Fleetwood's Chronicon Pretiosum*, in four tracts relating to corn: and, I think, in one of the volumes of *Museum Rusticum et Commerciale*. The fact is, if the average price of corn be taken from those tables, for twenty-five or thirty years before the bounty was enacted, and for the same term after, it will appear, that the price was considerably lower before the bounty, than it was after. This was the time for discovering the effects of the bounty; and the fact is, it advanced the price, nearly double, the first year.

We will now shew, that the natural and necessary tendency of the bounty is, to raise the price; and that it is impossible it should do otherwise; and therefore absurd to assert it. The advocates for the measure say, "It encourages the farmer to grow more corn, by providing a market abroad; this makes it more plentiful, and consequently cheaper." This, in fact, is saying, the farmer has more encouragement to grow corn, when the price is lower, than when it is higher. The market is nothing to him, abstracted from the price. When he sells his corn, he neither knows nor cares what becomes of it afterwards: he looks only to the price. If it affords him a reasonable profit, he proceeds with alacrity; and his diligence and industry will be excited in proportion to his gain. But, it seems, the bounty lowers the price and renders it cheaper, and, at the same time, encourages the farmer to extend its culture, and grow larger quantities, than he would otherwise do! This is the land-owner's argument; but where is the man, who can reconcile it to *common sense?* Repugnant as this is to the common sense of mankind, it is the great argument made use of, not only to continue the bounty, but to increase and extend it. I could, therefore, wish, as it is a question of very great importance, to be permitted to sift it to the bottom.

The farmer stands on the same ground as the manufacturer: every article of his farm stands him in a certain price; and, if he cannot sell it for a profit, sufficient to maintain himself and family, in time he must waste his capital, and come to ruin. Suppose he cannot grow wheat under four shillings a bushel, which is about the average cost: it is evident, he must sell it for more than four shillings, or he loses by that article. Now, if the bounty (as the advocates for it maintain) lowers the price, is it possible to conceive, that it should encourage the farmer to extend its culture? Or rather, is it not self-evident, that it would not only discourage his sowing corn, but necessitate him to discontinue the practice, to save himself from ruin? Put a similar question to any Gentleman here, who is versed in manufactures of any kind. Suppose a Velveret stands him in four shillings a yard: so long as he can sell it for four shillings and six-pence, or five shillings, he will be encouraged to make as much as he can: but let any measure be adopted which falls the price to three shillings and six-pence, would he not immediately relinquish that branch, and betake himself to something else? Surely he would. And, why should not the farmer, for the very same reason, abandon the planting of wheat, when the bounty has lowered the price so, that a bushel, which stands him in four shillings, he can only

only sell for three shillings and six-pence, three shillings, two shillings and six-pence, or even but two shillings; for, at all these prices has wheat been exported? It is plain then, if the price of grain is lower now, than it was in any former period, it must be owing to some other cause; for a bounty has a directly contrary effect.

Another argument for the bounty is, That it encourages exportation; and, as corn is the produce of our own lands, it greatly increases the riches of our country.

I answer—To object to the exportation of corn, or any other article of commerce, when it can be done on advantageous terms, would be extreme folly. But exportation, procured by means of a bounty, is so far from being advantageous, that it destroys, for the most part, all possibility of advantage: even of real, substantial advantage, which must, and would happen, if not prevented by the bounty. Every man is thoroughly sensible, that, if he pursues a business by which he is a loser, the longer he continues in it, and the larger his dealings, the more he suffers by it. Just so it operates in regard to the public; for the public and individuals only differ, as greater and lesser: and the loss of the one is in exact proportion to that of the other. To shew this, let us suppose, for example, as before, that wheat stands the farmer in four shillings a bushel: that the present market-price, however,

however, is no more than three shillings, and that there is not a sufficient demand even at that. The legislature, to relieve the farmer, and accommodate its members, gives a bounty of five shillings a quarter, or seven-pence halfpenny a bushel, to procure a market abroad. And is it not a *blessed* relief which it affords? In the first place, the farmer sells for three shillings what cost him four shillings; and, towards that three shillings, the public pay seven-pence halfpenny. The first is a loss of twenty-five per cent., and the latter of more than twenty; making together, above forty-five per cent.! What a glorious trade for *England*, attended with such immense advantages! But how much better for the sagacious Dutchman, who buys a commodity at forty-five per cent. below its real value, which, in the space of twelve or eighteen months, there is almost a certainty of selling again, sometimes in the same market, at a hundred per cent. profit.

But it may be asked, what is to be done, when the nation is so unfortunate, as to be overwhelmed with such an abundance: for it must be observed, such low prices never happen, but in consequence of a series of propitious seasons? I answer, we should then imitate the Dutch, and store up our corn when cheap, that, when unfruitful seasons come, we may, like them, sell it at a large profit without a bounty, with a saving of £200,000 a year to the public. This, I think,

think, is about the average sum we have annually paid for bounties, and is sufficient to purchase about a fourth of the corn, we have usually exported. But, giving a bounty of twenty per cent. to export corn, when the price is so low, leaves so little upon hand, that the first bad season which comes, raises the price to double; and then, when you should sell for a profit, you have no corn; but are forced to prohibit exportation, even without a bounty, or to import from abroad, at double the price you sold at. It is now about ninety-five years, since the bounty commenced, and thus it has operated from the beginning. The first unfavourable season, after a year of large exportation, hath constantly raised the price immoderately, as appears from the tables above-mentioned, and it is impossible it should be otherwise.

It has been also observed, that in *Italy*, and other places, where corn is not permitted to be sent abroad, it is always dear. Doubtless it is. We have no objection to exportation, when we have any corn to spare: on the contrary, we recommend the practice. But, is there no difference, between giving a bounty of twenty per cent. to force a trade, which reduces you to almost a famine, and selling at a fair average price, which obtains all over *Europe*? The former impoverishes and distresses you; while the other, if you had any corn to sell, would infallibly

bly enrich you. The exportation of corn, upon fair and juft principles, would be a very valuable article of commerce; and not lefs fo, in a national view, than a private one, to the land-owner and farmer: but fo execrable has been our management, by forcing a market with the lofs of from thirty to fifty per cent., that when a fcarcity comes, when the price advances, and we fhould gain fifty per cent., inftead of having corn to fell, we are forced to buy, and often to give double the price we fold at.

We quite miftake the matter, in fuppofing, the laws, in being, have provided a fufficient remedy: no law ever was, or ever can be, effectual to that purpofe, while a bounty fubfifts. It is in vain to think, that trade, like water, will find its own level, when fo large a fluice is opened to deftroy that level. We may as well throw a quarter of a hundred weight into one fcale, to preferve its equilibrium, as to give a bounty of twenty per cent., to put us upon an equal footing with the other corn-markets in *Europe*.

The impropriety of the bounty is not lefs apparent, in the influence it has on the farmer's conduct. It often tempts him to plant wheat on land, which is not fuited to it; and sometimes, two or three years together, on the fame land; which too often proves a great lofs to himfelf, and alfo to the public. For the farmer cannot

cannot suffer materially in the failure or loss of his crops, but the public will be affected by it: and, what is worse, while he plants wheat, for the sale of which the public are loaded with a heavy tax, he omits planting other grain, which *England* is obliged to import from abroad. At the same time that we have paid two hundred thousand pounds a year for bounties on corn exported, we have paid five hundred thousand pounds for oats imported, making together seven hundred thousand pounds. Can a more striking proof of the folly of the measure be desired, than giving such a sum to force a trade in one article, which necessarily obliges us to be purchasers for so large a sum in another, without any the least allowance whatever?

But, there are those who would persuade us, that to grow corn, or trade in it to any advantage, our ports should be always open, that the merchant might export or import, as best suited his interest. If the merchant were the only man in the kingdom whose welfare was to be considered, perhaps it might be right; or, if mankind considered all nations as brethren, among whom charity universally prevailed, the maxim might be just. But whilst neighbouring nations calculate their own interest, by the loss of it in others, the country which should be anxious to provide bread for its neighbours, would be sure to want it for itself. On this plan,

plan, what would become of the farmer and landowner? I answer, both would be totally ruined. In most countries in *Europe*, both land and labour are so much cheaper than in *England*, that, in fruitful seasons, grain would be poured in upon us in such immense quantities, and the price so far reduced, that the farmer must give up his business, and the land-owner cultivate his land, for the bare maintenance of his family. On the other hand, when the seasons proved unfavourable, and the crops were insufficient, our ports might be open to no purpose; no corn would arrive; the unavoidable consequence would be, a general famine; and under the influence of such an execrable measure, it would not be in the art or power of man to prevent it. It is not in corn only, that high customs, prohibitory and penal laws, are absolutely necessary, but in very numerous branches of manufactures; indeed, in manufacture almost the whole of linen, and silk. Vast quantities of the former are imported under duties of, from eighteen to twenty five or thirty per cent; and a vast variety of small wares at twenty-five; and one article at almost cent. per cent. Even fine broad-cloth, which is a staple commodity of this kingdom, I have known imported under an insurance of twenty-five per cent. *ad valorum*. In short, were our ports open to all, as some Politicians advise,

advise, the *English* mechanic must do as much work for three-pence, at least, as he now does for a shilling; and then I aver, he would be much better paid, than an ingenious workman now is in *France*.

But, as I find some Gentlemen, the most respectable in general for their judgment, think differently on this subject, I wish to give it a little further investigation. I remember Monsieur *Turgot* (who was, at least, as respectable for his humanity as for his penetration, and in neither, perhaps, much inferior to any man) thought it was a cruel measure to shut the ports, and keep back our corn, when so many provinces were starving for want of it. He contended, it was a narrow policy, and that general happiness requires, that the ports should be always open, and commerce left to those whose business it was to pursue it. This, I observe, was trying the question by the laws of humanity, and not by the policy of states; and particularly, not by the politics of the court of *France*, in one of the first departments of which he, at that time, filled a distinguished place, with much honour.

If the laws of justice and humanity universally prevailed, and every man, of whatever country or nation, esteemed every other man as his bro- brother and his friend, if all men had but
one

one common object of pursuit, viz. the general peace and happiness of mankind; and if each individual were content with his proportion of good, as it arose from the general stock, commerce and every thing else would put on a very different face.

It would be lost labour to attempt to prove, what every one is daily an eye-witness to. The present system of politics, not only among princes and states, but in small communities, and among individuals too, is not only to make the greatest advantages possible of the wants and distresses of others, but to create, as far as is practicable, those wants and distresses, as the most certain and direct road to such advantages. Hence, the accursed thirst of conquest, to feed the ambition of princes, and the atrocious spirit of monoplizing, to create scarcity in the midst of plenty, to distress, perhaps, ten thousand persons in order to gratify the insatiable avarice of one. Whoever may attend to the present system of things, as actually existing in a populous, industrious, fertile country, where the eyes of every individual are open to private advantage, will soon see the necessity of restrictive laws, to protect the weak and innocent against the fraud and abuse of those, who make artifice and cunning their study, to impoverish and enslave the rest of mankind. This is an affair of the last importance, which, I am afraid, is very far

far from being well understood. Some, I verily believe, from a generosity of temper, and benevolence of disposition, wish to see every means practised, which might probably reduce the price of commodities, especially the necessaries and conveniences of life. To this end, it has been thought, that if the ports were thrown open, and the flux and reflux of the articles of commerce might be as free as the tides, it would necessarily occasion plenty; and that this would as necessarily lower the price, which would be a convenience to all, and particularly, a great blessing to the industrious poor. This doctrine, plausible as it may seem, from the humanity of the spirit by which it is dictated, I regard as a sophism of the most dangerous kind. Nothing could sooner reduce this country, to the deepest poverty and distress.

What is it, that has raised this country to the state of affluence, ease, and happiness, it has long enjoyed? Not the natural fecundity of its lands: for, in that respect, it is very far inferior to many other countries. Neither our lands, their natural produce, nor the populousness of the country, could add one grain to its riches, without the industry and labour of its people: I mean those, who not only labour for their maintenance and support, but also, for the necessaries and conveniences of those, whose circumstances enable them to pay for what they are unable or unwilling to provide for themselves.

themselves. It is the well-directed industry of the labouring poor, which constitutes the riches of a country. They are, when beneficially employed, the true sinews of its prosperity; to promote and effect which, is the heighth of political wisdom. Numbers, unless usefully employed, are the bane and curse of every community.

Nature, in the most fertile soil and climate, can only provide the rough materials; it is the industrious and laborious man, who cultivates the earth, reaps the grain, shears the flock, fabricates the cloth, fells the timber, penetrates into the bowels of the earth, and navigates the seas. Upon the unremitting toil of these laborious people, do the riches, the prosperity, and the happiness of every populous country depend. A populous country, destitute of employment for its people, would soon exhibit a dreadful scene of wretchedness and misery. A people, enervated and dispirited for want of employment, and the means of a comfortable subsistence, to be procured by it alone, would soon become the scourge and curse of a country.

But let us make the experiment; like fighting a battle, it will be much more safe to do it on paper, than in the field. I am very far from pretending to have a perfect, or even a comprehensive view of the subject; but, I hope, without vanity it may be said, I have a practical knowledge of commerce, sufficient to enable

enable me to point out the inevitable ruin, that muſt attend the ſyſtem of eſtabliſhing free ports, for the importation and exportation of all kinds of commodities without reſtriction.

I will beg leave to premiſe a few propoſitions relative to this ſubject, the certainty of which, I perſuade myſelf, will not be diſputed.

1. If the labour and induſtry of a people are the ſources of the riches they poſſeſs, theſe ſources muſt dry up or abate, in proportion as the people want employment.

2. Both the land, and labour of *England* are very high, in compariſon with thoſe of almoſt any other country in Europe; conſequently, ſuch countries can under-ſell *England*, *cæteris paribus*, both in corn and manufactures, in any market in the world.

3. The produce of the earth, in its natural ſtate, and raw materials of all kinds, have their value exceedingly increaſed, by the ſkill and labour beſtowed upon them, in converting them into goods and wares, often in the proportion of, from five to twenty for one, and ſometimes a great deal more: therefore, where there are people to be employed, and ſuch goods and wares can be vended with advantage, it is extremely bad policy, to ſuffer the raw materials to be exported, on any pretence whatſoever.

4. Moſt countries have ſome advantages peculiar to them, ariſing from the ſoil, climate, ſituation,

situation, or natural productions of the same. The genuine and most warrantable policy of any country is, to accommodate such advantages to the good, the well-being, and prosperity of its people. Indeed, general policy renders it necessary, to put every state upon an equal footing with its neighbours; for it would be deemed weakness or madness, to neglect local advantages, when every state, and every individual around us, were availing themselves, to the utmost of their power, to profit by them.

5. If the exportation of raw materials is so impolitic a measure; how much more so is it, to encourage the manufactures of other nations, when they stand in competition with our own, and have a direct tendency to supplant us in our market at home, and in the consumption of our own manufactures, though infinitely better accommodated to the uncertain climate of *Great Britain?* This is most unpatriotic, and, to the last degree, culpable.

Now, sheep's wool is one of those peculiar local blessings, with which *Great Britain* and *Ireland* are favoured, beyond any other part of *Europe.* Its quality is such, that every ounce of it is capable of being wrought into useful clothing of some kind, which, it seems, is a rare and singular case. The value of wool, when wrought into cloth, upon an average, is reckoned to be in the proportion of, five or six to one.

one. The number of inhabitants is said to be somewhere from six to seven millions, and that one third of these are said to be employed and maintained by this manufacture. The proportion seems large; perhaps they are over-rated. Suppose only a sixth of the people to be employed in this branch, the object is important, so much so, that the wisdom of the legislature has always thought it necessary to encourage this manufacture by every means in its power. The question, it seems, is—" Have they judged and acted rightly?" The grazier, perhaps, will tell you, no; for if he were permitted to export his wool, he could sell it at double the price. This is very true, and would certainly be a great present advantage to him: but how long would it continue to be so? That, perhaps, he never thought of, nor of other consequences, which would certainly overbalance even his partial advantages.

If it be true, as it is generally believed, that one pack of *English* wool enables the *French* to work up two packs of theirs; and if labour in *France* is cheaper, by, at least, one half, than in *England*, they could afford to give a shilling for a pound of wool, that is now sold for sixpence, and sell their cloth at little more than half the price—say two thirds at most—that an *English* manufacturer could do. Where, then, must we send our cloth to market?

But it has been said—If the *French* would give us a double price for our wool, and supply us with cloth equally good, at two thirds of what we give for it now, that is, as good superfine cloth for twelve shillings a yard as what we pay eighteen shillings for now, and so for other sorts in proportion, is it not evident we should be very great gainers by the bargain? I answer: labour and toil are generally the effects of necessity, and not of choice. Few men would be at the pains of doing any disagreeable labour for themselves and families, if they had any sure means of doing as well, or better, without it: but what must the man do, who is destitute of such means? If he should sell his pound of wool to T. for a shilling, which E. would only give him six-pence for, would that enable him to give twelve shillings, or six shillings, to T. for a yard of their cloth? This is the true question; for at least nine-tenths of the people, perhaps ninety-nine out of a hundred, must earn their bread, and cloaths too, by their labour. It is not the case of the woollen manufactures only, but of almost all manufacturers and artificers whatever. It has been said, if that branch fail, let them betake themselves to some other! I should be happy to see the man, who could point out the means of employing a million of people beneficially, in any other branch whatever.

The linen manufacture comes the neareſt to the woollen: and the weaver of the latter, might ſoon be brought to weave the former. But here you are under a ſimilar dilemma: for not a piece could be made in *Great Britain* without great loſs, if foreign linens were not ſubject to cuſtoms, almoſt equal to a prohibition. The linens of *Sileſia, Pomerania, Saxony, Poland, Ruſſia, Flanders,* and *Holland,* pay cuſtoms from eighteen to thirty, and upwards, per cent.; and thoſe of *France* are prohibited. If you turn to the ſilk manufacture, you are there protected and encouraged by ſimilar means. *French* ſilks are abſolutely prohibited: thoſe of *Italy* pay too heavy a duty to be worn in common: the *Eaſt Indian* are prohibited under very ſevere penalties. Were it not for very heavy duties and prohibitions, not a piece of any of theſe goods could be made here.

Where, then, ſhall we find employment for ſo many millions of people, who, upon the ſcheme of a free trade and open ports, would be deprived of their uſual means of ſubſiſtence? Our manufactures of lace are upon the ſame footing: black and blond ſilk laces are prohibited: thread lace pays a duty, upon low goods, of four or five hundred per cent. The ſmall wares of *Harlem* are under the ſame predicament. Filletings, tapes, bobbins, threads of all kinds and denominations, pay duties from twenty to thirty per cent., and some much more; and, notwithstanding all this, the *English* manufacturer is often puzzled to sell goods in our market at home, upon terms equally low with the foreign manufacturer.

From hence it is easy to see, that the laws of this country, respecting commerce, are absolutely necessary to its very existence. Repeal the laws, open the ports, and invite all the world to a free correspondence with you, and you, at one stroke, deprive millions of people of the means of subsistence. What will you do with them then? Maintain them you cannot: for the whole income of the lands bears but a small proportion to the amount of the produce of their labour. The plain answer is—Many would be hanged, more would be starved, and many more would emigrate into other countries, as they did formerly into this, in hopes of employment.

The grazier, by this time too, would begin to feel the effects of his error: for having no market to go to, but *France*, with his wool, and that being glutted, it is more than probable, he would fall short of the price he now so much complains of at home. For wool, and corn, and all commodities whatever, are subject to, and governed by the same law. Every man, and every state, that is in want of any articles whatever, are ready to buy at a fair price: but the seller must submit to very disadvantageous terms, to prevail upon the buyer to purchase a commodity, he has no occasion for, and knows not what to do with.

I would beg leave just to mention, by way of illustration, that the grazier is now under the very same predicament, that the farmer was near one hundred years ago. Wheat was then at little more than three shillings a bushel; exportation was encouraged by a bounty to enhance its price. The experiment succeeded, as it infallably must; and the very next year it was nearly double. The grazier's hopes are equally well founded. Were he permitted to export his wool, the price would immediately advance, not only for exportation, but for home-consumption too; and were it not for the ruinous effects I have described, the measure would certainly be just and politic. But if the price hereafter should, by any means, fall a penny or two-pence a pound below what it is now, is it possible to conceive, that this circumstance could encourage the grazier to increase the quantity; or can we reconcile it to common sense, that a circumstance happening to a man, in any profession, by which he is a sufferer to a very considerable amount, should animate him to extend and increase his trade? Yet this is the very argument used by the advocates of the bounty. A bounty, say they, encouraged exportation; exportation encouraged the farmer to plant; and planting lowered the price; the price is, therefore, lower than it was before the bounty took place; the fall of price is owing to the bounty; *ergo*, the fall of price encouraged the farmer to plant more corn! But this is a sophism, as dangerous as it is absurd.

Were it true, that the average price of wheat has been cheaper since the bounty than it was before, it is clearly demostrable, that could not be the cause. From 1730 to 1750 there were twenty such years of plenty as were never known; consequently, the average price of those years was lower than was ever known before or since. But it seems to have been forgotten, how necessarily and how largely the price must have been affected, by the great improvements which have been made in agriculture during the last century. Clover, turnips, and potatoes, are such an acquisition, as ultimately, by means of general improvement, affects the price of *all* the produce of a farm. Potatoes alone contribute, in most families, to lessen the consumption of bread; and in dear times, in several counties, among the poor, they almost totally supply the use of it. It scarcely admits a doubt, that this useful root alone has lowered the average price of wheat, at least six-pence a bushel.

What has occasioned the loud outcry of the fall of price in coarse wool? The very same cause

cause, that would have lowered the price of corn, if exportation had not kept it up—that is—IMPROVEMENTS. In countries, which have been drained, the lands inclosed, and the turnip-culture adopted, the pasture has been amazingly increased, and the size of the sheep also; so that a double quantity of wool has been raised upon the same extent of land, and the grazier would be no sufferer, though he should sell for half the former price: for the loss in quality is more than compensated by the increase in quantity.

On the Natural History *of the* Cow, *so far as it relates to its giving* Milk, *particularly for the* Use *of* Man. *By* C. White, *Esq. F. R. S. &c. Read March* 12, 1783.

NATURALISTS seem to lay it down, as a general principle, that neither animals, nor parts of animals, are primarily intended for the use of man, but are only capable of a secondary application to his purposes. It must, however, be allowed that, in many instances, the secondary use is so manifest and important, that it cannot, with propriety, be excluded from the original designs of the all-wise Creator. And it appears to me, that the *Cow* in its faculty, of giving in such abundance, and with so much ease, its *Milk*, which forms so excellent an article of aliment for the human species, is a striking example of this subordination to the interests of mankind. For this animal differs in some parts of its organization from most others, having a larger and more capacious udder, and longer and thicker teats, than the largest animal we know; and she has four teats, whilst all other animals of the same nature, have but two.

She

She also yields the milk freely to the hand, whilst most animals, at least those that do not ruminate in the same manner, refuse it, except their own young, or some adopted animal be allowed to partake.

This is a subject which, one would have thought, had long since been exhausted; but I have not been able to find any thing satisfactory in the few authors I have read. I must confess, indeed, that my knowledge in Natural History is very confined, and should therefore wish to hear the sentiments of those learned Members of this Society, who have made the history of nature their more particular study.

In the first place, the Cow is of that class of *horned ruminating animals*, which have *cloven hoofs, four stomachs, a considerable length of intestines*, are furnished *with suet*, and have *no dentes incisores in the upper jaw*. From the different structure of the stomach in these creatures, a ruminant animal will be served with one-third less food, than another of equal bulk. Graziers are sufficiently acquainted with this. The reason is, that ruminating animals have many and strong digestive organs; and every thing capable of being converted into chyle, is extracted from the food; which therefore yields a greater quantity of milk: but a horse's and an ass's stomach is not fitted for this; so that they require a much a much greater quantity of food to extract the same nourishment.

A Cow's udder is so capacious, that it frequently contains ten quarts of milk, which it will yield twice a day; and it is not only remarkable for its quantity, but its quality, as some cows will afford twelve or fourteen pounds of butter in a week. The size and form of the teats appear, at the first sight, as if they were made on purpose for the hand to draw off the milk. But this is not the only advantage they possess; the thickness permits the lactiferous tubes to be of a larger diameter, and the length of them makes the syphon so much longer, and the extraction of the milk of course so much more easy.

The Cow having four teats is a striking peculiarity, the number in all other animals, bearing some proportion to the number of young ones, they bring forth at a time, as in the bitch, the cat, the sow, &c. But the Cow does not bring forth, at a birth, more young ones, than those animals who have but two teats.

The Cow will yield her milk to the hand as freely, and will continue to give her milk for as long a time, without any calf coming near her, as if it were permitted to suck her constantly. This is not the case with the ass, which, next to the Cow, is the animal we are most accustomed to have milked in this part of the world.

world. For it is well known, that an afs will foon grow dry, if her foal is not permitted to fuck part of the milk every day, but fhe is not a ruminating animal.

The human milk cannot long be preferved in the breafts, without the child be permitted to fuck. It otherwife foon acquires a bad faltifh tafte, and, in a fhort time, leaves them entirely; and this will happen, if the child alone fucks, if it be not permitted to fuck four or five times a day. Three times a day I find is, in general, not fufficient to keep the milk good, and in proper quantity. I do not mean to fay, that it is impoffible, in any fubject whatever, to keep the milk without a child fucking conftantly. I believe there have been inftances of fuction by perfons, above the age of infancy, and even by puppies, keeping the milk for fome time; but thefe may, in fome meafure, be confidered in the light of adopted children. What I would wifh to inforce is, that the moft dexterous and moft fkilful women, who draw breafts, do not keep the milk without the affiftance of the child; and when I have particularly defired them to do it, they have not been able, though they have fwallowed the milk, and repeated the fuction four or five times a day.

Capivaccius, it is faid, faved the only heir of a noble family by ordering him to lie between

two

two nurses, in the flower of their age, and suck their breasts.

Forestus tells us, that a youth at Bologna, of twenty-nine years of age, labouring under a true marasmus, lived upon the milk of a beautiful young nurse, of eighteen years of age, who lay in the same bed with him, by which means his emaciated body was well restored. In both these instances, I suppose the milk was preserved, without the child being permitted to suck. I am informed that goats, sheep, and rein deer will give milk freely to the hand, without the kid, lamb, and the fawn having access to them, but they are ruminating animals of the same kind with the Cow.

Upon the whole, I believe we may infer, that the property of yielding milk, without the young one, or some adopted animal, in some measure partaking of it, is confined to that class of *ruminating horned animals* who have *cloven hoofs, four stomachs, long intestines*, are furnished with *suet*, and have no *fore-teeth in the upper jaw*. That cows, sheep, goats and deer are of this kind, and no others; and that the Cow has this property in a more eminent degree than the others, owing to the capaciousness of her udder, and the size, form and number of her teats. There are other ruminant animals, besides those
I have

I have mentioned, some of which are without horns or cloven feet, and without suet; some have only two, some three stomachs, and some are furnished with fore-teeth in the upper jaw; but I cannot learn that any of these are possessed of the property I have mentioned.

It may, perhaps, be said, that the Tartars ride mares, upon their excursions for plunder, in order to live upon the milk, and probably do not take their foals with them. But this will not disprove the doctine I have advanced; as the milk will hardly desert them in so short a time, as one of these excursions might last.

Is there not, therefore, some reason to conclude that the Cow was, by the omniscient Author of nature, intended to give milk, particularly for the use of man?

On the Natural History *and* Origin *of* Magnesian Earth, *particularly as connected with those of* Sea Salt, *and of* Nitre; *with* Observations *on some of the* Chemical Properties *of that* Earth, *which have been, hitherto, either unknown, or undetermined. By* Thomas Henry, *F. R. S. &c.*

NATURALISTS and Chemists formerly divided the different kinds of earths into five genera, viz. the Siliceous, or Vitrifiable, the Calcareous, the Gypseous, the Argillaceous and the Talcky. But recent discoveries having proved the Gypseous, to be a compound of Calcareous earth and vitriolic acid, and the Talcky, to consist of a mixture of Argillaceous with other earths, the genera were reduced to three. M. Baumé has even attempted a farther reduction;* and has endeavoured to prove, that two of these are merely modifications of the other; argillaceous earth being, according to him, a vitriolic salt,

---

* Baumé, Chymie Experimentale et Rationée, vol. I. *sar la Terre.*

formed by the union of vitriolic acid with siliceous earth; and the calcareous, a combination of the same earth, with certain portions of air and water, effected by the operation of various marine animals: and he supposes, that when calcareous earth is deprived of air and water, it will return to its primitive state, viz. that of siliceous earth.

This theory is, perhaps, rather fanciful, than just. The operations of Nature, it must be allowed, are generally simple—but we may simplefy too far; and, in forming systems, we should not suffer our imaginations to carry us beyond those bounds, which our senses, and experiment, warrant.

Calcareous earth, indeed, in the form in which we commonly find it, is a compound, consisting of earth, air, and water; and is not considered as *pure*, till it be deprived, by fire, of the two last elements. It is then, properly, *pure calcareous earth*; but it does not appear that longer calcination, though it may divest it of some of the properties of *calcareous*, will ever reduce it to the nature of *siliceous* earth.

Every earth with which we meet, and which, when separated from those acids, or other accidental bodies, that are combined with it, resists every power we possess, to produce any farther decomposition, and yet differs in all, or any of, its properties, from the other known earths,

earths, may be admitted to form a new genus. And, on these grounds, two new genera have lately been added to the other three. The basis of some spars,* which had been generally deemed to be calcareous earth, has been proved to differ from it, in its affinities and some other properties; and has been admitted to form a distinct genus, under the title of *Barytic* or *Ponderous* Earth: and another kind of earth, which though rarely, if ever, found pure in nature, yet abounds, in great quantities, in various forms of combination, from which it may be separated by chemical means, has been allowed to form a fifth genus, under the appellation of *Muriatic*, or, *Magnesian* Earth.

This earth was also, for some time, confounded with calcareous earth, of which it was supposed to be a modification; for by the earlier modes of obtaining it, it was mixed with such

---

* 1. Marmor Metallicum, *Cronst*. 182, Gypsum Spathosum, Spathum Fusibile, *Margraf*. &c. Terra ponderosa vitriolata. *Bergman. Sciagraphia.* Ponderous Spar.

2. Marmor Metallicum, *Cronstedt. Min.* § 18. B. Calk or Cauk.

3. Gypsum crystallisatum capillare, *Cronstedt. Min.* § 19. B. Radiated Cauk.

4. This earth has been also found of a sparry appearance, and combined with aërial acid only, at Alston Moor, in Cumberland; *Terra ponderosa aërata*. See Dr. Withering's *Experiments and Observations on the* Terra Ponderosa. Phil. Transf. vol LXXIV. p. 293.

a quantity

a quantity of calcareous matter as to disguise its distinguishing features, and even make it assume some of the characteristics of calcareous earth. But the accurate experiments of Messrs. Black and Margraaf, soon removed the obstacles, which impeded our more perfect acquaintance with its nature, and they procured it pure from the mixture of other earths; in which state they found it so different, from what it had been represented, that it was declared to be an earth, *sui generis*. But though Dr. Black went thus far, he did not proceed to set it at the head of a distinct genus; but placed it, with all those earths, which he has classed together, under the general generic head of *Absorbent Earths*, of which he was content to make this a species. It has since obtained a more honourable rank, and forms a separate genus.

M. Fourcroy, who follows the arrangement of his predecessor M. Bouquet, has placed calcareous, ponderous, and magnesian earths among the salts. There should seem to be strong objections to this arrangement, even with respect to the two former; though *their* being sapid, and soluble in water, may give some countenance to it. But the insipidity and total insolubility of *pure* magnesia, together with its not being fusible, by the strongest heat we can apply, as will presently be shewn, are proofs of its being a real earth.

Though magnesian earth is rarely found pure, in nature, it is contained, in a saline form, in all nitre heaps, from the mother ley of which salt, it was formerly extracted; in the water of several medicinal springs, and even in our common wells. But the sea is the great source from which we obtain it; in the waters of which, it is united to the marine acid, in which form it remains, after the crystallisation of the sea salt, and is afterwards separated from the marine, and united to the vitriolic, acid, by a particular process. It is then called *Sal Catharticus Amarus*, and, from this salt, the magnesian earth may be precipitated. One hundred parts of the salt yield, on precipitation by a mild alkali, forty-two of magnesia, united with aerial acid. But, if a caustic alkali be employed, the product amounts to only twenty-five parts. But a portion of this last may be driven off by calcination, and consists of water, and, perhaps, *some* aerial acid, for it is difficult to procure the alkali quite free from that gas. The Magnesia is then said to be *pure*. One hundred parts of sal catharticus amarus contain only nineteen of *pure* Magnesia, and according to Bergman, thirty-three of vitriolic acid, and forty-eight of water. But Mr. Kirwan, who reckons only on the *real* acid, makes the proportion of acid twenty-four, and of water fifty-seven, parts.

Sir T. Bergman relates,* that he procured a salt, similar to the sal catharticus amarus, by lixiviating the earthy matters, separated by washing from the silver ore of Sahlberg, on the surface of which the salt forms, by exposure to the air. One hundred weight of the earth yielded sixty-five pounds of this salt. M. Monnet, also, discovered a kind of Schistus, which on calcination, and lixiviation, furnished a small portion of the same salt.

Magnesian earth may also be separated, by means of vitriolic acid, from some spars, marbles, and other earthy and stony bodies of which it forms a component part.

The compound spar, described by Mr. Woulfe,† contains, in 100 parts, 60 of mild calcareous, 35 of mild Magnesia, and 5 of iron.

One hundred parts of Creutzenwald stone contain 12 of mild Magnesia.

The *Kolmord marble*, the *Pietra Talchina*, the *Verde Antico*, and the *Griotte*, a red marble from *Autun*, all contain small portions of Magnesia.

The *Spuma Maris*, an earthy substance, from which the Turkey tobacco-pipes are made, is said to consist of equal parts of magnesian, and siliceous, earths.

---

* Bergman de Magnesia.

† Phil. Transf. vol. LXIX. p. 29.

Steatite, or Soap-rock, contains, according to Sir T. Bergman, 17 of mild Magnesia in 100 parts of that compound.

A loose earth, found in Silesia, and described by Margraaf, contains $\frac{1}{3}$ of its weight of Magnesia.

Fibrous Asbestos contains, in 100 parts, from 12 to 28, and, Coriaceous Asbestos, from 22 to 26 parts of magnesian earth, united to aërial acid. Amianthus affords 18, 6, Lapis Nephriticus 33, and Venetian Talc, an undetermined number of parts of the same earth.

Colourless Mica affords, on analysis, 20 parts, in 100, *blue Schistus* 8, *black Hornstone* 16, and *Killas* 6 parts of Magnesia.

Magnesia is also contained, in small quantity, in Chrysopathium, Felt-Spar, Schoerl, and Basaltes: and Pumice-stone yields of it, from 6 to 15 parts in 100.

A martial muriatic spar, found by *M. Monnet*, at St. *Marie aux Mines*, and, by him, named *Pisolites*, is constituted of 50 parts of Silex, the remaining parts consisting of mild Magnesia and Iron, the proportions of which are not determined.*

Such are the compounds under which magnesian earth is principally found; and I have

---

* Vide Kirwan's Elements of Mineralogy, passim.

collected them under one view, as it may be useful to some artists, particularly those concerned in the potteries, to know what earths and stones contain it, and in what proportions. Magnesia, as prepared for the shops, would be too expensive for the purposes of manufactures, which may perhaps, often, be equally answered by using it in these combined forms.

It may seem extraordinary, that a substance, so plentifully diffused in a state of combination, should so rarely occur pure.* But the case is the same, as the celebrated Bergman has observed, with Clay, which is always found, in nature, combined with other substances.† Siliceous earth is indeed, sometimes, found *pure* in the form of *Rock Crystal*; but Bergman detected small portions of both argillaceous and calcareous earth, in the specimens which he examined. Ponderous earth is generally combined with vitriolic acid, and the most pure state, in which it has been observed, is its combination with aërial

---

* I have been assured by Mr. Fabroni, that Magnesia has been found pure, in the Pyrenees. This, however, was, probably, not *pure*, in the present acceptation of the term; but pure from any other admixture, than that of aërial acid, for which magnesian earth has a strong attraction.

† Clay, commonly so called, does not, in general, contain more than from twenty-five to forty-eight parts, in one hundred of pure argillaceous earth.

acid.

acid. Calcareous earth has indeed been discovered, in the neighbourhood of Bath, in the state of quicklime, though, probably, not wholly divested of aërial acid. But they are all more frequently found combined with other substances, forming saline compounds, or, one or more, mechanically mixed with each other, constituting species and varieties.

The late Dr. Lewis, has considered the earth which is obtained from vegetables, after incineration, and washing, as of the same nature with Magnesia: and if we endeavour to trace the origin of magnesian earth, it may appear not improbable that, as all calcareous earth is the result of the destruction of testaceous animals, so the magnesian arises from vegetables, which have perished, and undergone some process in the great laboratory of nature; whereby they are reduced to this state. By putrefaction they are altered to a fine black Mold. And it may be that, Nature, who often operates by slow and secret steps, may make such further changes, as to convert this Mold into magnesian earth.

But the origin of magnesian earth is so connected with that of sea salt, which it always accompanies, that it may not be improper to consider them together; as it is probable that they are both formed under similar circumstances, and at the same time.

Philosophers have been much puzzled to account for the original saltness of the Sea. Some have imagined it must have been furnished by rivers, which, flowing from the land, conveyed with them such quantities of salt, from accumulations of that mineral, formed within the bowels of the earth, as to communicate, and continually supply saltness to the Sea; while others have attributed its impregnation to rocks of salt, situated at the bottom of the Ocean. To both these opinions, objections have been made; and the learned Bishop of Landaff,* has chosen to adopt another, viz. that the Sea was *originally created* salt. In support of this theory, and in objection to the others, especially to that which asserts the origin and supply from the land, it has been advanced, that a great part of the finny inhabitants of the ocean cannot exist in fresh water, and therefore it is not to be supposed, that they should ever have been placed in a situation unsuited for their support. It might also have been added, that, there is as much difficulty in accounting for the origin of the salt, which the rivers are supposed to wash down, as for its formation in the Sea. But might not the great Creator, by whose FIAT all things were produced, accommodate the first inhabitants of the Sea to their temporary

* Watson's Chemical Essays, vol. II.

situation; and gradually produce such changes in their constitutions, as to make the saltness of the water necessary to their support? Changes, equally great, appear to have taken place in the human habit. The duration of life, in particular, was protracted, in the earlier ages, to a length convenient for the speedy population of the world; and when that end was accomplished, to a certain degree, Providence assigned limits to the existence of mankind, at the utmost of which we seldom arrive, and beyond which we never pass.

Notwithstanding what I have here advanced, I must confess myself inclined to join in the opinion, that the Sea was originally created salt. But all saline substances, with which we are acquainted, are subject to gradual decay, decomposition, or volatilization, in long process of time, and when exposed to the action of air, moisture and heat. Nature has established an universal system of alternate destruction and recomposition in her works; and is continually carrying on processes in her grand laboratory, which art is unable to imitate. Animals and vegetables perish and decay; and, when corrupted, contribute to the support or accommodation of each other; and many mineral substances, though more permanent than those which constitute the other kingdoms, are liable to to confiderable changes, are frequently decompofed, and forced to enter into new combinations. It is not therefore to be fuppofed, that the fame individual falt has been contained by the ocean, from the creation to the prefent time. We know that the waters are continually evaporating into the atmofphere, forming clouds, defcending again in rain, replenifhing the earth, and, after forming rivers, returning to the fea. Sea falt rifes, by a moderate heat, with the vapour of water, and is often carried by ftorms to confiderable diftances. By thefe and other means, it is probable, there muft be a continual wafte of falt, which Nature muft have fome mode to fupply.

The ocean is replete with animals and plants. The deftruction and corruption of thefe muft furnifh much matter, fitted for the formation of faline fubftances, much earth, much of the principle of inflammability, and of air; and, if water were not a part of their compofition, the fea would plentifully fupply that elementary ingredient. By the putrefaction of fimilar fubftances, mixed with calcareous earth, moiftened with water, and expofed to the gradual action of the air, Nitre is formed. May not the fame fubftances, under different circumftances, covered by the depth of the ocean, and feparated thereby from immediate communication with the air, produce Sea-Salt. It has lately been

difcovered

discovered, by an ingenious chemist,* that though Nitre is produced by the above substances, with the access of air, yet if they be so placed that the air may be excluded, and the situation perhaps not too moist, Sulphur, and not Nitre, is the result. So that the three mineral acids should seem to have a similar origin, and it is not without good grounds, that they are said to be modifications of each other.

But it may be said, that the analogy in the production of Sea-Salt and of Nitre is not complete. That, in the one, both the alkaline and acid parts of the salt are formed; whereas, in the other, the acid only is produced in the beds, and it is necessary to add an alkaline salt to constitute the basis of the Nitre. I cannot however allow of the force of this objection. Though the addition of the alkali be necessary, in these northern latitudes, yet, in warmer climates, where Nature is more vigorous and active, there is no doubt but she forms, or devellopes, both the acid and alkali of Nitre, at the same time.

---

* M. Fougeroux. vide Memoires del' Academie Royale des Sciences pour l'année 1780.

The Sulphur, produced under the above circumstances, was found, amidst the ruins of an old house which had been built in a very filthy place, contained in a mass of earth, and, in part crystallized; and constituting, in several of the large portions of the earth, a third of the whole mass.

To the evidence adduced by Dr. Wall, in his ingenious paper, on the origin of the Fixed Vegetable Alkali, and of Nitre, I have to add that of Baron Dillon, the intelligent translator of Mr. Bowles's Travels in Spain, who has, personally, assured me of the authenticity of the fact; and of a Gentleman who resided, during several years, in the East Indies, as superintendent of the manufactures of the Company, and fully confirms the account, that Nitre is procured, from the soil of certain places in that country, merely by lixiviating it, and evaporating the water, without the addition of any alkaline salt. The Duke de Rouchefoucauld also obtained one ounce of nitre in the pound, from chalk of Roche Guyon: and it is said, by M. Fourcroy, to be found quite pure in chalk beds.

Indeed the relation between the production of these two salts is very striking; for at the same time that Nitre is formed in the beds, a considerable quantity of Common Salt seems to be produced; and, during the evaporation of the nitrous ley, such quantities of it are separated, that we cannot suppose the whole to have pre-existed, as such, in the urine and other animal matters, used in the nitre heaps, but must regard it, in some measure, as a new product.

Nor does the analogy stop here. Together with the Nitre, which is formed in the beds, and with the Sea-Salt, which we suppose to be

formed

formed in the ocean, another salt consisting of marine acid and magnesian earth, is always produced, or, at least, is always found mixed with these, and is left in the mother ley, remaining after their crystallisation. It should seem, therefore, highly probable, that Nature, at one and the same time, fabricates from the constituent parts of animal and vegetable substances, not only the alkaline and acid salts, but the mild and tasteless earth of Magnesia—and that this earth is the result of the decomposition of vegetables, whose other component parts, combining with animal matters with which they meet, and aided by the concurrence of air, water, and heat, constitute the different acids and alkalis, necessary to the formation of Sea-Salt and of Nitre.*

Messrs.

---

* M. Baumé is of opinion that the constituent parts of fixed alkaline salt, are calcareous earth, water, and phlogiston: and he asserts that he has produced this salt, by calcining together equal portions of powdered marble, and the charcoal of oil of hartshorn; and that the quantity of salt was always diminished by a diminution of the inflammable matter, employed in the experiment. He attempts to account for the formation of saline substances, in the humid way, in the following manner. " Les testacées croissent et perissent dans la mer. La Nature, par le mouvement des eaux, brise et reduit en poudre impalpable beaucoup de coquilles de ces animaux, et met la terre calcaire en etat d' être dissoute par l'eau. L'eau

Messrs. Black and Margraaf, and particularly the former, have thrown great light on the Chemical History of Magnesian Earth. The Essay of the former, in particular relates a number of experiments made in the most accurate manner, and of deductions the most clear and satisfactory, of any treatise extant. An essay the more valuable, as besides the discrimination of that earth from the Calcareous, it has laid the foundation of the many valuable discoveries relative to the nature of fixed air and the various Gases, which have been the sources of the most valuable improvements in Chemistry. Happy I must esteem myself if, following such great masters, I have been able to add any new or useful information.*

The

---

de la mer dissout de même la matiere inflammable, non seulement des corps dont nous parlons, mais de tous les corps organisés qui croissent et perissent dans son sein: elle elabore à son gré la matiere inflammable, et la reduit dans la etat convenable pour former différentes matieres salines. De cette union il résulte différents sels, suivant l'etat des substances, et les proportions dans lesquelles ces substances se sont combinées. Je pense que les sels contenant de l'acide vitriolique et ceux contenant de l'acide marin, sont les sels que la nature forme le plus abondamment dans la mer; ils sont, l'un et l'autre, des sels primtifs. Chymie Experimentale et Raisonnée vol. I. p. 205.

* The principal improvements, which I ventured to suggest, in Dr. Black's process for preparing Magnesia Alba; those, I mean, of employing a larger quantity of

The late Sir Torbern Bergman has pursued the subject with great success. He has satisfactorily explained some of the phenomena of the process for the preparation of Magnesia; has ascertained its affinities with all the acids, to many of which Dr. Black had not extended his inquiry, and described the Salts formed by their union with this basis. And he has given an account of the result of various experiments, made with a view of determining the degrees of fusibility, which Magnesian Earth exhibits, when exposed to a strong heat, either mixed with other earths, or *per se*.*

water, for the first washing, and of throwing the mixture, of the Saline Liquors, into boiling water, and continuing the coction, instead of boiling the mixture, previous to the addition of the water, have been adopted, in the later editions of the Edinburgh Pharmacopœia.

* This excellent Chemist has done me the honour to quote my discoveries relative to the difference of the septicity of Magnesia Alba, when applied to flesh and to bile; and subjoined my name in a marginal note to the passage. He then proceeds, in the next paragraph, to cite the antiseptic properties in both cases of Calcined Magnesia, and its power of rendering resinous substances soluble in water, in which passage he has used my own words. Yet M. Fourcroy, and after him, his translator Mr. Elliot, have mentioned M. Bergman, only, as the relater of the latter facts, without noticing the author from whom he had taken them. My Essay was published in May, 1773, whereas the date of that of Sir Torbern Bergman, which like most of his other excellent Tracts, was written as a Thesis for one of his Pupils, is December 23, 1774.

Magnesia, says M. Bergman, exposed to a long continued, and very violent, fire, agglutinates and begins to shew signs of fusion, especially if the Magnesia has been prepared, by calcination, from the mother leys. Monf. Darcet, on the contrary, had averred, that the earthy basis of Epsom Salt resisted the action of a fire equal, in continuance and force to that of a Porcelain furnace. And M. Macquer, in the new edition of his Chemical Dictionary, declares, that he has exposed the Earth of this Salt to the greatest heat, that could be formed in the focus of M. de Trudaine's large lens, without the least appearance of a tendency to fusion. M. Morveau had operated on Magnesia separated from the mother ley of Nitre, and had concluded it to be, not only in itself, the most fusible of all earths, but that it even decided the fusion of other earths. But on making his experiments with Magnesia, precipitated from Epsom Salt, he found, that on separately exposing two Hessian crucibles, the one containing Chalk, and the other an equal portion of Magnesia, to the strongest degree of heat, that could be produced in M. Macquer's furnace, the chalk was fused into a beautiful transparent glass, and had attacked and dissolved the crucible, for more than half its thickness, wherever the Calcareous Earth had reached. But the Magnesia was formed into a round, white, opake, solid, mass, not having the appearance even of the semivitrification of

Porcelain, and without the least adhesion to the crucible.*

This experiment seems to coincide with that of Bergman, but to differ, in some degree, from that related by Macquer. Mr. Magellan, whom we have very deservedly ranked among our honorary members, has lately favoured me with an account of some curious experiments, made in London, which may serve to clear up this point. I shall therefore comply with his request to lay an extract of his letter before the Society; and then beg leave to add a few remarks on the subject, and on some other of the chemical properties of Magnesian Earth, which are either unknown or undecided.

"I have a fact," says Mr. Magellan, "to
"relate, which may be agreeable to you, con-
"cerning the portion of Calcined Magnesia you
"favoured me with. On my return to London,
"many experiments were making with a most
"powerful burning lens, executed by Mr.
"Parker. Among these, was a very striking one,
"which puzzled me much, made with Calcined
"Magnesia, caked, by pressure, into a cubic
"form, of $\frac{1}{4}$ of quarter of an inch per side.
"This, exposed to the focus of the lens, was
"reduced from $\frac{25}{100}$ to $\frac{8}{100}$ on each side of the
"cube. On hearing this I was struck with the
"fact, which is contrary to the known property

* Opuscules Chymiques et Physiques de M. T. Bergman, traduits par M. de Morveau, tome. I. p. 398.

"of Magnesia, viz. of not changing its dimen-
"sions, nor receiving any alteration in its con-
"sistence, by the strongest heat. I therefore
"went, the first fair day, to the place where
"the lens was at work, carrying with me the
"very same bottle with which you favoured me.
"I made a similar cube of your Magnesia, with-
"in the same metallic box that had been used
"in the former case; but I found that, by ex-
"posing it, even for a longer time, to the force
"of the lens, than the other Magnesia had been,
"this of yours was not sensibly diminished in
"bulk, nor did it become harder, as the other
"had done, which must have had a considerable
"portion of Argillaceous or Siliceous Earth in
"its composition, to occasion it to shrink in
"such a manner. I was told it was bought of
"a very good and reputable Chemist. But, very
"probably, he may precipitate his Magnesia,
"with uncrystallised Tartar, or with any other
"Alkali, whereas Bergman prefers the vola-
"tile. Or, perhaps, crystallised Tartar has
"always some siliceous or other earthy sub-
"stance, which, mingling with the Magnesia,
"prevents its adhering to its specific character.
"I wish to know whether I am right in this way
"of accounting for the difference; for as I am
"now preparing for the press, a second edition
"of Cronstedt's Mineralogy, I wish the fact to
"appear in its true and proper light."—So far
Mr. Magellan.

It is very probable that the Magnesia, used in the experiments of Messrs. Bergman and Morveau, was pure, as the former recommends, and the latter actually employed, the Volatile Alkali, to effect the precipitation of the earth. The difference, therefore, between their experiments and that of M. Macquer, most probably depended on the communication of some portion of Siliceous or Argillaceous Earth, from the crucible in which they were made. Whereas M. Macquer's experiments, being made in a metallic box, and the heat directed immediately to the Magnesia, no tendency to vitrification would appear.

In regard to the difference between the Magnesia, which was first exposed to Mr. Parker's lens, and my own, I can only speak from conjecture. I have been particularly careful to have my Alkaline Lixivium, which is a solution of the finest pot-ash, perfectly purified: and have frequently observed, that after it has been freed from all Neutral Salts, and from all the earthy matter, that the filter could separate, the solution, on long standing, has become again turbid, and deposited a copious white sediment, Bergman, who describes a similar sediment, declares it to be Siliceous Earth, that had been held in solution by the Alkali, and is precipitated by the fixed air, attracted by the salt. This fact is adduced by him, as a proof a proof of the acidity of that gas. Perhaps the ingenious Chemist, who prepared the other portion of Magnesia, not adverting to this circumstance, or justly not considering it as materially affecting the *medicinal* properties of the Magnesia, though it would greatly alter its *chemical* qualities, might have used his Lixivium, soon after filtration, and, by this means, the extraneous Earth might have been introduced into the Magnesia, and have affected its fusibility.

Dr. Black had said, in his excellent Essay on Quicklime and Magnesia, that Calcined Magnesia, dissolves in the vitriolic, nitrous, marine, and acetous acids, and forms with them Salts, similar to those produced by the uncalcined earth with the same acids. But Mr. Mönch, a German apothecary, has asserted, that though he poured half an ounce of strong vinegar on twenty grains of Calcined Magnesia, and suffered the mixture to stand for twenty-four hours, only seven grains of the Magnesia were dissolved; and that he was unable to dissolve more than the same quantity, by digesting, in a moderate heat, an equal portion of Calcined Magnesia, in half an ounce of a mixture consisting of one part of strong vitriolic acid and six of water, for twenty hours. And, what is still more extraordinary, he could dissolve only nine grains out of twenty by boiling for a confiderable time, in an ounce of the same diluted acid. But in the

the nitrous and concentrated marine acids, he acknowledges, they diffolved entirely.*

Mr. Kirwan, alfo fays,† that this earth, perfectly dry and free from fixed air, could not be diffolved in any of the acids without heat. But that in a heat of 180°. thefe acids, diluted with four or fix times their quantity of water, attacked it very fenfibly. There is no doubt but Calcined Magnefia diffolves much lefs rapidly than the mild. The aërial acid, contained in the latter, while it is expelling, keeps up, as Bergman has juftly obferved, an inteftine motion, whereby the particles of the earth are agitated and feparated, fo that frefh furfaces are continually prefented to the Magnefia. Whereas, if an acid be added to this earth, when divefted of air, this motion is wanting, and that part of the acid, which becomes faturated with the earth, envellopes the remaining earth, and prevents the immediate action of the free acid on it.‡ Continual agitation, however, will greatly promote the folution.

Mr. Mönch, feems not to have been aware of the greater quantity of acid, requifite to diffolve Calcined Magnefia, than would be neceffary for the uncalcined. Nor indeed to

---

* Vide London Medical Journal, vol. III. p. 97.
† Philofophical Tranfactions, vol. LXXII. p. 193.
‡ Bergman Opufc. de Magnefia. § XIX.

have known the quantity required for the solution of the latter. I have found twenty grains of mild Magnesia require an ounce and half of distilled vinegar for its solution. This may seem a large quantity; but let it be remembered that, " the quantity of each basis, " requisite to saturate a given quantity of each " acid, is directly as the affinity of such acid " to each basis."* 100 grains of real vitriolic acid require 215 of vegetable fixed alkali to neutralise them; whereas the same portion of acid would be neutralised by 80 grains of Magnesia; and the proportional quantity of this earth to that of the alkali, necessary to saturate a given quantity of acetous acid, would be still smaller.

But Mr. Kirwan's experiments are more worthy of attention. His accuracy in every thing he undertakes is undeniable; nor would he probably have erred, but in a case in which the most faithful Experimentalist might be liable to deception.

I do not know any thing more subject to variety than the solubility of pure Magnesia in acids. I have dissolved 12 grains of aërated Magnesia in sufficient quantities of each of the four principal acids, when I have found the earth neutralised. Five grains of pure Magnesia, which is equal to twelve of the aërated has

* Kirwan in Phil. Transf. vol. LXXIII. p. 38.

dissolved, without heat, in the same quantity of the vitriolic, and even with smaller quantities of the nitrous and marine acids, than were necessary for the solution of the aërated. The action of the acetous acid was somewhat less complete, on the pure than on the aërated. The acids were previously diluted with about five times their weight of water, except the acetous which was concentrated, and the Magnesian Earth was intimately mixed with half an ounce of water, and continually agitated with a glass tube, till the solution was finished.

Thus I have often made complete solutions of pure Magnesia. But at other times I have found it obstinately to resist solution, though prepared, previous to calcination, in every respect, similar to the other, and, though, apparently, perfectly calcined. This for some time puzzled me exceedingly; till at last I discovered it to depend on the state of calcination, and that by continuing the fire for a longer time, this insoluble Magnesia acquired its customary solubility. Another circumstance, attending the calcination of Magnesia, I have always been unable to explain. In a certain period of the process, though the Magnesia were ever so tasteless before calcination, and though it, at this time, shews no effervescence with acids, yet it has acquired a disagreeable, bitter, pungent taste, somewhat resembling lime. But it does not, like lime, or Magnesia containing that earth,

form

form a lime-water. This obnoxious taste is also destroyed by a further extension of the calcination. On what can this property depend?

Magnesia has been described as throwing out a phosphoric light, in the latter periods of the calcination. This is a phenomenon which neither I, nor any of the persons I have employed, in the calcination of Magnesia, have ever been able to observe. Indeed I do not see how it could happen, except the Magnesia contained vitriolic acid or alkaline salt. M. Fourcroy, who mentions the fact, cites the authority of Messrs. Butini and Tingry, of Geneva;* and the process, which he has given, from the former of these Gentlemen, is very ill adapted to free the Magnesia, from the whole of the vitriolated tartar, formed in the mixture. Now, supposing aërial acid to be a compound of Air and Phlogiston, the last portions being separated with difficulty from the Magnesia, a decomposition of the Gas may take place, and a new combination ensue. The Phlogiston, quitting its aërial basis, may unite with the Earth and Vitriolic Acid, and, by this union, a Pyrophorus be formed; and, probably, from this cause, the appearances, described by these Chemists, may have proceeded.

* Fourcroy's Lectures, vol. I. p. 163, and 292.

END OF VOL. FIRST.

INDEX

TO THE

FIRST VOLUME.

A.

	Page
ACADEMUS, ancient, described	305
Acids, their use in bleaching linen, by Dr. EASON	240
ADDISON, Mr. quoted	145
AIKIN, Dr. senior, his character	76
——— junior, on attempts to winter in high northern latitudes	89
AKENSIDE, Dr. his beautiful description of distressing scenes accompanied with pleasure	151
Amusements, literary ones recommended	13
Animal substances regenerated	325, 338
——— bones, 329; nerves, 333; arteries, 334; crabs and worms, 335	
Ancients, knew that water would cool more easily, which had been heated	262
——————— that the evaporation of fluids produces cold	265
——————— that air is dissolved in water, by means of heat and agitation	266
——————— why the lower air is more heated than the higher	268
——————— why hail-stones suddenly concrete	268
——————— that air is separated from water by freezing	269

INDEX.

	Page
Ancients, knew that water will rise to its level in pipes	269
—— compared with moderns as to the imitative arts	405
ARTHUR's seat, pebbles found there	37
Arts, a general acquaintance with them necessary to excellence	77
—— plan for extending them	84

B.

BARNES, Dr. on poetry	54
—— on the affinity subsisting between the arts	72
BARROW, Dr. his observation on general scholars	72
Basaltes	38
BAUME, quoted	32, 33, 449, 462
Beauty in the imitative arts, defined, and accounted for	121
BELL, Dr. on the generation of cold	1
Bismuth, forms striæ on its surface	40
BLACKLOCK, Dr. an account of him	166
Blindness, observations on by Mr. BEW	159
BRINDLEY, what advantage he might have received from education	83
BROWN, Mr. of Virginia, his method of making saltpetre	203
—— Mr. author of the Essay on the Characteristics, quoted	230

C.

CAREW, his account of aged persons in Cornwall	359
CAVALLO, his account of the electricity of the atmosphere	398
Causeway Giants, described	38
Charades, riddles, &c. why agreeable	113
Chemistry recommended to the commercial student	24
—— adopted the symbols of astronomy	254
CHESELDEN, Mr. couched a young man born blind, with success	178
Chiaro-scuro, a modern invention	410
Chrystallization, by Dr. EASON	29
CICERO, his account of the effect of Carbo's Oratory	69
Colours, instances of persons who cannot accurately distinguish them	182

Conflict

INDEX.

	Page
Conflict of feelings, the cause of pleasure	157
Contrast, in poetry, painting and music, agreeable	119
Copper, why it has the symbol of Venus	256
Corn, a bounty upon it improper	413
Cow, adapted to the use of man	442
—— has four stomachs, long intestines, &c.	443
—— has four teats, gives her milk to the hand, &c.	444
Curiosity, one cause of pleasure in viewing scenes of distress	157
Customs, necessary in the present state of Europe	431
Cylinder-wire, its application to corn, bark, sand, &c.	78

D.

Diversions, of hunting, shooting, &c. reconcileable with humanity	341
———— the human mind naturally inclined to them	343
———— they conduce to health and pleasure	346
———— do not diminish the pleasure of the animals	349
———— often pursued by persons the most humane and benevolent	353
Dreams, of a blind man respecting visible objects	181
Dyers, but few of them *chemists*	27

E.

Earth, magnesian, its origin	455
——— *calcareous*, not convertible into siliceous	449
——— division of, into five genera	450
Eason, Dr. on chrystallization	29
East, the beautiful patterns from thence, accounted for	275
——— its poetry fine, because describing natural scenes	276
Electricity, its influence in evaporation	398
——————— in suspending vapour	400
Engraving, a modern invention	412
Epic poem, demands unity of action	126
Evaporation, from a heated human body	3
——————— in vacuo	396

INDEX.

                    Page

Execution of malefactors, why attended by so many persons - - - - 148

Exercise, its effect in preventing the scurvy - 106

———— of the mind, pleasant - - 110

———— a cause of the pleasure felt in contemplating scenes of distress - - - 156

F.

Fish—oil and fat, used by the Samoides, Esquimaux, &c. as food - - - - 103
Fixed air, machine for impregnating water, &c. with it 52
Flint, probably compounded of water, and an acid 33
Fly-shuttle, not yet used in the Norwich manufacture 84
Fogs, causes of them - - - 404
FORDYCE, Dr. experiments on cold - - 1
Fulham, account of salt-petre works formed there 201
Future state, differently represented by different people 286

G.

Gardening, its style and taste among the ancients 297
Gardens, hanging ones, of Babylon, described - 301
———— of Lucullus, described - - 308
———— of Pliny, his Laurentine Villa, described 312
———— modern, described and recommended - 322
Gentleman, the importance to him of a taste for literature 9, 10
GLAUBER, his attempts to make salt-petre - 198
Greenland, account of seven Dutch sailors who wintered there 1633 - - - - 93
Gypsum, five sorts of - - - 32

H.

HALL, Rev. Mr. on the influence of taste on morals 223
HAYGARTH, Dr. his machine for impregnating water, &c. with fixed air - - - 52
Heat, latent, not unknown to the ancients - 267
Heathen religion, favourable to sculpture - 407
HENRY, Mr. on the advantages of literature and philosophy, and their consistency with commercial pursuits - - - - 7

INDEX.

HENRY, Mr. on the prefervation of fea water by quicklime   41
——— on the natural and chemical hiftory of magnefian earth   - - - - 448
Hiftory, particularly Englifh, ufeful to a tradefman   16
——— requires a good imagination, in order to be read with pleafure   - - - 391
HORACE, his defcription of a true poet   - - 59
Hudfon's Bay, wintered in by Monck, and James   90, 92

J.

JAMES, captain, winters in Hudfon's Bay   - 91
Ice, modern way of making it in the Eaft Indies   - 266
Imagery, how far it conftitutes the effence of poetry   56
Imagination, neceffary to correct judgment   - 378
——— defined   - - - - 382
———amazingly ftrong in children   - 393
Indians, American, their mufic and poetry plaintive   285
JOHNSON, Dr. remarks on his criticifms upon Milton 66, 71
Iron, why it has the fymbol of Mars   - - 257
Iflands, more healthy than continents   - 366
Italy, peculiarly favourable to longevity   - 358
Jupiter, his fymbol accounted for   - - 247
——— why applied to exprefs tin   - - 258

K.

Keeping, in painting, little underftood by the ancients 411
KIRSHAW, Mr. on the comparative merit of the ancients and moderns   - - - 405
KIRWAN, Mr. quoted   - - - 454, 470
Knowledge, general, neceffary to particular   - 73
——— mathematical, its connection with imagination   - - - 387

L.

Landaff, bifhop of, quoted   - - - 457
Landfcape painting, ancient, very bad   - - 411
Language, originally poetical   - - - 58

LAOCOON,

INDEX.

	Page
LAOCOON, statue of, described	123
Laplanders, account of their diet by LINNÆUS	99
Linen, bleached by acids	240
———— manufactures, the duties they pay when imported	437
LINNÆUS, his account of the diet of the Laplanders	99
Literature and philosophy, soften the rigours of war	8
———————————— multiply the sources of pleasure	9
———————————— are useful to the gentleman	10
———————————— to the merchant	11
———————————— furnish agreeable amusement	14
London, bills of mortality, quoted from 1728 to 1758	362
Longevity, observations on by Dr. FOTHERGILL	355
———— tables of	357, 358, 360

———— depends on air, &c. 365; foods, &c. 367; motion and rest, 369; secretions, &c. 369; affections of mind, 369

M.

Machine, for impregnating water, &c. with fixed air	52
Machines, generally invented by persons not educated to mechanic employments	82
MAGELLAN, Mr. his letter to Mr. Henry on the infusibility of magnesia	466
Magnesian earth, its natural and chemical history	448
———————— various combinations in which it is found	452
———————— its origin	455
———————— infusibility ascertained	465
———————— solubility in acids when calcined proved	469
———————— not phosphoric	473
Manners, rude and ferocious, in mountainous and uncultivated countries	281
Manufactures, cotton in particular, depend upon machines	80
Mars, his symbol explained	253
Medici, the family of, their character by lord ORRERY	238
Memory, peculiarly strong in blind persons	175
Merchant, importance of taste for literature in him	11

METCALF,

INDEX.

	Page
METCALF, JOHN, though blind, a celebrated surveyor and projector of highways	172
MILTON defended	71
———— superior to Homer and Virgil in unity of action	130
Mind, human, improperly said to consist of several distinct powers	377
Miners, in general hardy and ferocious	283
Modulation, regular, essential to poetry	60
———— different in different languages	68
MONCK, captain, winters in Hudson's Bay	90
MOYES, HENRY, Dr. account of him	168
Muriatic acid, recommended for bleaching linens	242

N.

NEWTON, Sir ISAAC, possessed a vigorous fancy	389

O.

Oratory, capable of imagery and elevation, as much as poetry	61
Osiris, the supreme deity of the Egyptians, his symbol	246

P.

PALLAS, Mons. his account of islands between Kamskatka and America.	98
PARRY, the blind musician, account of him	167
Passions, their influence and use in directing the judgment	381
Pebbles, produced by irregular chrystallization	37
PERCIVAL, Dr. his tribute to the memory of CHARLES DE POLIER, Esq.	287
Physician, what necessary to constitute a skilful one	386
Plan, for extending arts and manufactures at Manchester	84
Pleasure, of contemplating scenes of distress accounted for	144
POLIER, Mr. DE, on the pleasure of mental exercise	110
———— tribute to his memory	287
Polite Arts, taste in, necessary for a manufacturer	28
Pot-ash, use of in making salt-petre	217

INDEX.

Q.

	Page
Quicklime, applied to the preservation of sea water	41
———— quantity requisite	49
———— its action accounted for	49

R.

Registers, œconomical, recommended	134
———————— to know the state of population	137
———————— to discover thieves, &c.	138
———————— to know the quantity of corn annually produced	143
REID, Dr. quoted	160
Rein deer, their blood drunk warm, how it acts as a preservative from the scurvy	104
Religion, how far influenced by the scenery of a country	279
REMBRANDT, character of his paintings	410
Repository, proposed for chemical and mechanical arts	85
REYNOLDS, Sir JOSHUA, quoted	409
Rhyme, why agreeable	115
ROI, Mr. DE, his theory of evaporation	396

S.

Saturn, his symbol explained	252
——— why used to represent lead	257
Salt-petre, treatise on by Mr. MASSEY	184
———— causes of the ill success of trials for making it in England	185, &c.
———— what principles enter into its composition	188
———— how the peculiar acid, necessary to form it, is generated	191, &c.
———— the influence of putrefaction in forming it	193
———— causes of its abundance in India	195
———— the old and approved method of obtaining it	205
———— makers of, in Paris, incorporated	208
———— account of the author's experiments	209
———— method of making it in Paris	211

Salt-petre

INDEX.

	Page
Salt-petre, translation, on the use of pot-ash in making it	217
———— procured, ready formed, upon the earth, in warm climates	461
Salt-sea, its natural history as connected with that of magnesian earth	456
———— or *bay*, better than that made from rocks or springs	43
Samoides, drink the warm blood of rein deer	98
SAUNDERSON, Dr. account of him	163
Scenery, of a country, its influence upon the inhabitants	271
Scurvy, occasioned by salt meats, and spirituous liquors, in cold climates	100
Sculpture, promoted by the heathen religion	407
Sea-water, its composition	42
SMITH, Dr. on the wealth of nations, quoted	82
Spar, Derbyshire, how compounded	33
Spectator, No. 411, quoted	9
SPITSBERGEN, account of seven Dutch sailors who wintered there 1638	93
——————————— eight Englishmen ditto	94
———————— East, four Russians winter there	96
Spirituous liquors, unfavourable to the scurvy	104
STANLEY, Mr. the blind musician, account of him	167
Steam, a powerful principle, lately applied to different uses	79
STERNE, quoted	390
Stones, precious, originally in fusion	34
———— contain three principles	36
SULLY's Memoirs, extract from, relating to an intended cabinet	87
Sun, the origin of its astronomic symbol	246
Symbols, used first by astronomers, and afterwards by chemists	245
Sympathy, the source of many noble pleasures	154

INDEX.

T.

	Page
Taste, its influence upon the strong poetic character	65
——— its analogy to the moral feelings, asserted	134
——— its influence not favourable to morals	223
——— distinguished from the moral sense	226
——— may shew the beauty of virtue, without giving the power	228
——— its connection with genius	232
——————————— with religion	233
——— instances in which it produces misfortune or immorality	234
——— effects of it at Athens	236
Tempest at sea, agreeable to behold from the shore	149
Towns, large, unfriendly to longevity	362
Turgot, Monf. his letter to Mr. Wimpey	135
——————— his remarks on preventing the exportation of corn	429

U.

Understanding, influenced by the imagination and passions - - - - 381
Unity, of action in painting and poetry, why agreeable 126

V.

Vapour, eight hundred times lighter than air	397
——— quicker from water electrified	398
Venus, the same with Isis; her symbol accounted for	250
Verse, regular, its origin accounted for	64
Volta, Mr. his remarks on electricity	399

W.

War, its horrors softened by literature	8
Whale's-fritters, eaten by persons wintering at Spitzbergen	95
Wheat, its price in 1687	418
——— often sown injudiciously, and why	426

WHITEHURST,

INDEX.

	Page
WHITEHURST, Mr. his inquiry into, &c. quoted	367
WIMPEY, Mr. againſt the bounty on corn	413
Windſor tables, quoted	420
Woollen manufacture, the numbers employed in it	435

Y.

Youths, two, reſtored from conſumptions by human milk — 446

www.ingramcontent.com/pod-product-compliance
Lightning Source LLC
Chambersburg PA
CBHW080232170426
43192CB00014BA/2449